KB038737

한국영화의 풍경 *1945-1959*

Traces of Korean Cinema from 1945 to 1959

한국영화자료총서 01

한국영상자료원(KOFA) 지음

한국영화의 풍경 *1945-1959*

Traces of Korean Cinema from 1945 to 1959

문학사상사

일러두기

1.

이 책은 올해로 30주년을 맞은 한국영상자료원이 발간하는 한국영화자료총서 『한국영화의 풍경』 시리즈의 첫 번째 권입니다. 해방 이후 1946년부터 1950년대 말까지의 한국영화 사진과 포스터와 함께 이 시기를 다룬 글들을 함께 실었습니다.

2.

실린 글인 "해방 직후의 한국영화계와 영화운동" "1950년대의 한국영화"는 한국영상자료원장인 이효인이 과거에 썼던 「해방직후의 민족영화운동」(『해방전후사의 인식 4』, 한길사, 1989)과 「1950년대 영화」(『한국현대 예술사대계 II』, 한국예술종합학교 한국예술연구소, 2000) 등을 토대로 각각 다시 쓴 글이며 「동란기의 한국영화」는 한국영상자료원 영화사연구팀 정종화의 석사논문 「한국영화 성장기의 토대에 대한 연구」(중앙대학교 첨단영상대학원 영상예술학과 2002.6)를 바탕으로 다시 쓴 글입니다.

3.

해외 한국영화 연구자와 한국학 연구자를 위한 영문 번역은 호주 울롱공^{Wollongong}대학교 예술대학 연구조교인 심애경이 담당했고 역시 호주 울롱공대학교 예술대학 커뮤니케이션&문화학과 교수인 브라이언 예시스^{Brian Yecies}가 감수를 맡았습니다. 영문 표기는 번역자와 감수자의 의견을 전적으로 따랐음을 밝힙니다.

4.

이 책에 실린 적지 않은 부분의 포스터는 상명대 영화학과 조희문 교수가 소장하고 있는 자료임을 밝힙니다.

5.

맞춤법과 띄어쓰기는 "한글 맞춤법"을 따랐으며 부호는 영화명 〈 〉, 논문 「 」, 도서 『 』, 인용 " ", 강조 ' '의 방식으로 사용했습니다. 별도의 설명이 필요한 경우에는 괄호와 각주를 사용했음을 밝힙니다.

1.

This book is the first book of the series, 「Traces of Korean Films」. The Korean Film Archive has started working on this project to celebrate its 30th anniversary this year. This book deals with the films from 1946 to the late 1950s, and includes images of posters and stills that help us understand Korean films.

2.

This book contains a collection of previously known articles such as: the Head of the Korean Film Archive, Yi Hyo In's 「The Korean Film Community and Film Movements during the Post-liberation Era」, and 「1950s Korean Cinema」. It also includes a revision of his previously known article, 「National Film Movement after the Liberation」 from 「Understanding the Pre & Post Liberation Korea 4」(Hangil-sa, 1993), and 「The Films in the 1950s」 from 「The Overview of Art History in Modern Korea Ⅱ」(The Korea Research Institute of Arts at the Korean National University of Arts, 2000). 「Korean Films During the Wartime」 was written by Chung Chong Hwa, who is a staff member of the research team under the Research & Programming Division of the Korean Film Archive. This article is based on his Master's thesis, 「The Analysis and Development of Korean Film and its Foundation」, from the graduate School of Advanced Imaging Science, Multimedia & Film of Chung Ang University(Department of Film & Multimedia, June 2002).

3.

For overseas Korean film and Korean studies scholars, an English translation of this book is available. Shim Ae Gyung, a research assistant in the Faculty of Arts at the University of Wollongong in Australia, provided the translation work. Dr. Brian Yecies, a lecturer in the Faculty of Arts and an affiliated researcher with the Centre for Asia Pacific Social Transformation Studies(CAPSTRANS) at the University of Wollongong, proofread and edited the translated work. Phonetically spelled Korean words are provided here to help better recognize the original sources. In some cases, the originally known names of some Korean organizations have been preserved, such as the Esperanto spelling of KAPF(Korea Artista Proleta Federatio).

4.

A good portion of the posters included in this book was reproduced with the permission of Prof. Cho Hui Moon of Sang Myung university's Film Department.

5.

The rules of the Korean spelling and spacing follow the current Hangul spelling. The symbols used in this book are: 〈 〉 for film title;「 」 for thesis; 「 」 for book; " " for citation; and ' ' for emphasis. Parenthesis and footnotes are used when additional explanations are needed.

차례 | Contents

1

해방직후의 한국영화계와 영화운동

The Korean Film Community and Film Movements
during the Post-liberation Era

1—

해방 직후 우리 영화계의 시설이라고는 일제가 남기고 간 기자재와 시설이 고작이었다. 게다가 생필름의 품귀현상 때문에 영화를 제작하는 일은 대단히 어려웠다. 또 미국의 직접배급회사인 중앙영화사가 국내 극장가를 거의 장악하고 있었기 때문에 한국영화의 입지는 더욱 좁아지게 되었다. 해방 직후 우리 영화계에는 연간 극영화 24편, 문화영화 6~7편, 뉴스영화 월 1~2편을 제작할 수 있는 시설 정도가 남아 있었다. 그러나 이 수치는 모든 영화시설이 체계적이며 합리적으로 운영될 때에 가능한 것이었다. 또한 일제가 남긴 조선영화사가 화재를 당했고 국내의 생필름 생산이 불가능한 데다 수입조차 변변치 못했기 때문에 영화 제작시설은 대단히 열악했다. 해방 후부터 1948년 8월까지 남한에서 제작된 영화는 극영화 약 15~16편, 문화영화 3~4편, 기록영화 5~6편 그리고 해방뉴스 등의 뉴스영화들이 있었다.

이들 극영화 중 무성영화가 절반을 차지했는데, 지방에는 유성영화의 영사시설이 부족했기 때문이기도 했다. 또 16밀리 영화가 성행하게 되었다. 해방 후 1년 사이에 영화를 제작한 곳으로는 조선영화사, 서울키노, 고려영화협회, 극동영화사, 남일영화사 등이 있었다. 1948년의 한 기록에 따르면, 서울에만 제작소 10여 개가 있지만 실제 제작을 할 수 있는 능력을 가진 곳은 절반에 불과하다고 적혀 있다. 또 생필름의 값이 하루 사이에 엄청나게 변하고 현상비, 자재비 등 모든 것이 지나치게 비쌌다고 한다. 당시 영화를 상영했던 서울의 주요 극장으로는 국제극장(전 명치좌), 국도극장, 우미관, 수도극장, 단성사, 중앙극장, 제일극장, 동양극장, 서울극장 등이 있었는데, 이 극장들에는 35밀리와 16밀리 영사시설이 갖춰져 있었다.

2—

한편 미국영화의 국내 직접배급방식은 전국을 완전히 장악했다. 미국영화의 세계 진출은 제1차 세계대전 때부터 시작되었고, 제2차 세계대전 중에는 전략적인 역할까지 수행하는 등 본격적인 기능을 발휘했다. 미국영화는 영국을 시작으로 프랑스, 이탈리아 등 서유럽 일대를 전부 장악하는 것과 동시에 전 세계로 발을 뻗치게 되었는데, 1946년도 기록에 따르면 미국영화의 외국 배급수익은 총 9억 달러로서 전체 수익의 17퍼센트에 이르고 있다. 한국과 일본에 대해서 그들은 미국 8대 영화사의 대표기관과 미육군성, 국무성 3자 합작에 의한 미국영화 직접배급회사인 중앙영화배급사Central Motion Picture Exchange(이후 중배)를 일본에 먼저 설립해 8대 영화사의 수출에 관한 업무를 담당하도록 했다.

이후 그들은 한국에 출장소를 두고, 계약을 맺은 극장과 수익금을 배분하는 과정에서 그중의 반을 차지해 국내 극장업자들의 반발을 사기도 했으며 극장 날짜를 잡는 데 있어서도 횡포를 부렸다. 서울 시내의 개봉관들은 거의가 한 달 중 3주 이상을 중배가 갖다 준 외국영화를 상영하는 데 할애했으며, 심지어 수도극장 등은 아예 중배영화의 전용관이다시피 했다. 그러나 중배를 통해 들어온 미국영화들은 제2차 세계대전 중에 만들어진 작품이 주종을 이루었다. 〈마음의 행로〉, 〈위대한 완쓰〉, 〈유혹의 봄〉, 〈아메리카 교향곡〉 등이 바로 그런 것들이다.

3 ―

이처럼 남한의 극장 96개소를 손쉽게 독점하다시피 하여 해방 전의 재고품과 새로 들여온 것을 합쳐 약 100여 편에 달하는 영화를 통해 전국을 장악한 중배는 영화 1편으로 약 450만 원의 수익을 거두었다. 따라서 중배는 1947년 한 해만 해도 4억 5천만 원을 가져간 셈이 된다. 당시 우리 영화의 평균 제작비를 250만 원으로 본다면 그 금액은 엄청난 것이었다. 즉 미군이 가는 곳에 미국영화는 반드시 대규모로 따라갔고, 미국영화는 경제·문화 면에서 침탈의 첨병 역할을 했던 것이다. 뉴욕의 영화수출협회를 본점으로 둔 중배는 1949년 10월까지 국내에서 활동한다는 조건으로 해방 후부터 들어왔는데, 1948년에 들어서는 국내제작 영화의 2배에 해당하는 45편의 영화를 보급해 국내 영화시장을 완전히 장악했다. 이러한 현상은 반제반봉건 민주주의혁명을 열망하는 민중들의 의지를 무마시키고 미국에 대한 숭배심을 조장하는 경제 외적인 기능까지 발휘했다. 미국이 이런 중배에게 갖가지 특혜를 준 것은 당연한 일이었다. 따라서 이에 대한 조선영화동맹을 중심으로 한 국내 영화인들의 반발도 거세었다.

한국영화진흥조합에서 발간한 『한국영화총서』에 따르면 한국영화는 1946년 4편, 1947년 13편, 1948년 22편, 1949년에 20편이 제작되었다. 그러나 조선영화사와 조선영화동맹에서 만든 〈해방뉴스〉 10편과 서울키노의 〈민족전선〉, 〈메―데―〉, 10월영화공장의 〈10월영

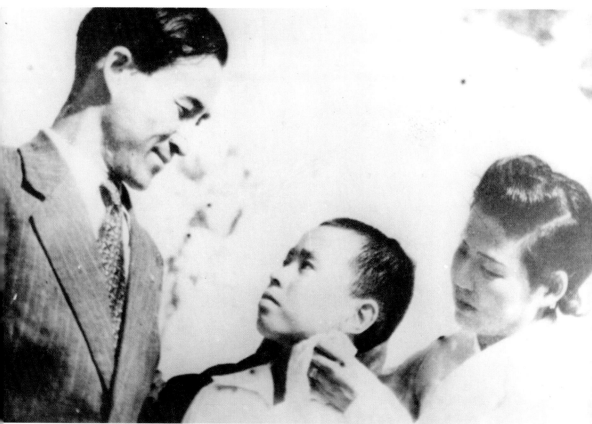

똘똘이의 모험 | 이규환 | 1946 | The Adventure of Ttolttori(Ttoltttori-ui Mohum) | Lee Kyu Hwan

화뉴스〉 2편, 미군정청이 만든 〈군정청 뉴스〉, 미육군 502부대(국립영화제작소의 전신)가 매월 2편씩 만든 〈전진대한보〉, 〈전우〉 등도 이 시기의 산물로 포함해야 할 것이다. 1945년에 만들어진 주요 영화로는 〈해방뉴스〉(1~4보)를 들 수 있다. 이는 8·15 대시위, 일본 사람들의 당황상 등과 조선의용군들의 위용 등을 담은 것으로 기록되어 있다. 물론 이해에 제작된 극영화는 없다. 1946년에 접어들자 극영화로는 〈자유만세〉, 〈똘똘이의 모험〉, 〈안중근 사기〉 등이 나왔고 〈해방뉴스〉(5~8보) 등의 기록영화도 나왔다.

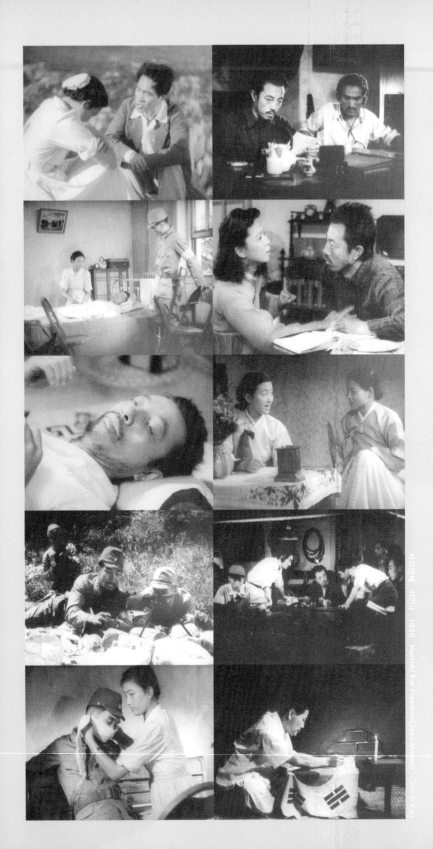

1 —

After the liberation in 1945, the extant film production facilities and materials in Korea included old and basic equipment left behind by the Japanese Empire. Using leftover facilities, the Korean film community had the capacity to produce twenty-four feature films and six to seven cultural and educational films a year, as well as one to two newsreels a month. However, these production figures depended on the continual support and the systematic operation of the facilities, which were actually lacking. For example, the Chosun Film Company(Chosun Younghwa-sa), formerly a Japanese company, burnt down, and the domestic production and adequate supply of raw film stock was impossible to attain. Furthermore, the Central Motion Picture Exchange(Chungang Younghwa-sa), the single and only direct distribution company from the USA, monopolized the exhibition market making the survival of Korean films in the Korean market extremely difficult. The meagre infrastructure, the shortage of raw film stock, and the disadvantaged film market and the film industry's subsequent lack of profits kept the Korean film community from improving its status. During the liberation period, between August 1945 and August 1948, the South Korean film community produced about 15 to 16 feature films, 3 to 4 cultural films, 5 to 6 documentaries, and many newsreels such as ⟨Liberty News⟩.

Among the number of feature films at this time, half were produced as silent films because of the shortage of sound-equipped film projectors in most Korean cities. At the same time, 16mm films became popular. Film companies such as Chosun Film Company, Seoul Kino, Koryo Film Association(Koryo Younghwa Hyuphoi), Kukdong Film Company(Kukdong Younghwa-sa), and Namil Film Company(Namil Younghwa-sa) produced films between 1945 and 1946. According to documents from 1948, there were ten extant film companies in Seoul. In reality, however, only half of them had the capacity to produce films. Prices for raw film stock fluctuated everyday, and costs for film

새로운 맹서 신경균 1947 A New Promise(Saero-un Maengse) Shin Kyong Gyun

수우 | 안종화 | 1948 | Sorrowful Rain(Soowoo) | Ahn Jong Hwa

development and other production resources were extremely prohibitive. As for the exhibitors, the main cinemas in Seoul were equipped with projectors that accommodated both 35mm and 16mm films. At the time, the list of cinemas in Seoul included: Kukje Cinema(Kukje Kukjang, formerly known as Myungchi Jwa), Kukdo Cinema(Kukdo Kukjang), Woomi Gwan, Sudo Cinema(Sudo Kukjang), Dansong Sa, Chungang Cinema(Chungang Kukjang), Jeil Cinema(Jeil Kukjang), Dongyang Cinema(Dongyang Kukjang) and Seoul Cinema(Seoul Kukjang).

2 —

The direct distribution of American films in the Korean market was so effective that they secured nearly the whole market. After American films were advanced into all the world's markets during the First World War, they were strategically placed to support the success of the Second World War. The exportation of American films began in the UK and other Western European countries such as France and Italy, and then gradually

검사와 여선생 윤대룡 1948 | A Public Prosecutor and a Teacher(Geomsa-wa Yeo-Sunsaeng) Yoon Dae Ryong

spread to all of the world's markets. According to documents from 1946, the profit of US film distributions to overseas markets was 900 million dollars, which was approximately 17% of the total profits in the US film industry. It was during this time that the US established an organization in Japan called the Central Motion Picture Exchange(CMPE). This organization was a collaborative body of representatives from eight US film companies, the US Department of the Army, and the State Department. The CMPE alone was in charge of exporting US films and directly distributing them in Japan and Korea.

The CMPE had a branch office in Korea. It absorbed half of the profits from all of the cinemas showing its films and it was known to act so arrogantly about the releasing dates of the films that exhibitors expressed repulsion toward this organization. The foreign films distributed by the CMPE occupied the majority of the screen time in most Korean cinemas. Some cinemas such as the Sudo Cinema exclusively screened films from the CMPE. However, the majority of films exported through the CMPE were mostly produced during the Second World War. Examples of these were: ⟨Random Harvest⟩(1942), ⟨The Great Waltz⟩(1938) and ⟨Rhapsody in Blue⟩(1945).

3

Without having to exert much effort, the CMPE seized control of South Korea's ninety-six cinemas by distributing about 100 old and new films, gaining an average of 4.5 million won profit out of one film. This means that in 1947 the CMPE must have gained about 450 million won in profit for the US film companies. These figures are significant, given that the average production capital of a Korean film at the time was 2.5 million won. Wherever the US army headed, US films always followed as a supporting guard of American culture and economy. The CMPE was actually a sub-group of the Motion Picture Export Association(MPEA), which was located in New York City, and the organization assembled in Korea with the intention to operate until

October 1949. However, with the distribution of 45 US films in Korea in 1948, which was double the number of Korean films produced the same year, it ruled Korea's domestic film market. Ironically, this phenomenon seemed to appease Korean audiences who longed for anti-imperialism, anti-feudalism and democratic revolution. The US films promoted admiration toward America to audiences and the CMPE received preferential treatment from the United States Army Military Government In Korea(USAMGIK), which aroused resistance from the Korean film community, especially by those who were members of the Korean Film Union(Chosun Younghwa Dongmaeng).

According to the 「Korean Film Collection(Hanguk Younghwa Chongseo)」, published in 1977 by the Korean Motion Picture Promotion Corporation(MPPC), the number of films produced in 1946 was four. There were thirteen films produced in 1947; twenty-two in 1948; and twenty in 1949. However, during this time, the Chosun Film Company and the Korean Film Union produced ten ⟨Liberty News⟩ newsreels. Seoul Kino made ⟨National Frontline⟩ and ⟨May Day⟩. The October Film Factory(Shiwol Younghwa Gongjang) made ⟨October Film News⟩. The USAMGIK produced a bimonthly newsreel called ⟨The USAMGIK News⟩. Finally, the US Army 502nd military unit, the predecessor of the National Film Production Center, produced ⟨Report of Korea's Progress(Chunjin Daehan-bo)⟩ and ⟨Fellow Soldiers(Jeon-woo)⟩. These important documentaries and films produced by the military should be considered as a product of this time. The major documentary produced in 1945 was ⟨Liberation News⟩(no. 1 to no. 4); they include coverage of the great demonstrations on Liberation Day, images of confused Japanese people and grand appearances of Chosun militiamen. There were no feature films produced in 1945. In 1946, however, ⟨Hurrah! For Freedom(Jayu Manse)⟩, ⟨Adventure of Ttolttori(Ttolttori-ui Mohum)⟩, ⟨The Life Story of the Patriot⟩, ⟨Ahn Jung Keun(Ahn Jung Keun Sagi)⟩ were produced as feature films, and ⟨Liberation News⟩(no. 5 to no. 8) was continuously produced.

1—

8 · 15 직후부터 1950년 한국전쟁이 일어나기까지 한국영화는 혼란과 갈등의 집합체였다. 일본의 침략전쟁에 강제로 동원되어 패전국의 식민지 상황에 처해 있는 시기였기에, 한국영화계 역시 그만한 곤란을 겪고 있었다. 한국이 처한 혼란과 갈등은 자주적인 단일국가로 가느냐, 그렇지 않으면 비자주적인 분열국가로 가느냐 하는 것이었다. 어떤 것이든 현실에서 자유로울 수 없었던 그 당시의 상황에서, 한국영화계 또한 예외가 아니었다. 1920년대 말부터 1930년대 초까지 조선영화가 성숙할 수 있었던 기간이었다면, 이후 해방까지는 일제에 의해 강제된 몰락기였다. 이후 겨우 해방이 되었으나 이 또한 재몰락의 과정이기도 했다. 당시 영화계는 영화인들의 노력이라든가 영화계 고유의 동력에 의해 움직이고 있는 것이 아니었다. 그 시기의 정치 · 사회적 동향에 따라 좌우되었다고 해도 결코 지나친 말이 아니다. 이런 현상은 비단 해방공간에서만 해당되는 사항이 아니다. 이는 대중적 파급력이 높고 자본주의적 이윤 추구에 따라 제작 · 배급되는 영화예술의 고유한 운명인지도 모른다. 특히 당시는 모든 분야에서 좌파와 우파가 다른 입장을 지닌 채 첨예하게 대립해 있던 급박한 시기였으므로 정치 동향에 따른 영화현실의 가변성은 더욱 컸던 셈이다.

〈똘똘이의 모험〉(1946)은 〈임자 없는 나룻배〉(1932)의 감독인 이규환 연출작으로서, 창고에서 쌀을 훔쳐 북으로 가려는 도적들을 추적해 일망타진하는 똘똘이와 복남이의 이야기인데, 당시의 평문들은 하나같이 이 작품을 비판했다. 〈안중근 사기〉(1946)는 이구영 연출로서 안중근 의사의 일대기를 극화한 영화인데 주목을 받지 못한 것으로 기록되어 있다. 마지막으로 〈자유만세〉는 친일영화를 만든 대표적인 감독인 최인규의 출세작이기도 하다. 이 작품은 관객들의 큰 지지를 받았으며 해방 후 독립영화의 대명사로 꼽힌다. 반면 조선영화사에서 제작하고 조선영화동맹의 열성맹원들이 주축이 되어 만든 〈해방뉴스〉는 급박하고 중요한 시대상황들, 예컨대 민전결성대회, 3 · 1운동 기념행사 등을 차례로 담아나갔다. 즉 조선영화동맹의 구성원들은 당장 극영화를 만들기 위해 힘을 모으기보다는 자주독립국가를 만드는 데 일차적인 목표를 두고 이에 따르는 기록영화의 제작에 주력했던 것으로 볼 수 있다.

여명 이중화 1948 Daybreak(Yeo-myung) Ahn Jong Hwa

2 —

　〈자유만세〉는 대중들이 겪은 해방의 감격과 일제에 대한 분노를 극적으로 구성한 최인규의 대표작이다. 주인공 한중은 심상찮은 정세(해방을 눈앞에 둔 상황)를 감옥에서 감지하고 탈출하여 동지의 집에 숨어든다. 한중은 동지의 소개로 어느 여간호사와 그 어머니가 사는 집으로 거처를 옮기고 동지들과 무장봉기를 준비하면서, 이에 반대하는 동지들과는 심각한 논쟁을 벌인다. 이후 다른 동지가 일경에게 잡힌 것을 구출하다가 쫓겨 기생 미향의 방에 들어서게 되고 미향은 한중에게 반해 그의 아지트로 와서 일을 돕겠다고 한다. 반면 미향은 그의 정부였던 일경 남부의 추적을 모르고 있었다. 결국 남부의 공격으로 미향은 숨을 거두고 한중은 부상당한 채 체포되고 만다. 그러나 간호사 혜자의 도움으로 한중은 옥에서 탈출한다. 이 영화에서 우선 눈에 띄는 점은 독립을 꿈꾸는 한중의 행적을 그려나가는 동시에 한중이 위기를 겪으며 극복하는 과정은 전적으로 통속 애정물의 서술구조를 따르고 있다는 점이다. 즉 한중은 미향의 열정 때문에 체포되고, 혜자에 의해 구출된다. 물론 이것은 검열에 의한 것이라기보다는 매표수익을 노린 관습적인 서술방식이다. 이는 현재 필름으로는 남아있지 않지만, 다른 자료를 통하여 알 수 있는 많은 일제하 한국영화들이 지닌 공통된 특징이기도 하다.

　〈자유만세〉(1946)의 서술 속에서 우리가 또 하나 발견할 수 있는 것은 감정의 전개가 기계적으로 이루어지고 있다는 점이다. 앞서 기술한 장면에서 보듯 미향이 한중을 숨겨주는 과정이 조금은 기계적으로 이루어지고 있으며 이에 이어지는 장면은 더욱 비약적으로 전개된다. 즉 이후의 장면에서 미향은 한중의 영웅적인 모습에 감동하여 눈물을 흘리면서 자신의 삶을 반성한다. 현대영화에 익숙한 관객들이 보기에는 지극히 함량부족한 작품인 것이다. 〈자유만세〉의 감정비약과 상황설정의 비사실성은 한국영화의 고질적인 관습이 않나 생각한다. 이런 경향은 작품의 대세를 크게 흠잡을 것이 없다면, 세부묘사의 결점은 덮어두는 당시의 풍토를 보여주고 있는 셈이다. 또 한중과 무장봉기를 반대하는 동지들이 논쟁하는 과정에서 보이고 있는 정세관은 비현실적이며 맹목적이기조차 하다. 실제 일제 탄압의 말기에 그러한 무장조직을 국내에서 운영했다는 설정이 비현실적이며, 영화적 허구라는 사실을 감안하고서라도 당시의 항일운동을 침착하게 그려내는 데는 역부족이었던 것이다.

마음의 고향 윤용규 1949 The Hometown In My Heart(Maeum-ui Gohyang) Yoon Yong Kyu

3 ─

또 일제의 탄압에 관한 몇 마디 말과 부정확한 상황설정을 제외하고 간호사 혜자의 집(이 집에는 경제력이 없는 어머니와 딸만이 살고 있다)에는 일제 말기의 참혹한 경제적 고통이 전혀 드러나 있지 않을뿐더러 사람들이 평화롭게 교회를 다니거나 간호사들이 배구놀이를 하는 등 당시의 긴박한 상황과는 동떨어져 있다. 〈자유만세〉는 일제에 항거하는 정신을 나름대로 담은 좋은 작품인 것만은 틀림없지만 다른 한편으로는 해방의 감격을 적절하게 상업적으로 차용했으며 또 이를 표현하는 데 있어서도 앞에서 본 대로 많은 역부족을 드러내 보였다. 하지만 여러 결함에도 불구하고 〈자유만세〉가 지닌 항일영화로서의 가치와 열정과 이에 대한 구체적인 영화적 표현능력이 당시로서는 뛰어났다는 것을 간과해서는 안 될 것이다. 우리는 이러한 토대 위에서, 왜 최인규는 이런 식으로 작업을 했으며, 그것이 후대 한국영화에서는 어떻게 변모, 발전했는가를 밝혀야 할 것이다.

1947년에 접어들자 진보계열의 영화제작은 급속하게 자취를 감추게 된다. 뿐만 아니라 제작상황의 악화로 16밀리 무성영화가 다시 출현하는 등 퇴행현상을 보이기도 한다. 김영순의 〈불멸의 밀사〉, 윤봉춘의 〈윤봉길 의사〉, 〈3·1혁명기〉 등 민족정신을 고양하는 영화, 전창근의 〈해방된 내 고향〉, 이규환의 〈민족의 새벽〉, 신경균의 〈새로운 맹서〉, 김정환의 〈천사의 마음〉 등 사회계몽물과 이규환의 〈그들의 행복〉이라는 오락성 선도물, 임운학의 권선징악적 조선시대 야사인 〈그들이 가는 길〉 등 그다지 주목할 것 없는 작품들이 이 시기의 산물이다. 한편 〈해방뉴스〉(9, 10보)도 제작되었는데 이 속에는 여운형의 장례를 중심으로 그의 투쟁사를 수록한 것도 있는 것으로 알려져 있다.

1948년에 접어들자 진보계열의 영화는 물론 조선영화동맹의 사회적 활동도 거의 자취를 감추었다. 이때는 이승만을 중심으로 한 세력이 정국의 주도권을 잡아나갔던 시기이기도 하다. 이 기간에 나온 주목할 만한 작품으로는 공보처에서 제작하고 안경호가 연출한 〈민족의 절규〉가 있다. 이는 이승만의 연설과 업적을 수록한 기록영화다. 또 최인규는 미국공보원의 제작으로 국민들이 단정수립을 위한 선거에 참가할 것을 독려하는 계몽영화 〈국민투표〉를 만들었다. 이 영화는 미군정 측이 직접 국민투표의 정당성을 선전하고 참가를 독려하기 위해 제작한 것이었다. 윤봉춘은 〈유관순〉이라는 민족계몽물을 만들었는데, 한편 전창근

성벽을 뚫고 | 한형모 | 1949 | Breaking the Wall(Sungbyuk-eul Ttulgo) | Han Hyung Mo

은 〈그 얼굴〉이라는 순애보를 다룬 영화를 만들기도 했다. 1945년 8월 15일 단정수립 이전까지 제작된 영화들을 보면 우선 주제별로는 독립운동 관계물, 계몽물이 가장 많으며, 뚜렷한 정치적 입장을 가진 영화로는 조선영화동맹 측과 미군정 측 혹은 관에서 제작한 것으로 대별된다. 물론 그것들은 기록영화의 형식을 취하고 있다. 이렇게 어려운 상황에서도 윤봉춘은 계속 독립운동과 관련된 작품만을 만들었는데, 이러한 자세는 높이 평가할 만하다.

1 —

The films made during the post-liberation era, between the liberation(1945) and the Korean War(1950), reflected aggregated confusion and conflicts. Previously, the Korean film community had been forced to serve the Japanese imperialist war. After the liberation, filmmakers faced new hurdles in pondering their own existence. There were fierce debates about whether Korea should unify as one autonomous country, or whether Korea should be separated, remaining dependent on other countries. Although the quality of Korean films and the skills of individual filmmakers advanced between the late 1920s and early 1930s, the number of local productions shrank substantially under the more restrictive Japanese film regulations. This situation continued until the liberation of Korea in 1945, and, even after the liberation, this inferior status remained unchanged. The voluntary efforts of Korean filmmakers were not acknowledged. The film community at that time was largely influenced by the political and social trends in Korea. However, this may not be a unique situation only to be found in the liberated spaces of Korean culture. Perhaps it is a characteristic fate of the film art form, which has an extensive reach to mass audiences and films are primarily produced and distributed in order to make profit. At this time, in particular, Korea was experiencing sharp conflicts between left and right wing philosophies in every field, and this shifting of the political consciousness greatly influenced the films being made.

⟨Adventure of Ttolttori(Ttolttori-ui Mohum)⟩(1946) was produced by the director, Lee Kyu Hwan, who previously made the classic film, ⟨A Ferryboat without a Ferryman (Imjaumneun Narutbae)⟩(1932), under the Japanese rule. ⟨Adventure of Ttolttori⟩ was a story about two adventurous and mischievous kids named Ttolttori and Bok Nam. They happened to assist in the arrest of thieves who stole rice and tried to escape to North Korea. Most of the film's reviews were not favourable. ⟨The Life Story of the Patriot⟩, ⟨Ahn Jung Keun(Ahn Jung Keun Sagi)⟩(1946) was a dramatised biography of Ahn Jung Keun, the leader of the independence movement. This too did not attract much attention from the public. ⟨Hurrah!

운명의 손 한형모 1954 The Hands of Destiny(Woonmyung-ui Son) Han Hyung Mo

For Freedom(Jayu Manse)⟩ brought fame to the director Choi In Gyu, who had previously produced pro-Japanese films before the liberation. General audiences seemed to love ⟨Hurrah! For Freedom⟩ and it has been counted as a representative of independent films after the liberation. Apart from these feature films, ⟨Liberation News⟩ produced by Chosun Film Company and the members of Korean Film Union covered important events such as the forming of the Interim People's Committee and a Commemorative Congregation for the March 1st independence movement in 1919. Members of the Korean Film Union appeared to concentrate on making documentaries, which aimed at establishing an independent country rather than making feature films.

2

⟨Hurrah! For Freedom(Jayu Manse)⟩(1946) is the most well known film made by Choi In Gyu. It dramatically expressed the nation's elation from the liberation and it's indignation toward the Japanese Empire. The synopsis of this film is described here: The main character, Han Jung, is a prisoner who escapes after sensing the coming liberation. He hides in his friend's house first and then moves to a safer place where a nurse, Hye Ja, and her mother live. Han Jung tries to gather a crowd of people in order to stage an armed uprising against the Japanese but he finds that not all of the members of the crowd agree with him. He, nonetheless, remains with them and later on becomes a hero because he is able to rescue his friend from the Japanese police. In return, the Japanese police chase Jung. While running away, Jung happens to hide in a gisaeng house(geisha in Korea). Mi Hyang, a gisaeng who is attracted to him, volunteers to help Jung realize his plan. Drama builds as Mi Hyang's ex-lover, a Japanese policeman named Nam Bu, pursues Jung. Nam Bu and Jung fight, and Mi Hyang dies by coming between them. Wounded Jung is arrested. In the end, Jung escapes from prison a second time with the help of Hye Ja. The film's most outstanding and significant point is the fact that Han

Jung is an independence movement leader, and his ability to overcome his crisis progresses with the narrative's melodrama. For example, Jung is arrested because of Mi Hyang's passion toward him, and he is rescued because of Hye Ja's help. This kind of narrative was not only the outcome of the censorship policy at the time, but also an attempt to make a box office hit. It was one of the distinguished characteristics of Korean films produced under the Japanese rule. Only a portion of this film survives today.

The development of the emotions in each character from 〈Hurrah! For Freedom(Jayu Manse)〉 seems to be perfunctory. As mentioned above, the scene where Mi Hyang gives shelter to Han Jung is illogical and the continuing events are without reason. Mi Hyang is moved by Han's heroic deeds and is shown regretting her life by crying. The film lacks the standard quality required for a modern audience. This trend of jumping between emotions within an unrealistic background was an ongoing source of trouble for Korean films. It reveals that there was a tendency to ignore detailed descriptions in favour of a story that generally made sense. The situation that Jung shared with his friends in preparing for the armed uprising was unrealistic and reckless. Furthermore, the creation of an armed militia in Korea under the Japanese rule, though it was near the end of the colonial period, was a complete fabrication. Hence, the film was incapable of providing a portrait of the resistance movement around that time.

3 —

The miserable economic situation of the late colonial period was not portrayed well in 〈Hurrah! For Freedom〉 except for a few moments of dialogue referring to the oppression by the Japanese government. The background described in the film is also inaccurate. For example, nurses leisurely play volleyball together and others peacefully attend church. Hye Ja is responsible for making a living for her family, her mom and

춘향전 | 이규환 | 1955 | Chunhyang Story(Chunhyang-jeon) | Lee Kyu Hwan

구원의 애정 | 민경식 | 1955 | Affection for Salvation(Guwon-ui Ae-jung) | Min Kyung Sik

주검의 상자 | 김기영 | 1955 | **A Box for a Corpse(Jugum-ui Sangja)** | Kim Ki Young

herself. Though her mom has no financial means to support the family, she does not appear to be suffering from the terrible economic situation. All of the situations depicted in the film for that matter are different from what actually happened in reality. Though ⟨Hurrah! For Freedom⟩ exploits its content for commercial value by taking advantage of touching moments and portrayals of liberation from Japan, this film expresses the fighting spirit of Koreans against the Japanese Empire, and it is a respectable piece of a work in that sense. The level of specific description about the passion for independence was comparatively high in spite of many shortcomings noted as a well-made film. The film's greatest value is summarized as an anti-Japanese and Korean liberation film. However, important questions remain unanswered, such as why director Choi focused on this kind of narrative style and how the film influenced the films that came after it.

At the start of 1947, films from the progressive and more liberal filmmakers began to disappear rapidly. Production conditions were worsening and 16mm silent films began to show up again. Film culture in Korea began to degenerate. The films produced in 1947 included works that inspired a national spirit, such as ⟨Immortal Secret Envoy(Bulmyol-ui Milsa)⟩ by Kim Young Soon, and ⟨The Patriot, Yoon Bong Gil(Yoon Bong Gil Ui-sa)⟩ and ⟨March 1st Revolution(Sam-il Hyuck-myung)⟩ by Yoon Bong Chun. There were also a number of films that attempted to offer social enlightenment. These included: ⟨Liberated My Hometown(Haebang-dwen Nae Gohyang)⟩ by Chun Chang Geun, ⟨The Daybreak of Koreans(Minjok-ui Sae-byuk)⟩ by Lee Kyu Hwan, ⟨A New Promise(Saero-un Maengse)⟩ by Shin Kyong Gyun, and ⟨Heart of an Angel(Chunsa-ui Ma-um)⟩ by Kim Chung Hwan. Lee Kyu Hwan produced ⟨Their Happiness(Geudeul-ui Hangbok)⟩ as an entertaining educational film. ⟨The Way They Have Trodden(Geudeul-i Ganeun Gil)⟩, directed by Im Woon Hak, used the background of the Chosun Dynasty and told a simple story about how good deeds would be rewarded in the end.

피아골 | 이강천 | 1955 | Pia Village(Piagol) | Lee Kang Chun

〈Liberation News〉(no. 9 and no. 10) was also produced in 1947, including a retrospective of Yeo Woon Hyung, a well-known independence movement leader of Korea. This later film celebrated Yeo Woon Hyung's life with footages of his recent funeral.

In 1948, the Korean Film Union seemed to avoid all social activities as well as making the type of progressive films it was known for. During this time, Syng Man Rhee and his men began to take control of the political leadership in Korea. 〈The Cry of Korean People(Minjok-ui Jeol-gyu)〉, directed by Ahn Kyung Ho, was a noticeable film in this year. It was a documentary recording of Rhee Syng Man's activities and speeches produced by the Public Information Bureau. With the sponsorship of the United States Information Service, Choi In Gyu produced an educational film called 〈National Vote(Kookmin Toopyo)〉 in order to promote voting for the up-coming election. This directly facilitated the mobilization of the public's attitudes and awareness for the establishment of an independent government. More specifically, this film was designed and created by the USAMGIK to promote the righteousness of the national vote and to encourage Koreans to actively participate in it. Around this time, Yoon Bong Chun made 〈Yu Kwan Soon(Yu Kwan Soon)〉, which was a national enlightenment film about a young patriotic girl. 〈That Face(Geu Eol-gul)〉 was a love story produced by Jun Chang Geun. Between the liberation in 1945 and the establishment of the South Korean government in 1948, most films dealt with the subject of the independence movement and the process of social enlightenment. The Chosun Film Company and the USAMGIK produced mostly documentary films with clear political standpoints. One director in particular, Yoon Bong Chun, continued making films with scenarios concerning the liberation movement despite the difficult and changing political and social situation.

1

　　1945년 이후 한국영화사 연구에서 가장 큰 걸림돌이 되는 것은 당시의 상황을 객관적으로 보여주는 필름이라든가 체계적인 자료가 부족하다는 점이다. 게다가 전쟁을 겪고 난 후 정리된 자료들은 좌우 갈등에서 비롯된 편향적인 관점에서 서술된 것이라 그 신빙도와 객관성의 측면에서 온전하다고만 할 수는 없을 것이다. 따라서 이 시기의 주요한 사항들을 이해하기 위해서는 해방 전과 전쟁 직후의 한국영화계에 대한 일정한 정보와 해석력을 갖춰야 한다. 한국영화계의 초창기부터 해방 전 사이에 벌어진 조선영화계에 대한 견해가 없이는 해방 직후의 사정을 명확하게 헤아리기는 힘들 것이다. 1945년에 맞이한 해방은 30여 년 동안에 걸친 민중들의 간고한 투쟁과 파시즘에 대항해 공동전선을 편 미·소 양대국의 힘에 의해 주어진 것이었다. 따라서 당시의 조선 문제는 세계사적 흐름상 중요한 것이었으므로 갈 길이 바쁜 해방민중은 도처에 숨어 있던 많은 암초와 직면하지 않으면 안 되었다. 특히 해방은 주체적으로 쟁취한 것이 아니었기 때문에 해방이 곧 자주독립국가의 건설로 이어지지 못했고, 한반도는 두 강대국의 군사력에 의해 점령되어 분할되는 운명을 맞아야만 했다.

　　한반도 처리에 관한 구체적인 방침이나 강대국 간의 협정이 마련되지 않은 상태에서 일본은 패망했고, 소련이 북한지역에 진주하자 미국은 한반도의 가능한 한 부분이라도 자신의 영향권 아래 두어야 할 시급한 필요를 느끼게 되었다. 이런 조건 아래에서 38선은 미국이 만든 잠정적인 군사분계선이자 민족분단의 상징으로서 한반도의 운명을 좌우하게 되었다. 1945년 9월 8일, 미군의 진주는 당시 한반도 문제를 이해하는 결정적인 계기가 된다. 알다시피 미국은 해방 이후 구식민지 질서의 온존과 재편을 통해 자국의 기반을 강화하는 한편, 북한에 진주한 소련군에 대항해 한반도 남쪽에 '공산주의에 대한 방벽을 구축'한다는 임무를 충실히 수행하기 위해 미군을 진주시켰다. 미군정은 일본이 남긴 식민지 지배체제가 남한을 통치하는 데 대단히 유효하다는 사실을 직시한 후, 과거 친일 경력 등은 문제 삼지 않고 여러 인력들을 정부조직 운영에 동원하였다.

망나니 비사(막난이 비사) | 김성민 | 1955 | The Sad Story of Mangnani(Mangnani Bisa) | Kim Sung Min

교차로(일명: 청춘가) | 유현목 | 1956 | The Cross Road(Gyocha-ro) | You Hyun Mok

　　이런 과정 속에서 사회주의자들은 물론 많은 민족주의자들도 배제되었다. 미군정은 일제가 노골적으로 조선민족을 탄압하기 위해 만든 법령을 폐지하는 한편, 그 외 통치에 필요한 법들, 예컨대 보안법 등은 형식만 바꾼 채 그대로 사용했다. 결국 질서유지와 효율적인 통치라는 명분으로 실시된 미군정의 통치정책은 식민지 잔재의 완전한 청산을 요구하던 민족좌파 세력에게 불리한 것이었고, 민족우파들에게는 상대적으로 유리한 위치에 설 수 있는 계기를 가져다주었다. 이러한 어지러운 정국 속에서 대립과 각축은 문화예술계에서도 일어났다. 당시 대표적인 단체로는 1945년 8월 16일에 발족한 조선문화건설중앙협의회와 곧이어 9월 30일에 발족한 조선프롤레타리아예술동맹 등이 있다. 이 단체들은 좌익진영의 인사들이 주도한 것인데, 시국을 바라보는 견해 차이와 앞으로의 문화예술을 어떤 방향으로 진행할 것인가 하는 차이 때문에 결국 갈라지게 되었다.

　　여기에서는 문학인들이 주도적으로 활동했다. 이는 일제시대 카프운동 시절부터 생긴 전통이기도 했다. 조선문화건설중앙협의회(이하 문건중협)를 주도한 인물이 임화, 김남천 등이었다면 조선프롤레타리아예술동맹(이하 프로예맹)을 주도한 인물은 이기영, 한설야 등이었다. 이들의 분열을 일제시대 카프조직의 해소를 두고 카프 해소파와 카프 비해소파가 대립한 연장선상에서 파악하는 견해도 있다. 영화부문 역시 문건중협의 산하단체인 조선영화건설본부(이하 영건)와 조선프롤레타리아예술동맹 산하단체인 조선프롤레타리아영화동맹(이하 프로영맹)이 1945년에 만들어지고, 이후 1946년 초에 문건중협과 프로예맹이 조선문화단체총연맹(이하 문화연맹)으로 통합되자 영화조직들 역시 조선영화동맹으로 통합한다.

　　반면 이러한 좌익진영 문예인들의 활발한 활동에 비해서는 상대적으로 열세에 놓였던 보수적인 예술인들도 점차 그 모습을 드러내기 시작했다. 그 출발은 아무래도 신탁통치안을 놓고 논쟁이 벌어진 시기라고 볼 수 있을 것이다. 신탁통치안은 한반도 독립을 전제로 한 임시적인 한국 민주정부 수립이라는 구체적인 안까지 갖춘 것이었는데도 미국의 고의적인 왜곡 보도가 갈등을 촉발시켰다.[1] 한국역사연구회 편, 『한국사강의』(한울아카데미, 1989), pp. 346~347. 모스크바 3상회의의 내용이 국내에 알려진 것은 1945년 12월 27일이었는데 최초의 미국발 보도내용은 "미국은 즉시 독립을 주장하며 소련은 탁치를 주장한다"는 것이었다. 그러나 이것은 사실과 반대될뿐더러 탁치와 독립을 대립시키는 내용이었다. 이후 정국은 급속하게 신탁통치를 쟁점으로 좌파와 우파 간의 치열한 대립으로 발전하게 되었다. 우파로 분류할 수 있는 문예인들은 우선 단체를 결성함으로써 좌파 측에 맞서고자 했다. 전조선문필가협회의 결성(1946.3.13)과 그 별동대 형식으로 결성을 본 조선청년문학가협회(1946.4.4)가 바로 그것이다. 2 신기, 「해방 직후 문학비평의 흐름」, 「해방 3년의 비평문학」(세계, 1988), p. 17.

전조선문필가협회는 민주주의 국가건설, 완전자주독립, 세계평화와 인류평화의 이념을 구현하는 조선문화의 발전, 세계제패를 꾀하는 비인도적 경향의 배격을 강령으로 삼았고 정인보가 회장을 맡았다. 정인보, 박종화, 안호상, 양주동 등이 요직을 맡아 운영한 이 단체의 연예부장으로는 친일 영화감독인 안석주(본명 안석영)가 임명되었다. 3 조선문예사 편, 「재일조선문화연감」(조선문예사, 1949), p. 129. 조선청년문학가협회에서는 박종화를 명예회장으로 하고 회장 김동리를 중심으로 유치환, 박두진, 조지훈, 서정주, 박목월, 조연현 등이 활약했다. 이 단체의 강령이 전조선문필가협회의 그것과 비슷했음은 당연한 일이었다. 반탁을 쟁점으로 모인 문예인들의 공식적 출현은 당시 영화계에서도 표면화되었는데 조선영화극작가협회가 바로 그것이다. 조선영화극작가협회는 '새로운 시대의 구상과 진실성을 가지고 향기 높은 새 전통의 수립과 영화예술의 질적 향상'을 강령으로 내세웠다.

4 —

정치적 색채가 배제된 이러한 주장은 순수예술성을 전면에 내세움으로써 민족자주진영 영화인들이 내건 일제잔재와 봉건적 잔재의 청산이라는 정치적 강령에 우회적으로 대응하고자 한 의도를 내비치고 있다. 즉 1945년 12월 16일에 발족4 자유신문, 1945.12.19한 조선영화동맹에 자의든 타의든 가담하지 않았던 소수의 보수적이거나 친일 경력이 분명했던 영화인 및 문학인들인 안석영, 김광주, 조연현 등과 백범 김구의 영향권 아래에 있던 감독 전창근 등이 중심이 되어 1946년 11월 4일에 이 단체를 결성했다. 당시 남한의 영화인들은 영건, 프로영맹 그리고 조선영화극작가협회 등으로 집결되어 있었다. 영건은 1945년 8월 18일 문건중협의 산

단종애사 | 전창근 | 1956 | The Sad Story of King Danjong(Danjong Ae-sa) | Jun Chang Geun

구원의 정화 | 이만흥 | 1956
Purification and Salvation(Guwon-ui Chunghwa) | Lee Man Heung

격퇴(일명: 우리는 이렇게 싸웠다) | 이강천 | 1956
The Defeat(Gyok-twoe) | Lee Kang Chun

하기관으로서 이재명, 김정혁, 박기채, 이병일 등을 중심으로 발족했는데 주지하다시피 박기채와 이병일은 친일영화를 만든 감독들이고 이재명은 일제 말기까지 제작자로서 활동했으며, 김정혁은 일제가 조선영화인들을 탄압하기 위해 만든 영화인 자격심사위원회의 간사로 일했던 사람이다. 이후 9월 24일의 영건 주최 조선영화인총대회는 윤백남을 위원장으로, 서기장에 김정혁, 집행위원에 이재명, 서광제, 방한준, 김한 등을 선출했다.

윤백남은 일제와 긴밀한 관계를 가진 당시의 인텔리로서 한동안 영화계를 떠나 있던 사람이며, 서광제는 카프영화계의 대표적인 평론가로서 활동하다가 이후 친일적인 태도를 취했던 인물이다. 반면 같은 해 11월 13일에 결성된 프로영맹은 중앙집행위원장 추민, 서기장 정준락, 집행위원 김형기, 나웅, 홍현중, 강호, 이병일, 허달, 민정식, 정준락, 석일량, 맹원에 김한, 독은기, 김영화, 이명우, 유장산, 김성춘, 최칠복 등으로 구성되었다. 프로영맹이 영건에 비해 훨씬 더 진보적인 입장에 설 수 있었던 것은 카프영화운동의 주도적인 감독이었던 강호와 카프연극 등에 관계했던 추민 등이 주도했다는 사실로서 짐작할 수 있다. 하지만 그 외 대부분의 집행위원과 맹원들은 사실상 일제 말기 당시의 강압적인 분위기 속에서 친일적인 영화활동을 하지 않을 수 없었던 인물들과 영화적 소양은 물론 그 이후의 활동에서도 거취가 불분명한 인물들이었다. 이러한 분리활동은 영화계 단체들의 상부 조직이라고도 할 수 있는 문건중협과 프로예맹과의 의견 차이를 반영한 것이었고, 이 의견 차이는 1930년대 카프영화운동 시기의 의견 대립(강호 등과 서광제 등의 갈등)의 재현이라고 할 수도 있을 것이다.

5

문예계의 판도를 크게 좌우했던 문건중협과 프로예맹은 모두 「8월 테제」의 내용, 즉 반제반봉건 부르주아민주주의혁명을 문화예술운동의 정치적 과제로 인정했다. 따라서 영건과 프로영맹의 방침 또한 각 중앙 조직의 방침을 인정하고 존중하는 방향으로 나갈 수밖에 없었을 것이다. 영건과 프로영맹은 1945년 12월 16일에 조선영화동맹으로 통합하였다. 반면 조선영화극작가협회의 영화인들은 한국영화감독구락부를 결성한다. 이 단체는 후일 대한영화협의회로 바뀌고 또 이를 중심으로 오늘날의 한국영화인협회가 생기게 된다(이 단체들에서 활동한 안석영이 초기에는 영건 소속이었다는 기록도 있다).

처녀별 오발춘 1956 The Virgin Star(Chunyo Byel), Yoon Bong Chun

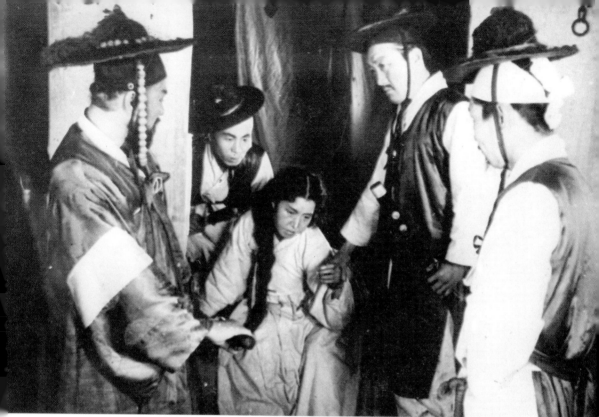

처녀별 | 윤봉춘 | 1956 | The Virgin Star(Chunyo Byol) | Yoon Bong Chun

여하간 안석영이 중심이 되어 1946년 11월 4일에 시나리오 작가들의 모임인 조선영화
극작가협회가 결성되었고 이후 1948년에 윤봉춘, 김소동, 이병일, 이구영, 신경균, 최인규 등
이 중심이 되어 대한영화협의회를 만들었으며 그 의장은 안석영이 맡았다.⁵ 약간 다른 기록으로는 경향
일보(1948.10.25)를 들 수 있는데 여기서는 대한영화협의회가 한국영화감독구락부를 중심으로 결성되었고 중심인물은 안석주, 김영화, 안철영 등이었
다고 기록하고 있다. 윤봉춘은 나운규의 친구로서 일제시대 때의 카프와 대립적인 위치에서 연기자
와 감독으로 활동했는데, 작품으로는 그다지 주목받지 못했으나 일제에 협력하지 않을 정도
로 강직한 성품을 지닌 인물이었다고 전해진다. 이구영은 초창기 영화인으로서 1930년대 중
반부터는 거의 활동을 멈춘 인물이며, 신경균, 최인규, 김영화는 친일영화를 만든 대표적인
감독들이다. 또 안철영은 과도정부 영화과장을 지내기도 한 인물이다. 이들 중 대부분은 조
선영화동맹에 가입했지만 이후 정국의 변화에 따라 처신을 달리한다.

　　한편 해방 직후 북한에서는 1945년 8월 20일 소련군의 진주와 더불어 각 지역에서 건준, 자치대, 치안유지위원회의 명칭으로 자발적인 조직들이 우후죽순으로 생겨났고 약 한 달간에 걸쳐 각 지역 혹은 도 단위로 인민위원회가 발족했다. 1945년 9월 21일 김일성이 '김일성 환영 평양시 군중대회'에 나타났고 조선공산당 북조선분국이 창설되고 북조선임시위원회는 20개 정강을 발표했다. 문예조직으로는 북조선연극동맹(1945.12.24), 평남지구 예술동맹(1946.1.26)이 결성되고 각 지방에 각 부문별 문예동맹체가 조직되었다. 이후 월북한 한설야를 위원장으로 하는 북조선문학예술가동맹(1946.3.25)이 결성되고 이후 이 단체는 이기영을 위원장으로 하는 북조선문학예술총동맹으로 개칭한다.

　　한편 영화계는 북조선문학예술총동맹의 한 동맹으로서 실제 창작은 당중앙위원회 선전선동부 소속 영화반의 형태로 있다가 최초의 장편기록영화인 〈우리의 전설〉의 완성과 함께 발족한 조선기록영화촬영소(1946.7.1), 조선예술영화촬영소(1947.2.6) 등이 발족했다. 동시에 남한의 조선영화동맹과도 관계를 유지해 조선영화동맹이 지부 결성을 할 때 평남지구영화동맹(1946.4.16)으로 참가하기도 했다. 북한 역시 남한처럼 영화제작의 어려움은 있었지만 특히 인력이 서울에 집중돼 있던 탓에 더욱 어려웠을 것으로 짐작된다. 하지만 소련의 지원은 남한과는 또 다른 풍토의 출발점이 되기도 했다. 이미 1945년 10월 29일에 북한과 소련의 첫 무역계약이기도 한 한·소 영화수입계약이 체결되고 기재 지원 등에 힘입어 촬영소 건설이 가능해졌다.

One of the biggest obstacles to studying and writing about Korean film history during the post-liberation era after 1945 is the lack of existing documents and films showing Korea as it was at that time. Though some of the documents remained after the Korean War, they were prejudiced because of the ideological conflicts between the left and right political parties. Therefore, they cannot be trusted entirely in terms of credibility and objectivity. Naturally, a certain amount of background information about the film community before and after the liberation as well as the ability to interpret it is required to understand what really happened. It is hard to understand the reality of the post-liberation period and the thinking of the members of the Korean film community without supporting information such as historical background of the development of Korean films under the Japanese rule. The liberation of Korea in 1945 came about after 35 years of fighting against Japanese fascism, and the USA and the USSR, the world's two superpowers, were key players in this fight. Hence, the hands of others attained the independence of Korea. As a result, the conflict in Korea became part of important world issues, and the Korean people once again encountered many unexpected setbacks by way of achieving its status as an independent country. The liberation was welcomed but it did not result in the establishment of a unified independent country. In the end, the Korean peninsula was divided into the North and South, two separate parts and governed by the USSR and the USA accordingly.

The Japanese Empire was defeated in the Second World War and left Korea immediately after surrendering to the US alliance. Neither talks nor agreements were made or held with Koreans about the way to handle the newly liberated Korean peninsula. All discussions had been privately arranged by the USA and the USSR beforehand. Troops from the USSR advanced into the Northern part of the Korean peninsula and the USA was pressured to maintain control of the Southern part of Korea. The 38 degree parallel was

청춘쌍곡선 靑春雙曲線 1956 Parallel Youth(Chungchun Ssang-goksun) Han Hyung-Mo

청춘쌍곡선 | 한형모 | 1956 | Parallel Youth(Chungchun Ssang-goksun) | Han Hyung Mo

suggested as a cut-off point and a temporary military boundary line was made by the US. The physical dividing line became a symbol of an ideologically separated country. The USA army advanced into southern Korea on September 8, 1945, and this became a crucial event in Korean history. The USA clearly wanted to strengthen its foothold in liberated Korea by securing and restructuring the old colonial system. It seems that the US felt that it had to confront the Soviet Union, which was occupying North Korea at the time. Hence, the goal of the US army was to 'establish a protective wall' for South Korea. In the meantime, the newly created governing body, USAMGIK, recognized that the Japanese colonial system was effective in governing South Korea and invited those involved with the previous Japanese regime to help the USAMGIK. Their previous pro-Japanese careers did not seem to be an issue for the USAMGIK.

자유부인 | 한형모 | 1956 | Madame Freedom(Jayu Buin) | Han Hyung Mo

Many socialists and nationalists were excluded from the talks concerning the initial rebuilding stages. The USAMGIK abolished most of the colonial rules that had been used for the last thirty-six years to oppress all Koreans. However, some important regulations needed for the US administration of South Korea, such as National Security Law, were kept with minor changes. The governing policies of the USAMGIK established the order and efficient control of South Korea. The situation was disadvantageous for the leftists who advocated the removal of all of the leftovers from the colonial time. In turn, this placed the rightists in a better political position. This type of conflict has also made an impact on the cultural field. Representative organizations established around this time include the Chosun Art Construction Headquarters (established on 16 August 1945) and the Chosun Proleta Art Federatio(established on 30 September 1945). These two organizations were both led by left-wing activists, but they clearly expressed different views of the social and political situation. The organizations especially differed on the best directions to pursue in the future development of Korean culture and art.

The leaders of the Chosun Art Construction Headquarters and the Chosun Proleta Art Federatio had literary backgrounds, which had been a traditional phenomenon originating from the Korea Artista Proleta Federatio(KAPF) movement under the Japanese rule. Im Hwa and Kim Nam Chun led the Chosun Art Construction Headquarters, and Lee Ki Young and Han Seol Ya led the Chosun Proleta Art Federatio. Some Korean scholars see their separation as a result of the break-up of the KAPF before the liberation. During the late 1920s and early 1930s, KAPF was separated into two groups, with pro-dispersion supporters on the one side and anti-dispersion supporters on the other side. In 1945, members of the film community formed a sub-organization of the Chosun Art Construction Headquarters called the Chosun Film Construction Headquarters and a sub-group of the Chosun Proleta Art Federatio called the Chosun Proleta Film Federatio. In the beginning of 1946, the Chosun Art Construction Headquarters and the Chosun Proleta Art Federatio were unified as one organization, which became known as the Chosun Cultural Headquarters. Each of their film sub-groups became unified as the Korean Film Union, which was established on 16 February 1946.

3

At the end of 1945, conservative right-wing artists, who had been considered less active than the left-wing artists, began taking an active role in the debates for the UN Trusteeship of Korea. The temporary Korean democratic government formed the structure of this Trusteeship on the premise of gaining independence. However, according to the Organization of Korean Historians(Hanguk Yeoksa Yeongu-hoi) in their edited book, 「Korean History Lecture(Hanguksa Kang-ui)」, published by Hanwool Academy Press in 1989(pp. 346-347), the American press intentionally reported slanted articles about this issue and triggered huge complications between the right and left wing people. Koreans first learned about the US agenda from the content of the Moscow Agreement discussed at the meeting in Moscow in late December 1945 among foreign ministers of the United States, Great Britain, and the USSR. On 27 December 1945, an American press reported that "the USA asserted plans for immediate independence and the USSR asserted the trusteeship." In actuality, this press report was not true, and its news instigated confrontations between the parties that either supported the trusteeship or independence. Koreans were thrown into a fierce debate over the trusteeship of their country. Right and left wing followers strongly opposed each other, and right-wing artists formed organizations to challenge the left-wing side. According to Shin Ki's article, 「The Flow of Literary Criticism after Liberation(Haebang Jik-hoo Munhak Bipyung-ui Hurum)」 published in 「Literary Criticism during Three Years after Liberation(Haebang Sam-nyunui

Munhak)』 by Segye Press in 1948, Seoul(p. 17), in accordance with this trend, right-wing artists formed the Chosun Literary Men's Association(Chun Chosun Munpil-ga Hyuphoi, established on 13 March 1946) and the Chosun Young Literary Writers Association(Chosun Chungnyon Moonhakga Hyuphoi, established on 4 April 1946).

The general principles of the Chosun Literary Men's Association primarily focused on the establishment of a democratic country, complete independence and world peace. The development of Korean culture and the denouncement of the inhumane disposition were also importantly considered as part of these goals. Jung In Bo was elected president of this organization, and Park Jong Hwa, Ahn Ho Sang and Yang Joo Dong offered their leadership together. Ahn Seok Joo, whose original name was Ahn Seok Young, became the manager of the entertainment sector. (According to the 『Chosun Cultural Annual Book(Jaeil Chosun Munhwa Yeon-gam)』 edited by Chosun Literary Art History(Chosun Munye Sa Pyun) in 1949(p. 129), the Korean film community knew Ahn Seok Young as a pro-Japanese filmmaker.) The Chosun Young Literary Writers Association was also formed at this time and it was guided under the honorary presidency of Park Jong Hwa and the presidency of Kim Dong Ri. Central members included: You Chi Hwan, Park Du Jin, Cho Ji Hoon, Seo Jung Joo, Park Mol Wol and Cho Yeon Hyun. The Chosun Young Literary Writers Association's main principles were similar to those of the Chosun Literary Men's Association. On 4 November 1946, other writers who supported the anti-trusteeship also gathered and established the Chosun Film & Theatre Writers Association(Chosun Younghwa Kukjak-ga Hyuphoi) and it was an engagement of the people who were not members of the Korean Film Union.

4

The Chosun Film & Theatre Writers Association pursued the establishment of a new tradition and the advancement of the quality of film art based on the concept of

포화 속의 십자가 | 이용민 | 1956 | A Cross under Gun Fire(Pohwasok-ui Sipjaga) | Lee Yong Min

벽락감투 홍일명 1956 Jackpot(Byorak Gamtu) Hong Il Myung

해정 박상호 1956 Love at Sea(Hae Jung) Park Sang Ho

fidelity, that is, pure art. Its members presented assertions that were far-fetched and unaligned with the political ideology of the time. Their ideas were meant to confront the political claims, such as clearing off the vestiges of Japanese imperialism and feudalism, which were made by the filmmakers from the national independence side. Members included Ahn Seok Young, Kim Kwang Joo, and Cho Yeon Hyun, all the people who were either conservative or pro-Japanese in the literary and film circles under the Japanese rule. Other members included those under the influence of the great independence leader, Kim Koo, such as director Jun Chang Gun. They were not related with the Korean Film Union which had been established on 16 December 1945(Freedom Newspaper(Jayu Shinmun), 18 December 1945). The whole of the Korean film community was engaged with the Chosun Film & Theatre Writers Association, Chosun Film Construction Headquarters or the Chosun Proleta Film Federatio. The Chosun Film Construction Headquarters was a sub-organization of the Chosun Art Construction Headquarters and was formed by Lee Jae Myung, Kim Chung Hyuk, Park Ki Chae and Lee Byung Il on 18 August 1945. Also of importance was a 24 September 1945 rally organized by the Chosun Film Construction Headquarters. Yoon Baek Nam was selected as the president of the Chosun Film Construction Headquarters while Kim Chung Hyuk became the chief secretary and Lee Jae Myung, Seo Kwang Je, Bang Han Joon and Kim Han became executive committee members. Among the people mentioned above, Park Ki Chae and Lee Byung Il had produced pro-Japanese films before, and Lee Jae Myung successfully sustained his status as a film producer during the late colonial period leading up to the Japanese defeat in the Pacific War. The Governor General of Chosun appointed Kim Jung Hyuk as the manager of the board that evaluated the qualifications of the Korean film community. It seems that this was a board, which the Japanese Empire used to suppress Korean filmmakers.

Yoon Baek Nam had close relationships with filmmakers and other officials in

천추의 한 안종화 1956 **Enmity Buried at Heart(Cheonchu-ui Han)** Ahn Jong Hwa

옥단춘 권영순 1956 **The Story of Okdanchun(Okdanchun)** Kwon Young Soon

Japan and had been away from the Korean film community for a while. Seo Kwang Je was probably the most well known literary critic from the KAPF movement in the late 1920s and early 1930s, but later on became a pro-Japanese supporter. The Chosun Proleta Film Federatio was composed of President Chu Min and Chief Secretary Jung Joon Rak. The executive board members of this organization included Chu Min, Kim Hyung Ki, Na Wong, Hong Hyun Jung, Kang Ho, Lee Byung Il, Hur Dal, Min Jeong Sik, Chung Chun Rak, Seok Il Rang. The other general members were Kim Han, Dok Eun Ki, Kim Young Ha, Lee Myung Woo, You Jang San, Kim Sung Chun, and Choi Chil Bok. The Chosun Proleta Film Federatio appeared more liberal than the Chosun Film Construction Headquarters because of its members'profiles. For example, Kang Ho was a leading director of the KAPF film movement, and Chu Min was involved with KAPF theatre projects in the past. However, most of the other members had involuntarily participated in pro-Japanese activities. As a result, their philosophical viewpoints about film and the future activities of the film community were not clear. This ideological separation was due to the differentiated opinions of the Chosun Art Construction Headquarters and the Chosun Proleta Art Federatio, which were their superior organizations. Their disparities could be seen as having originated from the 1930s when Kang Ho and Seo Kwang Je confronted each other regarding the direction of the KAPF film movement.

5

Both the Chosun Art Construction Headquarters and the Chosun Proleta Art Federatio were two of the most influential organizations in the art field. As indicated in the August Theses declared by Park Hun Hyung in 1945, anti-feudalism, anti-imperialism, and democratic revolution were their primary political motivations concerning all culture and art movements. As previously mentioned, on 16 February 1946, they merged into one organization and called it the Korean Film Union. Around the same time, members of the Chosun Film & Theatre Writers Association organized the Chosun Film Directors Club(Hanguk Younghwa Gamdok Gurak-bu), which was the predecessor of the Korean Film Council(Daehan Younghwa Hyup-ui Hoi). Later on, this organization was renamed again as the Motion Pictures Association of Korea(Hanguk Younghwa-in Hyup-hoi) in 1955, which is still actively operating in the film community. According to some documents, Ahn Seok Young was a member of the Chosun Film Construction Headquarters from the very beginning.

On 4 November 1946, Ahn Seok Young became the leader of the Chosun Film & Theatre Writers Association, which was formed as a gathering space for scriptwriters. In 1948, the Korean Film Council(Daehan Younghwa Hyup-ui Hoi) was organized by Yoon Bong Chun, Kim So Dong, Lee Byung Il, Lee Koo Young, Shin Kyong Gyun, and Choi In Gyu. Ahn Seok Young again became the president of this council. There exists a different opinion about how this organization was formed. According to an article in the Kyunghyang Daily Newspaper(Kyunghyang Ilbo, 25 October 1948), the members of the Chosun Film Directors Club created the Korean Film Council. Its central members were Ahn Seok Joo, Kim Young Hwa and Ahn Chul Young. Each member of the Korean Film Council seems to have lived completely different lives. For example, Yoon Bong Chun, who was known as a friend of the famous director Na Un Kyu, was once an actor and later became a director who opposed the philosophies and aims of KAPF. Though his works were not noteworthy, Yoon Bong Chun maintained his integrity by having worked before the liberation without assisting the Japanese. Lee Koo Young was known as one of the film pioneers, who gave up his filming activities in the mid 1930s. Shin Kyong Gyun, Choi In Gyu, and Kim Young Hwa were representative pro-Japanese filmmakers. Ahn Chul Young once served in the South Korean Interim Government. Most of the above men joined the Korean Film Union, but their views and attitudes shifted as the political situation changed.

왕자호동과 낙랑공주 김소동 1956 Prince Hodong and Princess Nakang(Wangja Hodong-gwa Nakrang Gongju) Kim So Dong

유전의 애수(일명: 집 없는 여인) 유현목 | 1956
Sad Inheritance(Youjeon-ui Ae-soo)　You Hyun Mok

장화홍련전 정창화 | 1956
The Story of Changhwa and Hongryon(Changhwa Hongryon-jeon)
Chung Chang Hwa

장화홍련전 | 정창화 | 1956 | The Story of Changhwa and Hongryon(Changhwa Hongryon-jeon) | Chung Chang Hwa

6

After the liberation, USSR Armies began advancing on North Korea as early as 20 August 1945. During this time, a plethora of voluntary organizations were formed with various names such as the New National Foundation Committee, Autonomy Council and Security Maintenance Board. Within one month, People's Committees(Inmin Wiwon-hoi) sprang up in every region and province. On 21 September 1945, Kim Il Sung established the Chosun Communist Party North Korean Branch(Chosun Kongsan-dang Buk-Chosun Bunguk) and appeared in Pyongyang for the "Welcoming Kim Il Sung Rally". The temporary North Korean Committee(Buk-Chosun Imshi Wiwon-hoi) announced a manifesto of twenty general principles. On 24 December 1945, the North Korean Theatre Union(Buk-Chosun Yeonguk Dongmaeng) was formed, and the formation of the Art Union(Yesul Dongmaeng) followed in the Pyungnam District on 26 January 1946. Regional art federation bodies were also formed in each province. The North Korean Writers Union(Buk-Chosun Munhak Yesul-ga Dongmaeng) was formed on 25 March 1946 under the leadership of Han Seol Ya, a writer who crossed the 38 degree parallel into North Korea. The name of the North Korean Writers Union was later changed to the North Korean Literary and Art Union(Buk-Chosun Munhak Yesul Chong Dongmaeng) under the presidency of Lee Ki Young.

The film community in Pyongyang was part of the North Korean Literary and Art Union. However, most filmmaking was carried out and supervised by the department of film in the Ministry of Promotion and Public Relations of the Central Party Committee. After the first documentary, 〈Our Legend(Woori-ui Chun-sol)〉, was completed, the Chosun Documentary Studio(Chosun Kirok Younghwa Chwalyoung-so) was established on 1 July 1946, and the Chosun Art Film Studio(Chosun Yesul Younghwa Chwalyoung-so) was also established on 6 February 1947. Their relationship with the South Korean Film Union continued and they met often. For example, the Film Federation of Pyungnam district sent a delegation to the Korean Film Union to partake in an event forming a new branch around 16 April 1946. Filmmakers on both sides of the 38 degree parallel had much in common in that they both had difficulties in making films. With most of the Korean filmmakers remaining in the South, it would appear that the difficulties in the North were greater than the South. However, the North Korean film community received a significant level of support from the USSR. On 29 October 1945, North Korea and the USSR signed their first trading contract between the two countries with a film importation agreement. The building of the North Korean studios was accomplished thanks in large part to the continuing support of the USSR.

1—

해방 후 영건과 프로예맹이 통합해 만든 조선영화동맹은 명실상부하게 조선을 대표하는 영화기구가 되었다. 이 단체는 그 강령으로 일본 제국주의 잔재 소탕, 봉건주의 잔재 청소, 국수주의 배격, 진보적 민족영화 건설, 조선영화와 국제영화 간 제휴 등을 내걸었고 또 진보적 민주주의 국가 건설을 향해 총력을 집중하는 시기에 일체 반동영화를 배격하고 민족영화의 획기적 발전과 완성을 기한다고 선언했다. 이 단체가 내세운 주요한 정책안은, 영화예술의 발전을 위해서는 적극적인 국영제가 수립되어야 한다는 것이었다. 이에 대한 구체적인 안은 다음과 같다.

- 영화제작 및 산업에 소요되는 기재시설을 국가적 견지에서 기획하여 수입 및 수출, 교재 · 문화 · 계몽 · 기록 및 극영화의 제작.
- 배급은 외래자본과 국가경제의 절약을 위하고 민족문화의 앙양을 위한 기획정책으로서 시행할 것이며 상설관 건설 및 경영.
- 이론기술진 확보 및 양성을 위해 영화과학연구소를 시설하고 영화인(예술가, 기술자)을 외국 파견.
- 사영(민간기업)에 대해서는 기술적인 조치와 문화적, 기획적인 측면에서 국가에서 적극적인 지도와 원조.
- 전문적인 영화학교의 설립과 학교, 직장, 공장, 농촌, 산촌, 어촌마다 영화실 설비.

이상에서 보듯 조선영화동맹은 국가차원의 지원 없이 조선영화의 획기적 발전은 불가능하다고 보았으며 이는 또 좌익 측이 큰 세력을 차지하고 정권을 창출할 수 있으리라는 기대감 위에서 이루어진 것이었다. 조선영화동맹은 조직선전부, 제작지도부, 배급지도부, 흥행지도부 등을 통해 각 하부단체를 독려하는 한편 사업을 추진했으며 소련영화의 일반상영, 해방기록사진전, 메이데이 기념행사, 6 · 10만세운동 기념주간 등을 실시했다. 한편 미군정은 중배에게 유리한 조건을 조성하는 한편 영건을 재조선미육군사령부 군정청 조선관계 보도부에 유치시켰다. 그러나 곧 조선영화동맹이 결성되자 1946년 4월 12일에 군정청 법령 제

물레방아 이현 | 1956 | The Water Mill(Mul-le Bang-a) | Lee Hyun

인생역마차 김성민 | 1956 | Life Like a Stagecoach(Insaeng Yeok-macha) | Kim Sung Min

68호 '활동사진의 취체'에 관한 포고령을 발표하고 곧이어 그해 10월 8일에는 군정청 법령 제115호인 영화에 관한 포고령(영화법)을 발표해 시행했다.

2 —

'활동사진의 취체'에 관한 포고령은 구 일제 영화법을 폐기하는 한편 검열 핵심을 그대로 이어받은 것이며 포고령 역시 상영 전 사전허가, 사전허가 미필영화에 대한 조치, 허가 수속방법, 허가와 불허의 경우에 관한 규정 등으로 짜여진 일제 영화법을 답습한 것이었다. 미군정청은 이 포고령의 목적이 최소한도 통제하에서 영화내용의 건전한 기초를 확립케 하는 데 있다고 밝혔지만 실제로는 일제 때와 조금도 달라진 것이 없었다. 또 사전허가를 위해 영문서류까지 준비해야 하는 것은 당시 영화인들에게는 대단히 치욕적인 일의 강요였다. 또 미군정은 일제가 남기고 간 극장을 조선영화인들의 의견에 따라 처리하겠다고 했지만 이는 일부 친일매판자본가와 친미자산가들의 손에 넘어갔다. 또 조선영화동맹이 하는 행사마다 제동을 걸거나 관련 책임자를 법적으로 옭아매기도 했다. 당시의 기록들은 조선영화동맹의 행사와 지방 이동영사시에 일어난 불법 방해와 테러 행위들에 대해 전하고 있다.

이에 조선영화동맹은 거세게 항의했으나 미군정에서는 답변을 아예 하지 않거나 대단히 소극적으로만 답변했다. 이후 미군정은 극장 입장세를 조정해 미국영화는 120원 정도면 들어갈 수 있도록 하는 한편 한국영화에는 200원 내지 300원의 입장요금을 내야 들어갈 수 있도록 만들었다. 이러한 미군정의 행패에 조선영화동맹은 적극적으로 대처했으나 현실적인 개선에까지는 이르지 못했다. 이러한 비극은 한반도 전체의 운명과도 흡사했다.

조선영화동맹의 조직체계는 다음과 같다. 중앙집행위원장 안종화, 서기장 추민, 중앙집행위원 이재명, 김한, 이병일, 이창용, 민정식, 강신웅, 이기성, 성동호, 문예봉, 독은기, 이명우, 허달, 윤상열, 서광제, 김정혁, 박기채 등이 포진했고 서울, 평남, 대구, 부산 등에 4개의 지부를 두는 한편 조선문화단체총연맹의 계몽동원본부 이동영사대에서 활동하기도 했다. 또 조선영화동맹에 소속된 단체는 흥행단체 1개, 제작단체 12개, 배급단체 12개, 기술단체 3개, 연구단체 1개 그리고 각 지부에 소속된 제작단체 4개, 배급단체 4개, 흥행단체 2개 등 전국적인 영역을 포괄하는 조직이었다.

애인 홍성기 : 1956 **Lover(Ae-in)** Hong Sung Ki

마의태자 전창근 : 1956
A Prince in Hemp Ciothes(Ma-ui Taeja) Jun Chang Geun

마의태자 | 전창근 | 1956 | A Prince in Hemp Clothes(Ma-ui Taeja) | Jun Chang Geun

3 —

　　민주주의민족전선에 가입된 조직임에도 불구하고 조선영화계 거의 전부에 해당하는 인원과 소속단체를 포괄했다는 사실로 미루어볼 때 당시 좌익의 세력판도와 지지도를 쉽사리 예측할 수 있다. 하지만 1946년 대구에서 일어난 10월항쟁 사건 이후 좌익 측의 활동이 대다수 불법으로 몰리게 되고 우익 측의 세력이 점점 미군정을 등에 업고 힘을 얻어가자 점차 그 결집력과 활동력이 줄어들게 된다. 조선영화동맹의 주요 인물들, 예컨대 중앙집행위원으로 있던 많은 인물들은 북으로 가거나 또 우익 측으로 자리를 옮겼다. 그동안 조직 확장과 국가수립 후 영화발전이라는 등식에 치중했던 노선은 점차 대중적 지지확보를 위해 이동영사대 활동과 민중들의 현장에 카메라를 갖고 가는 활동으로 옮겨가고 각 지부 건설 및 활동을 시작했다. 하지만 이미 그때 세력판도는 돌이킬 수 없을 만큼 기울어져 있었다. 친일 경력을 불문하고 서광제, 김정혁 등은 나름대로 각자 노력했고 서기장 추민은 힘겹게 조선영화동맹을 이끌어갔다.

　　그 외에도 김한, 독은기, 문예봉 등 친일 경력을 가진 배우들의 활약도 컸고 전혀 이

름이 알려지지 않은 서울지부 서기장 이기성, 문화공작단의 이현, 이용민, 이영준 등도 당시의 기록에 등장한다. 카프영화운동의 대명사였던 강호 감독은 이후 연극계에서 주로 활동했고 전쟁을 전후해 문예봉 등과 함께 월북했으며, 안종화, 최인규, 박기채 등 적극적인 친일 경력자들은 안석영, 윤봉춘 등과 함께 대한영화협의회를 결성해 오늘날 한국영화계의 주류를 형성하는 대열에 합류하게 된다. 이런 과정을 밟아 조선영화동맹은 미군정의 직접, 간접적인 방해공작과 역량상의 한계와 시대적 질곡으로 완전히 괴멸하게 된다. 하지만 자본의 논리와 사회적 여파력이 큰 탓에, 다른 예술에 비해 이중삼중의 고초를 겪어야만 했던 상황에서도 〈해방뉴스〉의 이동영사 등을 통한 대중적 보급 노력은 역사의 귀감으로 남는다. 사실이 시기 영화운동의 내부적 갈등은 사회운동과 예술운동의 양자 사이에서 겪는 갈등이기도 했다. 사회적 환경에 따라 종속적으로 결정될 수밖에 없는 것이 당시의 운명이었던 것이다.

4 —

하지만 일제잔재의 청산, 봉건잔재의 청산, 자주독립국가의 수립이라는 전 민족적 과제 앞에서 조선영화동맹을 중심으로 한 민족영화인들의 노력은 귀중한 것이다. 그들은 전국적인 조직 건설, 영화인의 통일된 대중조직 건설을 성취했을 뿐 아니라 문화공작대로서의 이동영사반 활동을 수행했고 그 간고한 시절에도 무려 20여 편에 달하는 반제반봉건 통일전선을 보도하는 기록영화를 제작, 상영했다. 또 정치·사회적 문제에 관한 판단력의 재고와 다른 문화단체와의 관계에서도 일정한 역할을 수행했다. 그렇다고 조선영화동맹의 과오가 없었던 것은 아니다. 당시 주도적인 노선이었던 부르주아민주주의 혁명단계의 실제 내용은 반제반봉건과 기층 민중 중심의 민주주의였어야 했다. 하지만 조선영화동맹의 지도부는 영화예술인 대중조직을 꾸리는 과정에서 기계적으로 이를 도입해 영화분야 속의 역할과 사회전체 속의 역할 모두를 제대로 수행하지 못하는 결과를 낳았다.

즉 무분별한 대중조직을 표방해 적극적인 친일파 사람까지 요직에 앉혀 실제 사업이 이루어지지 못했다든가, 영화창작에 대한 직접적이고 구체적인 계획을 갖지 못하고 전체 사회운동의 사업에 수동적으로 매몰되었다는 말이다. 그래서 결국 조선영화동맹은 반제반봉건의 과제와 기층 민중 중심의 민주주의 건설이라는 임무에 적극적으로 부응하지 못했다. 이후

1947년에서 1948년 초에 걸쳐 조선영화동맹은 과거의 오류를 시정하는 맥락에서 기층 민중 중심의 활동에 열중했지만 이미 조직은 거의 와해된 상태였고 또 전체적으로는 균형이 깨진 좌파적 행동에 그치고 말았다. 이런 오류는 당시 남로당 측의 오류와 일맥상통한 점이 있었고 또 운동의 한계와 상황을 반영하는 것이기도 했다.

5 ─

1949년에 접어들자 한국영화는 연간 20여 편이 제작될 만큼 일단 외형적인 성장세를 보였다. 그러나 바로 그 다음 해에 전쟁이 일어나 1950년 5편, 1951년 5편, 1952년 6편, 1953년 6편 등의 제작 편수를 기록하다, 전쟁이 끝난 1954년에는 18편, 1955년 15편, 1956년 30편, 1957년 37편 등의 회복세를 보인다. 이후 1958년 74편, 급기야 1959년에는 111편이나 제작하는 성장을 보이지만 이러한 회복과 성장이 한국영화의 온전한 출발과 성장이었는가에 대해서는 회의가 들지 않을 수 없다. 조선영화동맹에 대한 탄압과 전쟁으로 인해 많은 인력손실이 있었고 또 무엇보다 민족적 토양과 사회적 현실을 기초로 한 영화정신은 그 과정에서 실종되었기 때문이다. 나운규로 대표되는 민족정서라든가 김유영, 강호 등으로 대표되는 사회파 혹은 비판적 리얼리즘의 맥락은 이 과정에서 사라지고 이후 그들의 노력들은 비하되거나 금기시되어 왔다.

그 대신 윤봉춘의 애국물 시리즈가 그 자리를 메웠지만 전체적으로는 대단히 작은 것에 불과했다. 최인규, 임운학, 홍개명, 안종화, 이규환 등은 별다른 진전 없는 작품을 만들었고, 최인규의 조감독 출신인 홍성기는 〈여성일기〉(1949)라는 멜로성 계몽물을 통해 감독으로 데뷔했다. 또한 최인규의 조감독 출신인 신상옥은 전쟁 중에 〈악야〉(1952)로 데뷔하고, 이후 한국영화계는 하향곡선을 그리는 장년감독들과 영화를 오락으로만 생각하는 신진감독들의 각축장으로 변하게 되었다. 홍성기는 한국 멜로영화의 대부로 자리를 잡고 신상옥은 특유의 돌파력과 기행으로 한국영화의 중심에 진출한다. 물론 시대를 풍자하거나 작품성이 돋보이는 영화들이 1950년대 후기로 갈수록 만들어졌지만, 해방공간이라는 희망적이며 민족적이었던 시절을 생각한다면 그것들은 상대적으로 빈곤한 것이 아닐 수 없었다. 일제에 의해 뿌리를 뽑히고 전쟁을 치르는 과정에 있었던 한국영화는 크게 불행한 출발을 할 수밖에 없었던 것이다.

1 —

The Korean Film Union, which was an integrated body of the Chosun Film Construction Headquarters and the Chosun Proletariat Film Federation, became the primary representing film organization of South Korea in the post-liberation era. The Korean Film Union's general principles included: cleaning up the vestiges of the Japanese Empire and its feudalism, denunciation of ultra-nationalism, establishment of a progressive national cinema, and cooperation of Korean and international films. At the same time, it declared that it was devoted to building a democratic nation and excluding all types of reactionary films in its pursuit and development of a national cinema. In addition, the Korean Film Union made suggestions to the government regarding film policies and tried its best to help establish a strong national operating system that would develop film as art. Its recommendations included:

The Korean government should import the necessary filmmaking equipment required for a sustainable film industry. The government should also plan to produce films in a wide range of categories such as educational, social enlightening, cultural and feature films, and documentaries.

The distribution of all films should be conducted within the means of the national economy, and foreign investment should be used to enhance the national culture of Korea. Regular cinemas should be built, maintained and operated in order to achieve these goals.

A film research center should be established in order to educate and cultivate academics, researchers and filmmakers. Both artists and engineers should be sent overseas for professional training in the art of filmmaking.

The government should actively support and offer guidance to privately owned companies in the film industry and initiate programs that foster technical and cultural skills.

심청전 | 이규환 | 1956
The Story of Shimchung(Shimchung-jeon) | Lee Kyu Hwan

논개 | 윤봉춘 | 1956 | Nongae(Nongae) | Yoon Bong Chun

논개 | 1956 | Nongae(Nongae) | Yoon Bong Chun

Film schools and training centers should be founded and projection rooms should be built in urban and rural schools, work places, factories, as well as in farming and fishing villages.

As mentioned above, the Korean Film Union believed that it was indispensable to have government support for the development of cinema and film culture in general. This idea seemed to be based on the expectations that left-wing individuals would grow in numbers and strength and create a new government. The Korean Film Union helped organize all of the film industry and Korean film community personnel into different departments, which were individually responsible for the promotion, planning, distribution and exhibition of films in South Korea. It had also hosted a May Day celebration event, screened several well-known films from the Soviet Union and held an exhibition of still photographs of the liberation. The Korean Film Union also held a commemorative event for the June 10th movement. Around the same time, the USAMGIK created advantageous conditions for the Central Motion Picture Exchange in the Korean film market and placed the Chosun Film Construction Headquarters under the department of Korean press of the USAMGIK. On 12 April 1946 the USAMGIK promulgated the Military Government Ordinance No. 68, "Regulation of the Motion Pictures" and it was soon followed by No. 115, "Film Law" on 8 October 1946.

2 —

The laws outlined in the Military Government Ordinance No. 68 abolished most of the Chosun Film Laws promulgated by the Governor General of Chosun during the colonial period. However, the core censorship regulations remained in effect. The main contents of the regulations addressed the provisions for gaining exhibition permission before screenings and the follow-up measures for rejecting and accepting films. This aspect of Ordinance No. 68 mirrored the Chosun Film Laws under the Japanese rule. The USAMGIK explained that the new ordinance was intended to establish a foundation for sound film content with the least amount of regulations for it. However, in reality, the contents of the new ordinance were the same as those from the Japanese colonial period. Many Koreans were outraged and disgraced because of the new imperial implications under the American military rule. The Korean film community was additionally forced to prepare English documents in order to get permission to screening films. Though the USAMGIK had indicated to the Korean film community that they would have a say in how their own cinemas could be dealt with after the liberation, the cinemas were handed directly over to the hands of comprador and pro-US capitalists. Once again, Koreans had lost control of their own cinemas. Most of the film events hosted by the Korean Film Union during this time were hindered and censored by the USAMGIK, and often the temporary managers of the events were arrested. Newspapers published frequent reports about the terrors and obstructions, which troubled the events as well as the screenings of films at local villages.

Most of the members of the Korean Film Union protested against these incidents, but the USAMGIK did not seem to hear their concerns or provide solutions to the controversial issues. In fact, the USAMGIK did not show the slightest reaction to the complaints of the Korean film community. Later on, the USAMGIK changed the admission fee system by increasing ticket prices for Korean domestic films. American films were favoured in the new changes. Audiences had to pay 120 won to watch US films, but between 200 and 300 won to see Korean films. The Korean Film Union strongly opposed these changed admission prices but it was unable to make a difference or do anything about it. The Korean Film Union was as helpless against the occupied American military government as the rest of Korea was.

The Korean Film Union was structured in the following way: Ahn Jong Hwa as chief executive of the committee and Chu Min as chief secretary. Committee members included: Lee Jae Myung, Kim Han, Lee Byung Il, Lee Chang Yong, Min Chung Sik, Kang Shin Woong, Lee Ki Sung, Sung Dong Ho, Moon Ye Bong, Dok Eun Ki, Lee Myung Woo, Hur Dal, Yoon Sang Yeol, Seo Kwang Je, Kim Jung Hyuk, Park Ki Chae. There were four branch offices, which were dispersed in Seoul, Pyungnam, Daegu and Busan. The Korean Film Union frequently worked with travelling film shows, which operated under the department of the social enlightenment of the Chosun Cultural Association Headquarters. The Korean Film Union had several sub-groups with different purposes: one primary group in charge of entertainment, one in charge of research and three in charge of engineering. There were twelve production and twelve distribution groups as well. Each local branch office of the Korean Film Union also had four production and four distribution sub-groups and two entertainment groups. In this way, the Korean Film Union was spread nationwide.

랑의復讐! 그것을悲哀로만 끝일것인가!

製作 監督·金綺泳
脚本·安哲宗·撮影·金景·李燕
吳泰眛·有人·照明·李敏燁
錄音白龍珠·진行·李相万
音畫·鄭夜芳

風仙花

春秋映画社·作品

봉선화 | 김기영 | 1956 | Touch-me-nots(Bongsunhwa) | Kim Ki Young

韓國映畵史上初有의配役陣
梁金尹朱盧趙崔朱金李李金
美靜仁曾耕美戊善勝海鍾東
姬林子女姬鈴龍泰鎬浪哲園
特別出演
企一······愛子·民子·淑子
노래···········白一姬
N B C 樂團 세분스타一樂團

東海映畫社超特作
監督金漢日

女性의 敵

여성의 적 | 김한일 | 1956 | Enemy of Women(Yeosung-ui Jeok) | Kim Han Il

The Korean Film Union was a member of the Interim People's Committee and it governed and controlled almost the whole film organizations and manpower in Korea. This points to how influential the Korean Film Union was and how much support it had. After the political conflict at the October 1946 Daegu Revolution, all left wing activities became illegal. As a result, the Korean Film Union's power began to weaken gradually. Alternatively, the right wing groups were growing larger and getting stronger under the support of the USAMGIK. Many central committee members of the Korean Film Union either crossed the border to go to North Korea or migrated to one or more of the right wing groups. Despite these problems, the Korean Film Union maintained its general principles, which emphasized its expansion and advocated the establishment of the Korean nation. Rebuilding a strong country was its first priority and developing a film culture was its second priority. In this way, the Korean Film Union was attempting to gain the support of the public. One of the ways that the Korean Film Union branch offices tried was sponsoring travelling picture shows for remote communities as well as filming the normal everyday events that were happening in people's lives. However, even with all these efforts, the prominent and leading powers had already shifted toward the right. Seo Kwang Je and Kim Jung Hyuk, in spite of their backgrounds as Japanese collaborators, tried their best to regain the power of the Korean Film Union. Chu Min, the chief secretary, managed to run the organization with many difficulties.

Actors such as Kim Han, Dok Eun Ki, and Moon Ye Bong took active roles in the Korean Film Union. Lee Hyun, Lee Yong Min and Lee Young Jun(all from the Department of Culture) and Lee Ki Sung, the chief secretary of the Seoul branch, were names frequently associated with the Korean Film Union. Not everyone tried to stay in the American-controlled South. Kang Ho, the representing director of the KAPF movement, moved into the theatrical world and relocated in North Korea with Moon Ye Bong

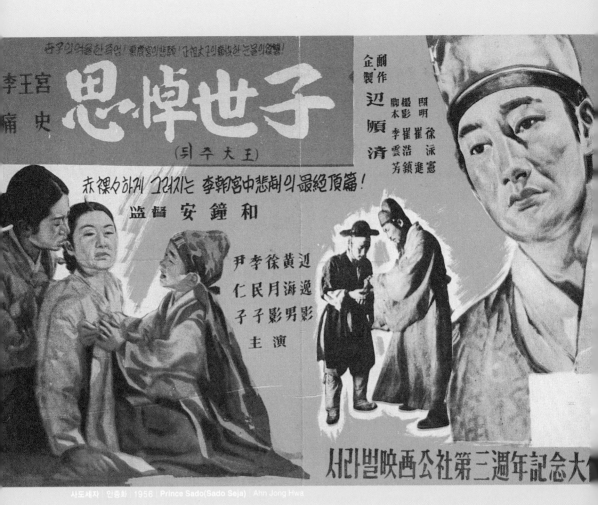

사도세자 | 안종화 | 1956 | Prince Sado(Sado Seja) | Ahn Jong Hwa

when the Korean War broke out. Those who did stay formed the Korean Film Council. The Korean Film Council included some of the Japanese collaborators such as Ahn Jong Hwa, Choi In Gyu and Park Ki Chae. This organization helped Ahn Seok Young and Yoon Bong Chun join the mainstream of the Korean film community. The dissolution of the Korean Film Union was caused by several reasons. There were direct and indirect disturbances from the USAMGIK, and the organization had its own self-imposed limitations due to the historical background situation in Korea. However, their activities, such as organizing, visiting, screenings of ⟨Liberation News⟩ as a way of spreading film culture in Korea should be well remembered, especially since the Korean Film Union was pressured heavily by the capitalist and social powers of the time. The same kind of internal conflicts found in the film movement were also happening in the social and art movements. Whatever the conflict was, in the end it was subordinated into the social context.

4 —

The ambitions and plans shown by the members of the Korean Film Union need to be highly evaluated. In addition to their general principles, such as sweeping over the vestiges of the Japanese Empire, the feudalism and the establishment of an independent country, what they had achieved was the establishment of a nationwide organization and the formation of a unified body of filmmakers. The Korean Film Union visited rural villages, screened films and produced about twenty documentaries. Their work promoted anti-Japanese ideals and feudalism, and unification of separated country. They also shared their views with the larger political and social fields, keeping on good terms with other cultural organizations. However, they had also made some mistakes. The true idea of a bourgeois democracy was for the general populace who believed in anti-imperialism and feudalism and it was not successfully pursued. The leading committee members of the Korean Film Union mechanically applied these ideas when they formed the public organization for the filmmakers. As a result, their influential roles in the film industry and in the larger society altogether were not carried out in a proper way because they did not seem to have practical grounding.

As a public organization, the Korean Film Union welcomed anybody with any type of background. The Korean Film Union even placed a previously well-known Japanese collaborator in an important position, which hindered some of their projects from being operated smoothly. While the organization looked well prepared on the surface, concrete plans for filmmaking and creating new projects did not exist. The Korean Film Union had buried itself under the strain of the social movement and, thus, it could not meet all of the goals that it wanted to achieve. Between 1947 and 1948, the Korean Film Union focused on activities that targeted the wider populace in order to compensate for their initial misdirections. However, the organization had been nearly collapsed because it could not balance all of its left-wing efforts. This fallacy was also evident within the South Korean Labour Party(Namro-dang) and it related to the limitations of the larger social movement and the reflection of the situation.

5

In 1949, the Korean film industry produced about twenty films. This level of productivity represented a green light for growth. However, within a year, the Korean War broke out and the number of films produced was reduced to five. Until the armistice in 1953, the number of film productions remained nearly the same: five in 1951; six in 1952; and six in 1953. After the war, the number of film productions regained their previous capacity. Eighteen were produced in 1954; fifteen in 1955; twenty in 1956; thirty-seven in 1957; seventy-four in 1958; and one hundred eleven in 1959. However, this growth in production was not the right index to evaluate all of the films or the state

시집가는 날(원작명: 맹진사댁 경사) 이병일 1956 The Wedding Day(Sijip-ganeun Nal) Lee Byung Il

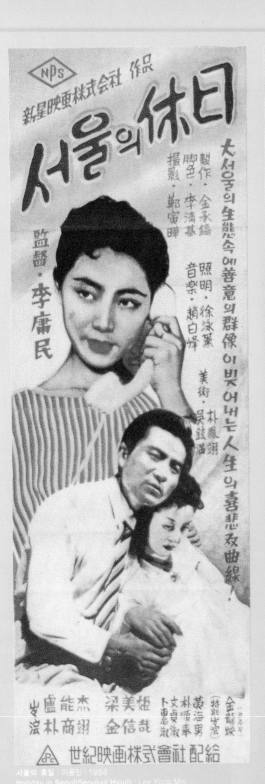

서울의 휴일 | 이용민 | 1956
Holiday in Seoul(Seoul-ui Hyuil) | Lee Yong Min

숙영낭자전 | 신현호 | 1956
The Story of Lady Sookyoung(Sookyoung Nangja-jeon) | Shin Hyun Ho

of the Korean film industry. A significant amount of manpower was lost during the war. The Korean Film Union was suppressed, and the larger efforts of the Korean film community, especially concerning national culture, spirit and social background, disappeared. The national sentiment best represented by Na Un Kyu's work in the 1920s and 1930s, and the critical social realism represented by Kim You Young and Kang Ho had vanished. The efforts to bring these ideas to life on the screen were degraded and avoided.

During this time, Yoon Bong Chun's patriotic series attempted to fill this void, but it was only a small part of the overall situation. Choi In Kyu, Im Woon Hak, Hong Gae Myung, Ahn Jong Hwa and Lee Kyu Hwan also produced minor films. Hong Seong Ki, who used to be an assistant director to Choi In Kyu, made a melodramatic social enlightenment film called 〈A Woman's Diary(Yeosung Ilki)〉(1949). Shin Sang Ok, who also used to be an assistant director to Choi In Kyu, debuted with 〈The Evil Night(Akya)〉 (1952). During the war, the members of the Korean film community began to compete with each other. Those who had once been in their prime were now declining. Younger filmmakers who considered filmmaking as amusement began to rise. For example, Hong Seong Ki became known as the father of Korean melodrama films, and Shin Sang Ok entered into the mainstream with his eccentricity and groundbreaking determination. Toward the end of the 1950s, high quality films with social satire themes began to appear. Films with good quality contents were still needed and expected in the post-liberation space with more freedom. As the Japanese colonial rule period and the Korean War riddled the country with turmoil, unlike most other countries in the world, the Korean cinema had been in poor shape for more than fifty years.

백치 아다다 │ 이강천 │ 1956 │ **Adada(Baekchi Adada)** │ Lee Kang Chun

동 란 기 의 한 국 영 화

Korean Films during the Wartime

1—

한국현대사에서 6·25전쟁만큼 민족공동체의 삶의 구조와 질을 변화시킨 것은 없을 정도로 그 의미와 영향력은 크다. 이는 한국영화사에서도 다르지 않다. 전 민족을 큰 비극 속으로 몰아넣은 전쟁이 한국영화도 비켜가지 않았음은 너무도 당연하기 때문이다. 그러나 6·25전쟁은 한국영화 제작을 중단시키지 않았고 영화인들의 제작 의욕은 소진되지 않았다. 온갖 악조건의 원시적인 시설이었지만 그들은 세계 수준의 영화를 지향하고 있었고, 보이고 들리는 영화를 만들기 위한 한국영화인들의 치열한 노력은 6·25전쟁 중에도 계속되었다.

동란기6 동란기란 1950년에서 1953년까지의 기간을 일컫는다. 한 시기의 문화인 영화를 다루는 글에서 굳이 1950년 6월 25일 전쟁 발발부터 1953년 7월 27일 휴전 성립이라는 정치적, 역사적 사건의 시간 구분을 따를 필요는 없다는 생각에서이다. '동란기'라는 용어를 사용하는 것은 『한국영화자료편람』, 이영일의 『한국영화전사』 등 기존의 기록들을 맹목적으로 따르고자 함이 아니다. 문화적인 시각에서 '동란기'라는 용어는 좁게는 한국영화인들, 넓게는 한반도 사람들이 겪었던 전쟁 당시의 분위기를 가장 잘 표현하고 있다는 것이 필자의 견해이다.를 단순히 소수의 기록영화와 극영화로 한국영화의 명맥을 힘겹게 유지한 시기로 보는 것은 매우 피상적인 견해이다. 6·25전쟁은 전전과 전후의 한국영화계와 단속적인 지점을 형성하지도, 한국영화를 공백으로 돌리지도 않았다. 동란기는 현대 한국영화사의 단순한 전사前史에 불과한 것이 아니라 한국영화 성장의 기점으로 다시 평가받아야 한다. 동란기는 전쟁의 혼란 속에서도 영화를 산업으로서 자각하고 모색했던 시기이자 한국영화 산업의 맹아들이 발견되는 중요한 시기인 것이다.

처와 애인 | 김성민 | 1957
Wife and Mistress(Chu-wa Ae-In) | Kim Sung Min

황진이 | 조긍하 | 1957 | Hwangjini(Hwangjini) | Cho Geung Ha

황진이 | 조긍하 | 1957 | Hwangjini(Hwangjini) | Cho Geung Ha

1

The Korean War was a national tragedy. It transformed the meaning and the quality of life for all Koreans, and it gave them a new sense and purpose in life. Likewise, films were also a part of a society that was influenced significantly by the war. However, one thing remained the same: the production of films continued as filmmakers never gave up their passion for telling stories during the war. The Korean film community attempted to meet world film standards even under the disadvantaged conditions with primitive facilities.

대춘향전 | 김향 | 1957 | The Great Story of Chunhyang(Dae Chunhyang-jeon) | Kim Hyang

사랑 | 이강천 | 1957 | Love(Sarang) | Lee Kang Chun

The wartime period generally refers to the three years from 1950, when the Korean War began, to 1953, when the armistice was signed. Korean War broke out on 25 June 1950 and it was suspended on 27 July 1953. However, it may not be necessary to define this time period based on these exact dates when the film community is examined. Here, the concept of a "wartime period" in Korean film history is not simply being used in the same way that others previously have applied the term, such as in Lee Young Il's 「The History of Korean Cinema(Hanguk Younghwa Chunsa)」 and in the 「Korean Film Material Collection(Hanguk Younghwa Charyo Pyunram)」. Hearing the phrase "wartime period" seems to convey the whole atmosphere of what all Koreans all over the country, including the film community, would have experienced at that time.

For the film industry it was also a time of survival with only a few documentaries and feature films made. However, the low number of productions should not suggest that the period was superficial or that one should think of the time in a superficial way. The Korean War itself was not responsible for disconnecting the pre and post war Korean film community nor did it create a vacuum in Korean cinema. It was more than a chapter in the history of Korean society and Korean cinema. The wartime needs to be re-evaluated as another starting point for the growth period in the history of Korean films. Korean filmmakers rediscovered filmmaking as a potential industry during the chaotic war. In truth, this was the time to find film industry prodigies growing up among the rubble of the national conflict.

1 —

동란기 한국영화의 제작 경향으로 특징지을 수 있는 것은 지방에서의 영화제작 열기, '코리안 리얼리즘'의 시도, 방첩영화와 군사영화의 제작, 극영화와 기록영화의 양식 혼용 등 이며 특히 기술적으로는 16밀리 발성영화의 시대로 정리할 수 있다.

6·25전쟁은 서울이 아닌 대구, 부산, 마산, 진해 등 피난도시에서 한국영화가 만들 어지는 계기를 마련하였다. 영화제작의 중심이 서울에서 지방으로 잠시 이동했던 시기로 당 시 대구와 부산에서는 지역 인력들을 주축으로 한 영화제작이 활발하게 진행되었다. 배우 이 민의 데뷔작인 〈화랑도〉(1951)는 6·25전쟁의 발발로 촬영이 중단되었다가 피난지인 대구에 서 완성되었다. 〈악야〉(1952) 역시 배우가 모이면 그때그때 몇 컷씩 찍는 방식으로 대구에서 완성되었다.7 신상옥 인터뷰, 2001.9.10. 당시의 지역 언론들은 "한국의 호리운드화" 영화 〈여성전선〉의 여 영남일보, 1952.6.21 라는 표현으로 피난지 대구의 영화제작 열기를 주목하였다. 길지 않은 기간이나마 대구지역은 한 국영화 제작의 중심으로 부각된 것이다. 신문 연재소설의 영화화도 시도되었다. 영남일보의 연재소설 「여성전선」의 영화화를 위해 전쟁 중임에도 불구하고 신인배우 공모 주인공 옥란 역으로 중등 이상 출신 19세부터 25세까지의 여성을 공모하였다. 이후 영화가 완성되지는 못했지만, 이는 대구에서의 영화제작 열기를 짐 작할 수 있게 해주는 대목이다. 영남일보, 1952.6.25. 등 세간의 흥미를 모았다.

대구에서의 영화제작 열기는 영화에 관심이 있었던 지역 사람들이 영화현장에 투신 하는 계기도 만들어주었다. 피난생활을 주제로 한 〈태양의 거리〉(1952) 제작에 자유극장의 미 술부장이었던 민경식과 기획자 변종근 등 지역 영화인들이 참가했던 것이 그 예이다. 전후 이들은 서울에서 활발한 활동을 이어갔다. 동란기 대구에서 〈내가 넘은 38선〉(1951), 〈공포의 밤〉(1952)을 연출한 손전도 주목할 만하다. 동향인 이규환 감독의 〈무지개〉(1936)에 주연으로 출연하면서 영화를 시작한 그는 연출작 4편 중 2편을 동란기에 만들었다. 6·25전쟁이 고향 에서 활동하는 계기를 만들어준 셈이다. 지방에서의 영화제작 열기는 부산도 예외가 아니었 다. 경상남도 공보과의 재정 후원을 받은 〈낙동강〉(1952)은 부산 문화예술인들의 모임이었던 '향토문화연구회'가 중심이 되어 제작하였다. 마산에서는 법인 만주영화사에서 영화 스틸을 하다 돌아와 사진관을 하던 김찬영의 사비로 〈삼천만의 꽃다발〉(1951)이 제작되었다. 마산 출 신의 무용가 최현과 〈자유만세〉(1946)의 황려희가 남녀 주인공으로, 기타인물들은 영화 애호

가인 마산의 지역 청년들이 출연했다고 한다. 10 복혜숙, 「나와 영화 반세기」, 『월간 영화』, 1974년 4월호, p. 72.

2

피난도시에서 제작된 영화들은 전쟁 중의 사회문제를 담아내었다. 이태리 네오 리얼리즘 계열의 작품들을 자양분 삼아 시도된 일련의 한국영화가 그것이다. 당시 영화계는 이태리적인 리얼리즘에 관심을 쏟았고 〈평화에 산다〉, 〈자전차도적〉, 〈무방비도시〉 11 대구 매일신문의 영화광고 중 이태리 영화들의 상영기록은 다음과 같다. 1952.1.1 자유극장 〈자전차도적〉, 1952.3.11 만경관 〈평화에 산다〉, 1952.3.13 자유극장 '이태리 2대 명화 동시상영' 〈자전차도적〉, 〈로마의 분노(일명: 무방비도시)〉. 같은 영화를 화제에 올렸다. 이태리 네오 리얼리즘 영화들은 전쟁이라는 비슷한 현실 속에서 이룬 성취로 한국영화가 나아가야 할 방향을 재고하는 계기가 되었다. 12 허백년, 서울신문, 1952.5.3. 한국영화인들이 받은 자극은 '코리안 리얼리즘'으로 표현되었다.

〈악야〉(1952)는 "코리안 리얼리즘을 시사하는 선구적 시금석" 13 장갑상, 민주신보, 1952.3.20. 장갑상은 부산대 영문과 교수로서 작고시까지 30여 년간 부산 영화평론계에 큰 업적을 남겼다. 이하 민주신보에 실린 그의 글은 저서 『영화와 비평』(삼신서적, 1970)에서 재인용했다. 이었고 연출수법이나 작품구성에 있어 '데 시카'적인 '로셀리니'적인 것을 찾아볼 수 있는 흥미로운 작품 14 이해랑, 「악야를 보고(하)」, 경향신문, 1952.3.20. 이었다. 이 영화는 『백민지 33인집』에 실린 김광주의 단편 「악야」를 원작으로 시작되었지만 6·25전쟁의 발발로 인해 감독 자신이 실제로 체험한 피난생활이 영화에 반영되었을 가능성이 크다. 뉴스영화 화면을 복사한 화면이 극영화에 널리 쓰인 당시의 경향을 생각해 볼 때 기록 화면들도 삽입되었을 것으로 추정된다. 신상옥 감독 자신도 피난 때 가장 큰 자극과 쇼크를 받은 것이 '데 시카'의 명작 〈자전차도적〉을 보았을 때라고 밝혔다. 15 정영일, 「주역을 통해 본 스크린 반세기 (10)신상옥·최은희」, 조선일보, 1966.6.26. 〈지옥화〉(1958)의 초입에 실제의 양공주와 미군이 나오는 댄스홀 장면으로도 이태리 네오 리얼리즘의 영향을 감지할 수 있다. 16 신상옥 인터뷰, 2001.9.10.

코리안 리얼리즘을 시도하는 영화들의 중요한 모티브는 '거리의 여인'이다. 전쟁이 길어지자 민중은 전쟁의 허무 속에 빠지고, 생활터전을 잃은 절망과 불안 속에서 사회윤리는 급속하게 퇴폐 경향을 나타냈으며 사치풍조가 늘어갔다. 전쟁을 계기로 소비물자가 범람하는 동시에 혼란과 무질서 속에서 나날을 영위하고 있던 사람들의 찰나적 생활태도와 결합되어 한국인의 새로운 소비풍조가 조장된 것이다. 이러한 흐름 속에서 성윤리 또한 문란해진다. 외국군 주둔과 전쟁으로 인한 생활난은 여성으로 하여금 몸을 팔아서 자신과 가족의 생존을 유지하게끔 강요했다.[17] 정성호, 「한국전쟁과 인구사회학적 변화」, 「한국전쟁과 사회구조의 변화」, pp. 34~41. 〈태양의 거리〉에서 등장하는 접대부 딸과 〈베일부인〉(1952)에서 자살 기도에 실패해 거리의 여자로 변하는 현옥이 그러하다.

3 ─

이만흥 감독의 〈탁류〉(1954), 정창화 감독의 〈최후의 유혹〉(1953), 〈유혹의 거리〉(1954), 한형모 감독의 〈운명의 손〉(1954)은 혼란한 전시사회를 배경으로 한 범죄 소재의 서스펜스 영화 제작 경향에 속하는 작품이다. 간첩 밀수배들을 소탕한다는 암흑가 활극 패턴은 동란기 미학의 하나이며 관객에게 서스펜스와 스릴이라는 흥미요소를 주려는 [18] 이영일, 「한국영화주조사」, p. 408. 장치였다.

사실 밀수단을 소재로 한 영화의 제작은 1947년 〈바다의 정열〉에서 시작되었다. 당시 밀수가 성행하여 사회문제가 되었고 밀수단을 소재로 한 작품도 다수 제작되었다.[19] 복혜숙, 「나와 영화 반세기」, 「월간 영화」, 1974년 4월호, p. 72. 1948년에는 〈밤의 태양〉, 〈수우〉, 〈끊어진 항로〉, 〈여명〉 등 4편이나 만들어졌다. 『한국영화총서』에서는 〈바다의 정열〉, 〈밤의 태양〉, 〈수우〉는 활극물로, 〈끊어진 항로〉, 〈여명〉은 계몽물로 분류하고 있지만 다섯 작품 모두 밀수 근절을 위한 정책영화라고 할 수 있다. 〈바다의 정열〉은 해양경비대 후원으로, 〈밤의 태양〉은 수도관구 경찰청 후원으로, 〈수우〉는 제1관구 경찰청 후원으로, 〈여명〉은 제7관구 경찰청 후원으로 각각 만들어졌다. 즉 해방 후 국민들에게 민주경찰이라는 이미지를 심기 위하여 정책적으로 제작된 계몽영화들이었다.[20] 「한국영화총서」, pp. 264~276.

밀수단을 소재로 한 활극 혹은 계몽물들은 6 · 25전쟁을 통해 '반공'이라는 소재를 가미해서 다시 등장하게 된다. 특히 '카바레를 아지트로 암약하는 대규모 밀수단을 민완형사들이 일망타진한다'는 내용의 〈밤의 태양〉과 〈수우〉는 '카바레를 거점으로 하는 간첩단을 방첩대원이 일망타진한다'는 내용의 〈탁류〉(1954)와 〈운명의 손〉(1954)으로 재생산된다. 두 영화는 카바레를 거점으로 하는 간첩밀수단이 간첩의 정부인 카바레 마담의 도움을 받은 방첩대원에

여성전선 | 김기영 | 1957 | A Woman's War(Yeosung Chunsun) | Kim Ki Young

의해 소탕되는 거의 유사한 줄거리의 영화이다. 〈탁류〉의 방첩대원은 이집길이, 〈운명의 손〉
에서는 이향이 연기했다. 〈탁류〉에서 여간첩 나타샤는 김신재가 연기했고 〈운명의 손〉에서는
윤인자가 여간첩 마가렛을 연기했다. '방공防共'을 유일한 국가이념으로 하는 당시의 시국에
국민의 방첩의식을 고취시키는 역할을 담당한 영화들이었다.²¹ '활기 띠는 우리 영화계』, 중앙일보, 1954.4.11.

　　반공영화라는 장르가 처음 등장한 것은 1949년으로 미공보원에서 제작한 홍개명 감
독의 〈전우〉,²² 1949년에 개봉한 〈전우〉는 〈성벽을 뚫고〉, 〈나라를 위하여〉와 같은 반공극영화이지만 1948년에 개봉한 〈밤의 태양〉, 〈수
우〉, 〈여명〉 같은 경찰 소재 영화의 연장선상으로도 파악할 수 있는 텍스트이다. 공산학정에 시달리다 월남한 두 형제가 형은 국군에, 아우는 경찰에
각각 투신하여 멸공전선에 앞장선다는 내용으로 경찰 소재와 군사 소재가 하나의 텍스트에서 만난 것이다. 한형모의 감독 데뷔작

〈성벽을 뚫고〉, 국방부 정훈국이 후원한 안종화 감독의 〈나라를 위하여〉 등 3편의 반공극영화와 이창근 감독의 〈북한의 실정〉, 윤봉춘 감독의 〈무너진 38선〉 등 2편의 반공기록영화가 있었다. 1949년에 개봉한 20편의 영화 중 5편이 반공 이데올로기를 주제로 한 영화였다. 동란기에 개봉한 〈화랑도〉(1951)와 〈내가 넘은 38선〉(1951)도 반공영화의 제작 추세에 따라 6·25전쟁 발발 전에 이미 제작에 들어간 작품들이었다. 사실 반공영화라는 명칭은 후대의 해석에 의해서 붙여진 것이다. 당시의 언론은 '반공영화'라는 명칭을 사용하지 않고 주로 '군(사)영화' 혹은 '경향영화'라는 명칭을 사용하였다.

6·25전쟁 전에 이미 뚜렷하게 발견되는 냉전적인 반공주의는 이데올로기적으로 국민을 통합하는 주요 기제였으며 일종의 시민 종교였다. 동란기에 제작된 대부분의 기록영화도 군의 후원하에 군사영화의 외양을 띠고 국민들에게 반공 이데올로기를 설파하는 역할을 담당했다. 전쟁이라는 사회상황은 극영화들도 군사와 반공이라는 소재를 적극적으로 차용하게 한다. 〈출격명령〉(1954)이 "북한 출신의 공군 대위(이집길)를 중심으로 우정과 연애를 통속적으로 취급하면서 내면에는 공군과 애국 의식을 강조하려는 정책적 의도가 가미된 멜로드라마"[23 장갑상, 『영화와 비평』, p. 251] 인 것처럼 동란기의 극영화들도 군의 적극적인 후원하에 제작되었고 자연스럽게 정책영화의 성격을 띠게 되었다.

6·25전쟁을 소재로 한 군사영화의 제작은 비단 한국영화에만 국한된 것이 아니었다. 할리우드에서는 이미 전쟁 중에 한국전선의 세트를 지어 6·25전쟁 영화를 제작하였고,[24 RKO 작품 〈0호작전〉은 부산교두보 작전을 묘사한 것으로 미국방성 후원으로 콜로라도 주 육군 연습지형에 대구시가와 네 개소의 농촌 전답 등 대규모적인 오픈 세트를 지어서 촬영하였다. 상당수의 동양인 엑스트라가 동원되었다고 하는 이 영화의 원제는 〈One Minute to Zero〉이다(「한국 전과 외화」, 영화시보, 1953.4.10).] 심지어 전쟁 중의 한반도에서는 프랑스 극영화의 로케이션 촬영이 이루어지기도 했다.[25 프랑스의 카메라맨 안리 로제의 잔 라비에, 연출가인 쟈크 듀론 세 사람이 5개월간 한국에서 로케이션하여 제작한 영화 〈비통〉이 그것이다. 사관학교를 졸업하고 한국에 출정한 육군사관의 무용을 그린 것으로 실제 군인인 가로세 사관이 주연하였다. 평양시가전의 실경도 삽입되었는데 원명은 〈creva coeur〉이다(「한국전과 외화」, 영화시보, 1953.4.10).]

4

〈총검은 살아 있다〉(1953)와 〈영광의 길〉(1953)은 『한국영화총서』에서 기록영화로 분

배뱅이 굿 | 왕주님 | 1957 | Babaengi Exorcism(Babaengi Gut) | Yang Joo Nam

그 여자의 일생 | 김한일 | 1957
Life of the Woman(Geu Yeoja-ui Ilsaeng) | Kim Han II

나는 너를 싫어한다 | 권영순 | 1957
I Hate You(Naneun Nureul Siruhanda) | Kwon Young Soon

산유화 | 이용민 | 1957 | A Wild Chrysanthemum(Sanyouhwa) | Lee Yong Min

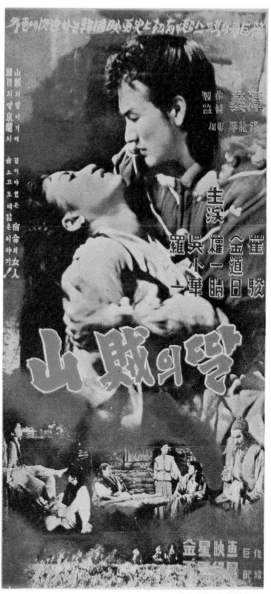

산적의 딸 | 윤예담 | 1957
Daughter of a Bandit(Sanjok-ui Ttal) | Yoon Ye Dam

류하고 있음에도 불구하고 직업 배우들이 출연한 것으로 알려진 영화들이다. 주지하다시피 상업극영화의 서사기법을 차용한 기록영화를 반기록영화 즉, 세미 다큐멘터리라고 한다. 영국과 미국, 캐나다를 중심으로 시작된 세미 다큐멘터리는 현실이 그 어떤 허구적인 이야기보다 더 자극적이었던 제2차 세계대전의 산물이었다. 당연히 주요 소재는 전쟁이었고 임무를 수행하는 군인들의 모습을 담고 있었지만 사실상 모든 행위는 연출된 것이었다. [26] '영화용어해설 집」, 이승구·이용관 엮음, 집문당, p. 151. 동란기의 기록영화 중에는 육군포병학교 기간요원 및 생도들의 생활상과 교육과정을 드라마틱하게 수록 [27] 한국영화진흥조합, 「한국영화총서」, 1972, p. 301 했다는 〈육군포병학교〉(1951)가 반기록영화의 전형적인 작품일 것이다.

그러나 전거한 두 영화의 경우는 반기록영화의 테두리에 묶는 것을 유보해야 할 영화들이다. 기록영화임에도 불구하고 직업 배우들의 전문적인 연기로 극적 구성을 채우고 있기 때문이다. 말 그대로 극영화와 기록영화의 중간 지점에 위치한다는 의미에서 반기록영화로 지칭할 수도 있겠지만 동란기 기록영화의 독특한 제작 경향으로 조금 차별된 의미를 지닌다. 6·25전쟁으로 인해 소수의 극영화만 만들어지고 있었던 상황에서 기록영화에도 배우가 활용되는 등 극영화와 기록영화의 양식이 혼재되는 특이한 양상을 보이게 된 것이다. 동란기의 한국영화들은 기록 부분과 극 부분이 영화 전체에서 어느 정도를 차지하느냐에 따라 기록영화 혹은 극영화로 불려졌던 것으로 판단된다.

이러한 양식의 혼재는 순수 극영화에도 나타난다. 동란기 극영화의 특징은 직업 배우들이 출연한 극임에도 불구하고 극영화로 보이지 않고 기록영화로 보인다 [28] '국산영화계의 결산」, 중앙일보, 1953.12.6 는 것이다. 그것은 6·25전쟁이 직접적인 배경으로 등장하는 군사극에 제한되지 않는다. 대부분 로케이션 촬영으로 이루어졌던 극영화 제작환경을 고려할 때 동란기 사회상이 있는 그대로 드러나는 것은 당연한 결과였다. 로케이션 현장의 관중들이 무표정하게 등장 [29] 장갑상, 민주신보, 1952.10.15 했다는 〈태양의 거리〉(1952)처럼 극영화 화면들은 실제 사회상을 사실적으로 담아내는 기록영화 화면과 유사할 수밖에 없었다. 전쟁을 몸소 겪은 도시 혹은 일선 진지에서 한 대의 카메라만으로 촬영하는 방식이 영화적 리얼리티를 구축했을 리 만무하고 전쟁을 실제로 체험한 관객들의 공감을 이끌어내기도 힘들었을 것이다.

5 —

　　"뉴스영화의 복사와 단조한 실사는 기록영화의 감을 준다"[30 장갑상, 민주신보, 1952.1.13.]는 〈삼천만의 꽃다발〉(1951)처럼 삽입된 뉴스영화 장면들도 극영화를 기록영화로 보이게 하는 이유이다. 국방부와 미공보원의 협조를 얻어 실제의 낙동강 전투 장면이 삽입되었다[31 정봉석, 「부산영화사」, 「항도 부산」, 제14호, p. 334]는 〈낙동강〉(1952)처럼 뉴스영화 화면의 삽입은 동란기 극영화의 중요한 특징이었다. 실제 기록 장면이 극영화에 삽입되는 경우는 동란기 직후에 만들어진 영화에서도 계속된다. 〈운명의 손〉(1954)의 부두 장면에서 이향과 윤인자가 부두를 바라보는 숏[shot]들 다음에 미군들이 하역하는 뉴스영화 장면을 연결한 것이 대표적인 예로, 필름이 남아 있지 않은 동란기 영화양식의 혼용을 미루어 짐작할 수 있게 하는 대목이다.

　　극영화 화면이 기록영화와 유사하게 보인 것은 당시에 가능했던 영화기술 수준과도 연관이 있을 것이다. 필름의 형식으로 구분하면 동란기에 제작된 영화는 대부분이 16밀리 영화였다. 동란기에 개봉한 26편[32 동란기 한국영화의 제작 편수가 극영화 14편, 기록영화 8편이 아닌 극영화 17편과 기록영화 9편이라는 것은 연구자의 졸고 「한국영화 성장기의 토대에 대한 연구-동란기 한국영화 제작을 중심으로」(중앙대학교 첨단영상대학원 영상예술학과 석사학위 논문, 2002)를 통해 밝힌 바 있다.]의 한국영화 중에서 35밀리 작품은 극영화 〈삼천만의 꽃다발〉(1951)과 기록영화 〈정의의 진격〉 1, 2부(1951, 1952) 등 3편뿐이다. 이는 당시에 35밀리 필름을 구한다는 것이 얼마나 힘든 일이었는지를 여실히 보여주는 대목이다.

　　당시 영화평론가들은 성능으로 보아 시각적 미감을 애초에 기대할 수 없는 16밀리 필름으로 극영화가 제작되었다는 것은 비극을 지나 희극이라고 지적한다.[33 유두연, 「16밀리 영화의 맹점」, 경향신문, 1953.11.13.] 영화평에서도 16밀리인지 35밀리인지는 영화를 평가하는 중요한 척도가 된다. 화면을 밝은 것과 어두운 것으로 구분하는 것이 당시 영화기술 분석의 방법이었는데 전자는 35밀리 영화, 후자는 16밀리 영화였다. 〈코리아〉(1954)는 35밀리인 관계로 화면이 선명하여 내용과 대상이 감흥을 돋운다[34 박인환, 「한국영화의 전환기-영화 〈코리아〉를 계기로 하여」, 경향신문, 1952.5.2.]는 반면, 16밀리 영화인 〈삼천만의 꽃다발〉은 기재 조건의 불비로 화면의 암조를 가져왔다[35 장갑상, 민주신보, 1952.1.13.]는 식이다.

6

    기술 표준으로 인식되었던 35밀리 필름으로 제작된 영화가 동란기 이전에는 어느 정도의 비율을 차지하고 있었을까. 해방 이후 1946년에서 1950년 전쟁 발발 전까지의 제작 편수 62편 중 35밀리는 24편, 16밀리는 38편으로, 35밀리 필름으로 제작된 영화가 상당한 비율을 차지하고 있었다. 전 시기에 비해 동란기 영화 대부분이 16밀리로 제작되었다는 것은 기술의 퇴보보다 한국영화의 명맥을 유지하려는 노력이라는 관점에서 평가되어야 한다. 16밀리 필름은 동란기 한국영화인들이 창작활동을 멈추지 않은 절실한 수단이었던 것이다.

    하지만 전쟁 중에 힘겹게 만들어진 대부분의 한국영화들은 외국영화에 밀려 개봉할 기회도 잡지 못하고 있었다. 〈총검은 살아 있다〉(1953), 〈북위 41도〉(1953), 〈피난일기〉, 〈한라산에 봄 오다〉, 〈영광의 길〉(1953), 〈백만의 별〉(1954) 같은 영화들은 만들어놓고도 개봉을 못하는 형편이었다. 그 이유는 제작사 측과 극장 측의 미묘한 관계 때문이었다. 제작사 측은 "봉절영화는 봉절영화관에서 봉절하는 것이 영화의 가치도 있고 관객의 주목도 받게 된다"는 입장이었고, 서울 시내 봉절영화관(시공관, 수도극장) 측은 전쟁 중에 만들어진 16밀리 영화들이 예술성이 없기 때문에 35밀리 영화만을 상영한다는 원칙을 내세우고 있었다. [36] 서울특별시공관 운영위원회(제2회)의 시공관 사용허가요강 결의사항」, 평화신문, 1953.10.7. 결국 〈백만의 별〉은 35밀리에 국한한다는 규정에 대한 반발로, 화면의 흐려짐을 감수하고 35밀리로 확대하면서까지 개봉을 추진하기에 이른다. [37] 중앙일보, 1953.12.6. 〈피난일기〉, 〈한라산에 봄 오다〉 같은 영화들이 제작이 완성되었다는 기록 [38] 중앙일보, 1953.12.6. 에도 불구하고 『한국영화총서』에 누락되어 있는 것은 당시 개봉을 하지 못했던 것이 결정적인 이유로 추정된다. 16밀리 영화였으므로 시공관 같은 개봉관에서 개봉할 수 있는 기회를 놓친 것이다.

7

    무성영화와 발성영화라는 사운드 형식으로 본다면 동란기를 평가하는 양상은 달라지게 된다. 동란기를 기술이 퇴보한 시기로만 보기에는 무리가 있기 때문이다. 1948년에 제작된 한국영화 중 발성영화는 12편, 무성영화는 10편으로 무성영화가 무시할 수 없는 편수를 차지하고 있었다. 이듬해에 들어서면 발성영화는 18편, 무성영화는 2편으로 무성영화 시대

아리랑 | 김소동 | 1957 | Arirang(Arirang) | Kim So Dong

를 거의 벗어나게 되고 1950년에는 무성영화가 완전히 사라지게 된다. 1948년에 제작된 〈검사와 여선생〉이 6·25전쟁 발발 직후인 1950년 8월 부산에서 변사 신출의 해설로 상영되었다 39 부산일보, 1950.8.2(주윤탁, 『부산영화사』, 『부산시사』, 부산직할시사편찬위원회, 1991, p. 498의 재인용)는 것은 변사의 공연이 곁들여진 무성영화가 관객들에게 그다지 낯설지 않았음을 보여주는 대목이다. 다행히 동란기에는 영화가 발성이어야 한다는 원칙이 지켜졌다. 비록 자기 녹음기가 없어 생필름에 녹음하는 방식이었지만 무성영화로 다시 퇴보하는 현상은 일어나지 않았던 것이다. 그 원칙을 고수하는 데에는 협동영화제작소의 이경순 등 한국영화 기술인들의 활약이 뒷받침되었다. 이는 동란기가 해방기와 성장기를 이어주는 고리 이상의 의미를 가졌음을 시사하는 것이다.

1—

There are several specific production trends that we can identify from the wartime period. Cities other than the capital city of Seoul showed their attempts at making films. They followed the trail to revive "Korean realism." Counter-espionage and military films were produced as well as documentary and dramatic films. These genres were sometimes blended together and they were made mainly with 16mm sound film.

In essence, the War created an opportunity for smaller cities such as Daegu, Busan, Masan, and Jinhae, so called refugee cities, to take part in filmmaking projects. Refugee cities here meant places where refugees gathered for temporary protection away from the battlefields. As a result, the center of filmmaking was temporarily shifted away from Seoul towards these other locations. In particular, a number of filmmaking activities were conducted in Daegu and Busan in cooperation with the local workforce. For example, Lee Min, an actor, was working on his debut film, 〈Hwarang-do〉(1951), when the war broke out. Later, this film was completed in Daegu. Director Shin Sang Ok's 〈The Evil Night〉(1952) was also made in Daegu. According to an interview with Shin Sang Ok on 10 September 2001, it was a slow and piecemeal process. He filmed segment by segment whenever the actors could meet and shot as many scenes as possible whenever he could. As noted in many newspaper articles, the local press seemed to pay a lot of attention to the filmmaking fever in Daegu, and addressed the production activities as the "Hollywoodization" of Korea(Youngnam Daily Newspaper(Youngnam Ilbo): 21 June 1952). Though it was only for a short time period, Daegu became the center of film production.

Some films were based on serial novels from the newspapers as experiments with a new style. For instance, a serial novel from Youngnam Daily Newspaper, 〈Women Frontline(Yeosung Chunson)〉, was selected as a test case. There was a newspaper advertisement for the position of the lead female character, Ok Ran, by seeking only the minimum requirements of a woman aged between 19 and 25 who was also a middle school graduate. According to the evidence, though this project was never completed, its casting and production efforts are enough to guess how fervent the filmmaking in Daegu was(Youngnam Daily Newspaper: 25 June 1952).

The flurry of filmmaking in Daegu around this time opened many doors for local people who wanted to build film careers. The art director of Jayu Cinema(Jayu Kukjang), Min Kyung Sik, and the planning director, Byon Jong Geun and many more Daegu citizens were involved in the making of 〈Street of the Sun(Taeyang-ui Geori)〉(1952), which was a story centered around the lives of refugees. After the war, they moved to Seoul to continue their film careers. Around the same time, Son Jeon attracted attention for making 〈Thirty Eight Parallel I Have Crossed(Naega Num-eun Sampal-sun)〉 (1951) and 〈Night of Terror(Gongpo-ui Bam)〉(1952). Son Jeon started his film career as an actor in 〈Rainbow(Mujige)〉(1936), directed by Lee Kyu Hwan who came from Daegu. Half of the films in Son Jeon's filmography were completed during the wartime, and the war provided him with an opportunity to work in Daegu, his hometown. Busan also shared this filmmaking fever. The local Culture Research Center(Hyangto Munhwa Yeongu-hoi) was a gathering place for Busan-based artists. They produced 〈Nakdong River(Nakdong-gang)〉(1952) with the support of the Department of the Public Information of the Kyungnam Province. In Masan, Kim Chan Young personally financed and produced 〈Bouquet for All Koreans(Samchun-man-ui Kkotdabal)〉(1951). In the past, Kim Chan Young had worked for the Manchuria Film Association(Manchu Younghwa Hyuphoi) as a still photographer. Choi Hyun, a dancer from Masan, and Hwang Ryu Hee, an actor from 〈Hurrah! For Freedom〉(1946), were the main characters of 〈Bouquet for All Koreans〉, and, according to Bok Hye Sook (in 「Me and 50 Years of the Film」, 「Monthly Film(Wolgan Younghwa)」 published in April 1974 (p. 72)), the other members of the cast were all young actors also from Masan.

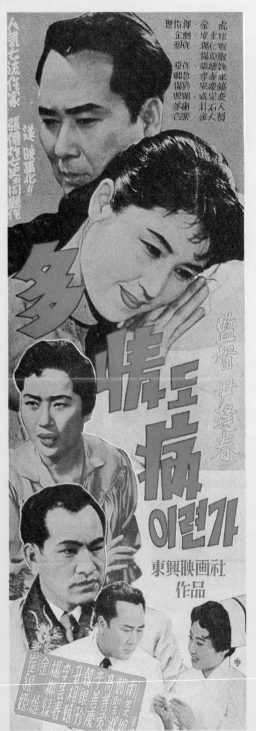

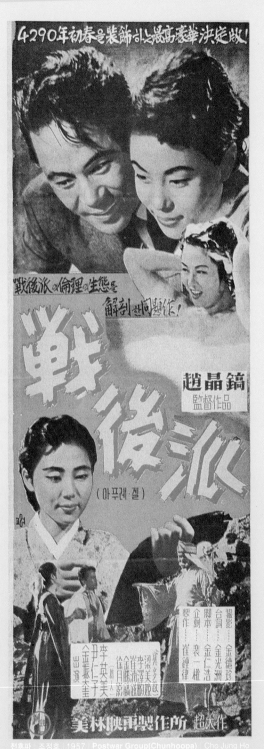

다정도 병이런가(다정도 병이런가) | 윤봉춘 | 1957
Sweet and Kind for You(Dajung-do Byong-iryon-ga)
Yoon Bong Chun

전후파 | 조정호 | 1957 | Postwar Group(Chunhoopa) | Cho Jung Ho

운명의 여인 | 강원주 | 1957
A Woman of the Destiny(Woonmyong-ui Yeoin) | Kang Won Joo

김삿갓 | 이만흥 | 1957
Wanderer Mr. Kim Satgot(Kim Satgot) | Lee Man Heung

The films made in these refugee cities mostly focused on social problems that developed during the War. Clearly, the Italian Neo-realism films influenced them. The film community was most interested in the Italian Neo-realism films such as ⟨To Live in Peace⟩(1946), ⟨The Bicycle Thief⟩(1948) and ⟨Rome Open City⟩(1945). The Daegu Maeil Newspaper(Daegu Maeil Shinmun) frequently advertised the screening of Italian films. For example, the ⟨The Bicycle Thief⟩ screened at the Chayu Cinema on 1 January 1952. ⟨To Live in Peace⟩ screened in Mangyung-gwan on 11 March 1952. There was also a double feature of classic Italian films(⟨The Bicycle Thief⟩ and ⟨Rome Open City⟩) at the Chayu Cinema on 13 March 1952. According to Hur Baek Nyon, from the Seoul Newspaper(3 May 1952), these Italian neo-realism films, which seemed to rise out of the ashes of war, provided momentum and new ideas for the Korean film community and other Koreans who were experiencing the harsh realities of the Korean War. The Italian films showed what life could be like when the War ended.

The new stimulation that filmmakers were receiving was expressed as "Korean Realism". For instance, a well known Busan film critic and an English professor at the Busan National University, Jang Kap Sang regarded ⟨The Evil Night⟩ as a "leading touchstone for Korean realism"(Manchu Shinbo, 20 March 1952: 「Film and Criticism (Younghwa-wa Bi-pyung)」, Samshin Publishing company, 1970). Lee Hae Rang was another important critic who mentioned that ⟨The Evil Night⟩ was interesting because it used the elements from the works of Vittorio De Sica and Roberto Rossellini in terms of the direction and the narrative structure(「After watching ⟨The Evil Night part 2⟩」, Kyunghyang Daily Newspaper, 20 March 1952). ⟨The Evil Night⟩ was based on the same titled short story written by Kim Kwang Joo. The story was originally published in 「Baekmin Magazine for 33 People」, but it may have contained the director's real refugee experiences from the Korean War. Considering that the trend of using footages of

마인 | 한형모 | 1957 | **The Devil(Main)** | Han Hyung Mo

newsreels in feature films was a new concept for filmmakers, documentary scenes were also inserted into his film as an experiment. Director Shin Sang Ok confessed that he was incredibly shocked and stimulated by watching Vittorio De Sica's 〈The Bicycle Thief〉(Jung Young Il, 「50 Years of Screen History From the Angles of the Kingpins Part 10」 Shin Sang Ok & Choi Eun Hee, Chosun Daily Newspaper(Chosun Ilbo), 26 June 1966). 〈Flower of Hell(Jiok-hwa)〉(1958), was one particular film made by director Shin Sang Ok that opened with real scenes of a dancing hall where prostitutes for foreigners(Yang Gongju) and American soldiers danced together. According to an interview with Shin Sang Ok from 10 September 2001, the Italian Neo-realism movement also influenced 〈Flower of Hell〉.

One of the key motifs of Korean realism films was 'the street woman'. With the prolonged war, the nation was lost in the nihilism of the situation. Obviously, people had experienced despair and anxiety from losing the very basis of their lives. At the same time, the morality of large parts of the society became decadent. A strange sense of extravagancy began to pervade through society. Korea was overcome with an overflow of consumer goods. A new propensity toward consumerism was formed as Koreans focused and affiliated themselves with momentary livelihood. People were living amidst confusion and chaos. According to Jung Sung Ho(「The Korean War and the Population Changes in the Social Science Context」, 「Korean War and the Changes of the Social Structure」, pp. 34-41), the ethics of sex also became corrupted. With these economic difficulties, women were forced to sell their bodies to foreign soldiers in order to support themselves and their families. This harsh reality was reflected in a number of films. For example, the daughter of a prostitute in 〈Street of the Sun〉 and Hyun Ok from 〈Veiled Lady(Veil Buin)〉(1952) had failed to kill themselves in the stories and ended up walking the street, mirroring what was really happening in the society at that time.

3

Other types of films began to set a trend of using action and suspense devices in the narrative story telling. 〈Muddy Stream(Takryu)〉(1954) by Lee Man Hung, 〈The Final Temptation(Choihu-ui Youhok)〉(1953) and 〈Street of Temptation(Youhok-ui Geori)〉(1954) by Chung Chang Hwa, and 〈The Hand of Destiny(Woonmyung-ui Son)〉(1954) by Han Hyung Mo portrayed the gritty background of the wartime and dealt with the crimes going on in the chaotic society. They were also action films, which dealt with seedy people from the underworld involved in espionage, gangs and smuggling. Films such as these appealed to audiences with their suspense and thrill. According to Lee Young Il(「Korean Film Making Story」, p. 408), these types of films were viewed as an aesthetic achievement during the wartime.

Films dealing with the subject of smugglers began with 〈Passion of the Ocean(Bada-ui Yeol-jong)〉(1947). An increase in the number of smuggling cases had become a serious social issue and concern. According to Bok Hye Sook(「Me and 50 Years of the Film」, 「Monthly Film(Wolgan Younghwa)」, April, 1974, p. 72), there were lots of films using this theme. Four films were produced in 1948: 〈Sun in the Night(Bam-ui Taeyang)〉, 〈Sorrowful Rain(Soowoo)〉, 〈Disconnected Route(Kkeuna-jin Hangro)〉 and 〈Daybreak(Yeomyung)〉. A fifth film, 〈Passion of the Ocean〉, was made soon after. According to the 「Korean Film Collection」, 〈Passion of the Ocean〉, 〈Sun in the Night〉 and 〈Sorrowful Rain〉 were categorized as action films, and 〈Disconnected Route〉 and 〈Daybreak〉 were considered as social enlightening films. However, all of the above five films were planned and produced by various public offices in order to promote new social policies that attempted to eradicate smuggling. The Maritime Guard supported 〈Passion of the Ocean〉 while the 1st district of the National Police Agency supported 〈Sun in the Night〉. Also, the 7th district of the National Police Agency supported 〈Daybreak〉. These were educational films produced for the wide general public. The

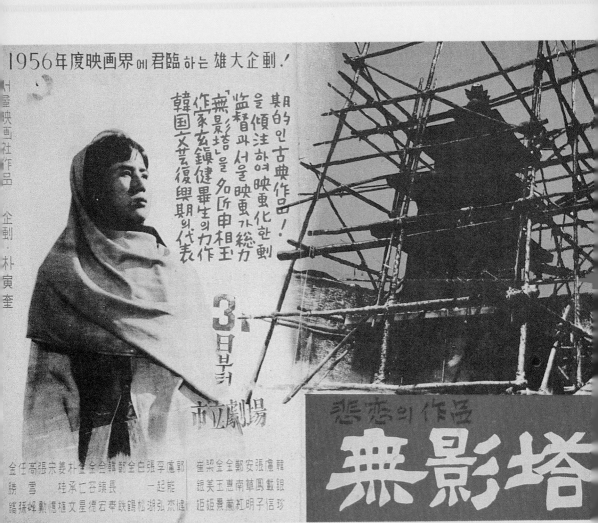

무영탑 | 신상옥 | 1957 | **A Pagoda with No Shadow(Muyoung-top)** | Shin Sang Ok

aim was to convey the image of a democratic police system and a society which both supported tougher smuggling policies(「Korean Film Collection」, pp. 264-276).

The action films as well as the enlightenment films of the late 1940s, which dealt with smugglers and social problems, reappeared during the war. However, the films now focused on a different subject: anti-communism. Two films in particular, 〈Sun in the Night〉 and 〈Sorrowful Rain〉 told stories about clever and competent police detectives who arrested gangs of smugglers. Each story took place in a cabaret, and the same ideas were reproduced in 〈Muddy Stream〉(1954) and 〈The Hand of Destiny〉 (1954). In these two films from 1954, police detectives were replaced with anti-espionage agents and the smugglers were replaced with covert communist infiltrators and spies. The cabaret-based spies were arrested by counterespionage agents with the help of the cabaret owner, who was also the mistress of one of the spies. Lee Jip Gil starred as the anti-espionage agent in 〈Muddy Stream〉 and Lee Hyang performed in the same role in 〈The Hand of Destiny〉. Kim Shin Jae played the female spy, Natasha, in 〈Muddy Stream〉 and Yoon In Ja played the role of Margaret, another female spy. Each film (and each actress) promoted an increased awareness of anti-espionage efforts, which served the anti-communism ideology of South Korea. According to an article in the Chungang Daily Newspaper(Chungang Ilbo), anti-communism sentiments seemed to be the primary ideology of Korea at this time(「Korean Film Community Becoming Active」, 11 April 1954).

4 ─

Hong Gae Myung and his work, 〈Fellow Soldiers〉, first introduced films dealing with anti-communism themes in 1949. The film was produced with the support of the United States Information Service. Though it was known as an anti-communism film, along with 〈Breaking the Wall(Sungbyuk-eul Ttulgo)〉 and 〈For my Country(Nara-rul

Wihayeo)〉, in reality, it could be understood in the context of and in connection with the same reasoning found in 〈Sun in the Night〉, 〈Sorrowful Rain〉 and 〈Daybreak〉, which were both made in 1948. 〈Sun in the Night〉 and 〈Daybreak〉 both dealt with the subject of the police. 〈Fellow Soldiers〉 was a story about two brothers who crossed the border and came to South Korea. Each brother became a policeman and a soldier who joined the anti-communism battle and actively stood guard against the 'red menace.' Subjects of the police and the military were mixed together as one concept through this film. In addition, there were others like 〈Breaking the Wall〉, which was the debut film of Han Hyung Mo, and 〈For my Country〉 by Ahn Jong Hwa. Both were anti-communism feature films and the Troop Information and Education Center supported 〈For my Country〉. Apart from the above feature films, there were two anti-communism documentaries called 〈Reality of North Korea(Bukhan-ui Siljeong)〉 by Lee Chang Geun and 〈Broken Down Thirty Eight Parallel(Moonujin Sampal-sun)〉 by Yoon Bong Chun. Five out of the twenty films released in 1949 dealt with the theme of anti-communism. The two films that were released in 1951, 〈Hwarangdo(Hwarangdo)〉 and 〈Thirty Eight Parallel I Have Crossed〉, had been planned for production before the Korean War started. It should be noted that the term "anti-communism film" was a label created after the War; it was not used at that time. Instead, terms such as "military film" or "tendency film" were the common words used by the press and the Korean film community.

This anti-communism ideology was the outcome of the Cold War, but it had been in existence even before the Korean War started. It was used as a mechanism to integrate people together and was treated almost like a civilian religion. The documentaries produced during the War were a disguised form of the military film and in actuality they were sponsored by the military as a way of preaching anti-communism ideology. The subjects of the military and anti-communism were actively exploited in notable feature films. 〈Attack Order(Chul Kyok Myongryung)〉(1954) was a melodramatic story of a captain from North Korea, portrayed by Lee Jip Gil, who became a member of the South Korean Air Force. According to Chang Kap Sang(『Film and Criticism(Younghwa-wa Bi-pyung)』, Samshin Publishing company, 1970, p. 251), the film's intention was to underscore the importance of the air force and inspire patriotism in the audience. The military headquarters actively sponsored these types of stories and filmmaking projects because they naturally supported the military and promoted the new government policies.

The subject of the Korean War was also used in a number of pictures made by Hollywood studios. Recreated locations of the frontlines of the Korean War were used as the background sets for a few Hollywood films. One film in particular, ⟨One Minute to Zero⟩(1952), was sponsored directly by the US Department of Defense. It was produced by RKO and filmed at the army manoeuvring grounds in Colorado. It portrayed the military operations of the Busan bridgehead. According to 「The Korean War and Foreign Films」(Film News(Younghwa Shibo), 10 April 1953), large groups of Asian extras were mobilized for this picture and large scale open sets were designed to look like the downtown of Daegu city as well as its surrounding farming villages and rice paddies. According to the same article, a French feature film crew visited locations in Korea to shoot their project called ⟨Creva Couer⟩, a film about a brave army officer in the Korean War. The cinematographers Henrie Roche and Jean Ravie and the director Jaque Duron actually stayed in Korea for five months to complete their production. This film contained real scenes of downtown Pyongyang and casted an actual army officer, Garce, as the main character.

5 —

Other war films included documentaries. ⟨Bayonet is Alive(Chong-gum-un Saraitda)⟩(1953) and ⟨The Road of Glory(Young-gwang-ui Gil)⟩(1953) have been categorized

청실홍실 정일택 1957 Blue Thread Red Thread(Chung-sil Hong-sil) Chung Il Taek

실낙원의 별(실락원의 별) | 홍성기 | 1957 | The Star of the Lost Paradise(Sillakwon-ui Byul) | Hong Sung Ki

as documentaries according to the 「Korean Film Collection」. But in reality, professional actors starred in these two films. Hence, they should be labelled as semi-documentaries, which borrow the narrative structure of more commercial films. This semi-documentary style was more the product of the Second World War where real war stories were far more interesting than most fictitious ones. This style was especially popular in the UK, USA and Canada. The main subjects of semi-documentaries were war and soldiers on their missions. However, nearly all of the action projected on the screen was staged and directed in advance(「Film Terminology」, Ed. Lee Seung Ku and Lee Yong Gwan, Jimmundang Press, p. 151). According to the 「Korean Film Collection」, 〈The Artillery School(Yook-gun Pobyong Hak-gyo)〉(1951) was a typical wartime semi-documentary, which described the school activities and private lives of key military personnel as well as the students in training(MPPC, 1972, p. 301).

Seeing that 〈Bayonet Is Alive〉(1953) and 〈The Road of Glory〉(1953) contained professional actors, there can be doubt about which category or genre of films they belong to: Should they be grouped as semi-documentaries or not? Though they followed the typical structure associated with and found in most documentaries, the use of actors had a significant impact on the art of expressing dramatic elements. In this sense, they should be differentiated from typical semi-documentaries. 〈Bayonet Is Alive〉(1953) and 〈The Road of Glory〉(1953) should be considered as examples of a unique filmmaking style found during the wartime, when the war allowed only a few films to be made and provided starring roles for a few actors in documentaries. It can be said that during this time the structure of documentary and feature films were all confounded. A film's genre depended on which narrative quality or strategy was emphasized more in the film.

Feature films also witnessed the mixing of narrative styles and storytelling structures. Films shot with professional actors often looked like documentaries rather than feature films(「Closing the Domestic Film Community of the Year」, Chungang Daily Newspaper, 6 December 1953). Many films were shot on location, capturing the live social atmosphere through the viewfinder. For example, the expressionless people, or the bystanders, who were in the location were filmed as part of the scene and projected on the screen without being edited. These characteristics were not only limited to the military feature film with the Korean War background(Jang Kap Sang, Manchu Shinbo, 15 October 1952). Many scenes in feature films were similar to those of the objective documentaries of the time. For example, 〈Street of the Sun〉(1952) contained real images of the society. It was hard to construct a totally fictitious reality considering that there was only one camera shooting in and around the scenes of ruined cities and battlefields. As a result, it was also more difficult to arouse sympathy from the audience who already had been exposed to the real war-torn streets and bleak realities of the period.

6

Feature films also made use of newsreels and monotonous actuality footage, which gave the impression of watching documentaries(Jang Kap Sang, Manchu Shinbo, 13 January 1952). For example, 〈Bouquet for All Koreans〉 inserted newsreels into the narrative, making it look like a documentary. Also, with the sponsorship of the Ministry of Defense and the United States Information Service, real battle scenes from the Nakdong River were inserted into the film(Jung Bong Seok, 「Busan Film History」, 「Harbour City Busan」(no. 14), p. 334). As found in the film 〈Nakdong River〉(1952), inserting newsreels was a significant characteristic of the wartime feature film. This trend also continued after the war. In 〈The Hand of Destiny〉(1954), scenes of a harbour were composed of two edited parts: actors Lee Hyang and Yoon In Ja watched over the harbour, and real newsreels showed American soldiers unloading materials from boats. Examples such as these help us to understand how a single film made during the wartime used a mixture of styles and staged formats to tell a story.

The film technology used around this time also influenced the look of feature films, making them appear like grainy documentaries. Twenty-six of the films released during the Korean War were mostly produced in 16mm film(See note). Only two of the films included in the statistics above were shot on 35mm film: the feature 〈Bouquet for All Koreans〉(1951), and the documentary 〈Righteous Attack(Jungui-ui Jin-kyuk)〉(1951 & 1952). This illustrates how difficult it was to secure 35mm film stock and equipment for filmmaking. Film critics of the time have pointed out that making feature films with 16mm equipment was not a tragedy. They considered the use of the 16mm format as a comedy since advanced visual aesthetics could not be expected from this inferior technology(You Doo Yeon, 「The Blind Points of 16mm Films」, Kyunghyang Daily Newspaper, 13 November 1953).

Essentially, there was a strong belief that a formal and mature cinema needed to

항구의 일야 | 김화랑 | 1957
One Night at the Harbor(Hanggu-ui Ilya) | Kim Hwa Rang

봉이 김선달 | 한홍열 | 1957 | Famous Mr. Kim Sundal(Bong I Kim Sundal) | Han Hong Ryol

선화공주 | 최성관 | 1957
Princess Sunhwa(Sunhwa Gongju) | Choi Sung Gwan

잃어버린 청춘 | 유현목 | 1957
Lost Youth(Iruburin Chungchun) | You Hyun Mok

involve the 35mm format in order to be considered advanced. In Korean film criticism, the use of 16mm or 35mm film changed the attitudes of the criticism. For example, the analysis of film technology was based on the brightness of the screen; 35mm films were considered to have the right amount of light and brightness while 16mm films were considered too dark. Here are a few more examples of this type of film criticism: On the one hand, Park In Hwan addressed that 〈Korea(Korea)〉(1954), which was made with 35mm equipment, contained clear pictures that animated the content and made the acting more enjoyable(「The Turning Point of the Korean Films: Korea as a Momentum」, Kyunghyang Daily Newspaper, 2 May 1952). On the other hand, 〈Bouquet for All Koreans〉 was made with a 16mm camera, and Jang Kap Sang mentioned that the film looked so dark because of a lack of proper facilities(Manchu Shinbo, 13 January 1952).

Note: It was found that the films released during the Korean War was composed of fourteen feature films and eight documentaries, which is different from what was previously calculated as fourteen feature films and six documentaries. (This new research comes from Chung Chong Hwa, 「Thesis on the Foundation of the Korean Film Development: Focusing on the Film Production during the Korean Wartime」, M.A. Chungang University, Graduate school of Advanced Imaging Science, Multimedia and Film, 2002).

7 —

Clearly, 35mm films were regarded as the technological standard for filmmaking. Before the Korean War started, between 1946 and 1950, sixty-two films had been made. Out of these, twenty-four films were made with 35mm cameras, and thirty-eight were 16mm films. Though the number of 35mm films decreased during the wartime, the trend of using the 16mm format demonstrated active efforts to continue the filmmaking tradition in Korea rather than accept its demise. The deterioration of the film technology did not hold the Korean film community back from making films and keeping their creative work and ideas flowing during the difficult period.

However, the films produced during the wartime with these difficulties did not even have a chance to be released due to the influx of imported foreign films. 〈Bayonet is Alive〉(1953), 〈41 Degree North Latitude(Bukwe Sasip-ildo)〉(1953), 〈Refugee Diary(Pinan Ilgi)〉, 〈Spring Comes to Mt. Halla(Hallasan-e Bom-oda)〉, 〈Road of Glory〉(1953) and 〈Star of One Million People(Baekman-ui Byol)〉(1954) were not released because of conflicts between Korean production companies and the cinemas. Production companies insisted that "the films should be released in the first-run cinemas for the value, and to better attract audiences". But, the first-run cinemas in Seoul, such as Shigong Gwan and Sudo Cinema, had their own rules that only 35mm films could be screened. The cinemas believed that the 16mm films produced during the war did not have any artistic value. (See the 「Articles of Resolution for Permitting the Use of the First-run Cinema Suggested by the Cinema Operating Committee of the Seoul Metropolitan City」, Pyunghwa Newspaper(Pyunghwa Shinmun), 7 October 1953). In response to this article, 〈Star of One Million People〉 was later released after transferring it to 35mm film in spite of losing much of its picture clarity in the process(Chungang Daily Newspaper, 6 December 1953). Other films such as 〈Refugee Diary(Pinan Ilgi)〉 and 〈Spring Comes to Mt. Halla〉 were not released. They were forgotten and even dropped off of the list in the 〈Korean Film Collection〉. They lost the chance to be released at a first-run cinema due to their 16mm format.

8

From the point of view of silent films and talkies, the technological capabilities of the wartime period was somewhat advanced. Back in 1948, among the twenty-two films produced, there were twelve talkies and ten silent films. Silent films continued to be produced in large quantities. In 1949, only two films were silent films and eighteen talkies

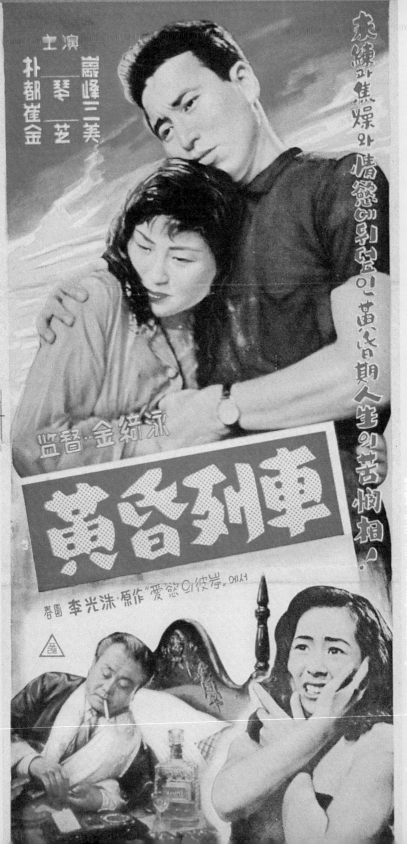

were produced. Starting in 1950, silent films were no longer produced. However, silent films were still screened even in the 1950s. For example, ⟨A Public Prosecutor and A Teacher(Geonsa-wa Yeo-Sunsaeng)⟩(1948) was screened in 1950. This film was shown with the performance of the byunsa, Shin Chul, in August 1950 after the Korean War broke out(Chu Yoon Tak, Busan Newspaper, 2 August 1950; 「Busan Film History」, 「Busan News」, Committee of Editing Busan City History, 1991, p. 498). People in the 1950s continued to enjoy silent films along with the byunsa performances. During the wartime, films were all produced as talkies. Though there was no electric recording machine, sound was still recorded on the raw films. Korean cinema did not have to regress back to the silent film period. Lee Kyung Soon from Hyupdong Film Studio, as well as other film engineers, was behind the scenes working to advance the sound industry. The achievements made during the wartime were not mere links between the post-liberation era and the growth of the film industry in the 1960s. Significant and long lasting advances had been made in film in Korea during this time.

1 ——

동란기 영화제작 지형을 그려보면 비교적 선진 영화 기재를 보유한 미공보원과 수공업적 환경을 사람이라는 테크놀로지로 극복한 국방부 정훈국 촬영대, 대한민국 공보처, 공군촬영대, 육군본부 촬영대, 해군 촬영대, 협동영화제작소 등의 국내기관으로 크게 구분해 볼 수 있다. 영화기술인들은 각 기관이 자리 잡은 진해, 부산, 대구 등의 피난도시로 분산되어 제작활동을 이어갔다.

미공보원[10 미공보원(United States Information Service), 약자로 USIS는 모두 미국 워싱턴에 본부를 둔 USIA(United States Information Agency)의 지부이다.]의 전신은 주한 미육군 제502부대이다. 해방 후 중앙청에 주둔했던 미 502부대는 디어든 대위의 책임하에 한 달에 두 번씩 내는 뉴스영화 〈전진대한보〉를 제작했다. 해방 직후 한국영화 현장에서 미첼 카메라, RCA 자기 녹음기, 무비올라 편집기, 제너럴 일렉트릭 노출계 등 서구의 선진 영화 기재를 보유했던 유일한 곳이었다. 녹음기사 이경순의 증언에 의하면 좌익 성향의 조선영화동맹에서 탈퇴한 우익 영화인들이 극동영화사를 만들어 미 502부대 산하로 소속되었다고 한다. 한국영화 기술인들로는 촬영, 녹음, 현상을 모두 담당한 이필우를 비롯하여 이명우, 유장산 등의 촬영기사, 이경순, 최칠복 등의 녹음기사, 김봉수, 김형근 등의 현상기사가 소속되어 있었다. 미 502부대는 뒤이어 촬영기사 김학성, 양세웅, 임병호, 홍일명 등을 보강해서 뉴스영화 제작의 중심 역할을 담당했다.

미 502부대의 영화기술인들은 한국영화 기술의 역사 그 자체인 이필우의 제자나 후배들이었다. 당시 한국영화 기술계의 핵심 인력들이 모두 모여 있었던 셈이다. 그들은 뉴스영화 〈전진대한보〉를 제작하는 한편, 미공보원의 시설을 이용하여 한국영화를 만들었다. 영화 기재는 미공보원이, 제작 인력은 한국영화 기술인이 담당하는 식이었다. 〈전진대한보〉는 동시녹음으로 제작될 정도로 미 502부대는 한국영화 영토에서 선진 영화 기술이 발휘되는 유일한 장이었고, 이후 동란기까지 미공보원의 최신 기재들과 선진 기술은 한국영화 기술인들에게 큰 영향을 주었다.

6·25전쟁이 발발하자 미공보원은 진해에 자리를 잡고 해군 장교 구락부에 녹음, 현상시설을 마련하였다. 이때는 촬영기사 임병호, 임진환, 배성학, 현상기사 김봉수, 김형근, 서은석, 이태환, 이태선, 녹음기사 이경순, 최칠복, 양후보, 편집기사 유재원, 김흥만, 김영희

가 소속되어 있었다. 41 이영일, 『한국영화전사』, p. 185. 편집기사 명단 중 유재원은 김영화(2001.11.16)의 인터뷰 결과 밝혀진 사실이다.
해방 후 미 502부대의 기술 인력들이 고스란히 이어진 상태에서 새로운 인력들도 더 확보되었음을 알 수 있다.

전쟁 발발 후 뉴스영화를 처음 시작한 곳도 미공보원이었다. 피난지 진해에서도 소규모로 진행된 부정기적인 뉴스영화 〈전진대한보〉는 해외편과 국내편을 수록, 1편당 30벌씩 복사하여 배포되었다. 이후에 국내 뉴스를 정기적으로 제공하기 위해 진해에서 가까운 창원군 상남면에 있는 구 일본 해군 통신소 건물을 개조하여 본격적인 제작 기반을 만들게 된다. 42 김원식, 「리버티 뉴스 15년의 영암」, 『신동아』, 1967년 7월호, p. 290. 원로 영화인들은 진해 미공보원 시절과 구별하여 상남 미공보원 혹은 상남 제작소 시절이라고 일컫는다. 〈전진대한보〉는 1953년 5월 1일 〈리버티뉴스〉로 개칭된다. 매주 1편씩 35밀리로 35벌씩 복사하여 43 〈리버티 뉴스〉는 16밀리 리버설 필름으로 촬영되어 35밀리로 확대되었다. 극장에서 〈대한뉴스〉와 교대로 상영했는데, 별도로 16밀리를 40벌씩 복사하여 이동 영사반을 통해 순회 상영도 하였다. 44 문화공보부, 『문화공보 30년』, 1979, p. 27. 당시 〈리버티뉴스〉 제1호에 수록된 내용을 살펴보면 국내 소식으로는 장택상의 총리 취임식과 리즈웨이 장군과 클라크 장군의 이 대통령 예방이 있고, 외국 소식으로는 미국의 신형 원자탄 실험 광경, 한국으로 발송되는 미국의 신형 탱크들, 트루먼 대통령 3년간의 수리를 마친 새 백악관으로 이사 45 김원식, 앞의 글, p. 291. 등 우방 미국에 관한 소식 일변도였다.

각 기관과 군에서 제작된 뉴스영화는 부산, 대구 등 피난지의 극장을 통하여 전선의 소식을 전하는 전시 시민들의 귀중한 매체였다. 뉴스영화를 제외하고는 복구된 라디오망과 피난도시에서 발행하는 신문 정도가 당시 매체의 전부였다.

2

국방부 촬영대는 한형모 46 한형모가 6·25전쟁이 발발하지마자 종군에 매우 적극적이었다는 것은 추후 그의 연구에서 꼭 주목해야 할 지점이다. 여순반란사건을 다룬 〈성벽을 뚫고〉(1949)로 감독 데뷔한 그의 작품 이력도 함께 고찰되어야 할 것이다. 감독이 흰 광목에 검은 글씨로 '국방부 촬영대'라고 쓴 완장을 만들어 차고 전선으로 촬영 나간 것으로 시작되었다. 47 1950년 7월 4일을 국방부 촬영대의 시작으로 삼은 것은 이날을 기념한 것이다. 6·25전쟁 발발 당시 한형모는 전남 목포에서 해군 본부의 홍보영화 〈사나이의 길〉을 촬영 중이었다. 전쟁 소식을 들은

애원의 고백 홍성기 1957
Confession of Imploration(Aewon-ui Gobaek) Hong Sung Ki

오해 마세요 권영순 1957
Don't Misunderstand Me(Oh-hae Maseyo) Kwon Young Soon

오해 마세요 | 권영순 | 1957 | Don't Misunderstand Me(Oh-hae Maseyo) | Kwon Young Soon

그는 촬영팀을 목포 해군 기지에 남겨두고 6월 28일 촬영하다 남은 필름 1만 자와 아이모 카메라를 들고 대전으로 올라간다. 당시 대전 도청에 내려와 있던 국방부의 승낙으로 한형모는 김보철, 김관수^{48 김보철은 반공영화 〈성벽을 뚫고〉(1949), 김관수는 경찰청 후원 영화 〈밤의 태양〉(1948), 반공영화 〈나라를 위하여〉(1949)의 제작자였다.} 와 함께 전지로 촬영을 나간다. 전세가 불리하여 대구까지 내려간 촬영대는 1950년 8월 〈사나이의 길〉 촬영기사 심재홍, 촬영부 양보환 등을 보강하여 국방부 정훈국 촬영대로 정식 발족한다.

9월 28일 서울 수복 후에는 을지로 4가의 허바허바사장에 '군영화 촬영대' 라는 간판을 걸어놓고 사용하다가 1951년 1·4후퇴로 부산 보수동에 자리를 잡게 된다. 목욕탕 건물을 징발하여 평양 촬영소의 노획품으로 원시적인 현상시설을 만들고 촬영기사 외에도 현상기사, 편집기사 등을 충원한다. 1952년 1월 군사영화촬영소로 승격될 정도로 전쟁의 기록을 남기는 데 중요한 역할을 담당하였다. 촬영기사로는 김학성, 홍일명, 심재홍, 양보환, 김보철, 이성춘, 변인집 등이 활동했고, 현상기사로는 김창수, 노희삼, 염화춘 등이, 편집기사로는 양주남, 김희수 등이 활동하였다. 국방부는 가장 늦게 뉴스영화 제작을 시작했지만 국방부 소속의 영화인들은 가장 활발한 활동을 보였다. 〈국방뉴스〉는 1952년 6월 27일 제1호를 시작으로 환도 전까지 총 49편이 제작되었다. ⁴⁹ 「군영화 40년사」, 국군홍보관리소, 1992, p. 528.

3 —

　　국방부 촬영대의 가장 큰 성과는 〈정의의 진격〉(1951, 1952) 2부작일 것이다. 동란기에 제작된 극영화와 기록영화를 포함해서 현재 유일하게 남아 있는 작품이다. 〈정의의 진격〉 1부 중 국군의 전황 기록 대부분은 국방부 촬영대 소속의 한형모, 김강위, 김종한 등이 촬영한 것이다. 김강위는 동해안 쪽 전투를, 김종한은 서해안 쪽 전쟁상황을, 한형모는 내륙의 전황을 기록했다. ⁵⁰ 한형모, 「국방부 촬영대 창설의 시대적 배경」, 「군영화 40년사」, p. 59.

　　어렵게 촬영은 진행되었으나 필름을 현상하지 못해 허바허바사진관에 쌓아두기만 하다가 ⁵¹ 양주남, 「촬영대 활동과 '정의의 진격' 제작을 회고」, 「군영화 40년사」, p. 81. 1·4후퇴 때 부산으로 옮겨 뒤늦게 후반작업에 들어간다. 목욕탕에 만든 현상실에서 네거티브 현상은 가능했지만 녹음시설이 없어 진해 미공보원에 의뢰하게 된다. 그러나 당시 녹음시설이 있는 유일한 곳이었던 미공보원은 외부의 일을 할 수 없다는 규정을 들어 국방부의 녹음 의뢰를 거부하고 한형모는 직접 〈정의의 진격〉 네거티브를 들고 일본으로 가게 된다.

　　극작가 오영진이 해설을 쓰고 아나운서 홍영보가 내레이션을 녹음한 〈정의의 진격〉은 후반작업을 마친 후 일본 UN 외신 구락부에서 시사회를 가졌고 외신기자들로부터 주목을 받았다. 판권을 사겠다는 일본 영화 배급업자들의 제의를 받고, 한형모는 〈정의의 진격〉 프린트 1벌과 20만불 상당의 영화 기재인 16밀리 현상기, 녹음기 1세트 그리고 프린트기 1대와 교환했다. 이렇게 판권 양도 대가로 받은 기재는 한국으로 가져와 촬영대의 후반작업에 바로 투입되었다. ⁵² 이성춘, 「한국영화촬영사(8)」, 「영상기술」, 제16호, 1996년 4월호, p. 76.

　　〈정의의 진격〉 1부의 제작에 참가했던 한형모, 김종한, 김강위는 이후 국방부 정훈국 촬영대를 그만두고 외신특파원으로 전황 기록을 이어나간다. 필름의 보급, 차량의 편의 등

촬영상의 좋은 조건 때문에^{53 이성춘, 앞의 글, p. 76.} 한형모는 I.N.S 특파원으로, 김종한은 M.G.M 특파원으로, 김강위는 워너브라더스 특파원으로 활동하게 되었다. 한형모는 틈틈이 〈정의의 진격〉 2부를 편집하였고 1부가 냉대를 받은 것과는 달리 2부는 상남 미공보원에서 현상과 녹음작업을 거쳐 완성하였다.^{54 한형모, 앞의 글, p. 59.}

　　〈정의의 진격〉 1부의 길이는 80분, 2부는 55분 정도로 실제 국방부 촬영대가 기록한 필름뿐만 아니라 미국 등 우방국의 뉴스영화나 북한군 측의 기록영화가 상당히 많은 부분 포함되어 있다. 국방부 촬영대원들이 기록한 촬영분으로는 6 · 25전쟁을 조망하는 기록영화의 전체 구성을 충당하기에는 부족했을 것이다. 북한군의 기록은 평양 촬영소에서 노획한 필름들로 알려져 있다. 〈정의의 진격〉 2부작은 현재도 6 · 25전쟁 자료화면으로 자주 활용되는 기록이다. 전후 극영화에도 자주 삽입되었는데 〈이 생명 다하도록〉(1960)의 초입에 김진규가 부상당하는 장면에 앞서 제시되는 전쟁 장면들이 대표적인 예이다.

　　〈정의의 진격〉 2부작의 제작기는 동란기 한국영화사에 대한 집약이라고 해도 과언이 아닐 것이다. 미 보병부대의 전투를 취재하던 김학성과 이성춘이 박격포탄에 맞아 부상을 입기도 하는 등 한국영화사에 다시없을 열악한 상황 속에서도 한국영화인들의 역량이 여실히 드러난 의미 있는 작품이다.

　　그 외 관과 군의 활동상황을 정리하면 다음과 같다. 공보처는 1952년 임시 수도 부산에서 뉴스영화 제작에 착수하여 〈특별전선뉴스〉를 부정기적으로 배포하다가 1953년 〈대한뉴스〉로 개칭하면서 월 1회 제작하였다.^{55 문화공보부, 앞의 책, p. 27.} 제작 주체는 공보처 산하의 대한영화사^{56 1948년 정부수립으로 공보처에 공보국 영화과가 설립되었고 1949년에는 국무총리령으로 영화과에 대한영화사가 설치되었다. 영화과는 기획과 촬영만을 하고 기타의 제작과정은 대한영화사가 담당하는 것으로 역할이 분리되었다. 현재 국립영화제작소의 전신이다.}였다. 경남 도청 지하실에 현상소를 만들고 아이모 카메라 2대와 인화기 1대로 뉴스 제작활동을 재개한 것이다. 안종화 감독이 영화과장이었고^{57 한성일보, 1950.5.17.} 소속 카메라맨들이 전후방에 파견되었다. 대구에는 공군 본부 정훈감실 공군 촬영대가 있었다. 촬영기사로는 홍성기 감독과 공군 현역 장교였던 정인엽이 활동했다. 이때 신상옥 감독, 함완섭 조명기사와 전택이, 김일해, 노경희, 황남 등의 배우도 소속되어 있었다.^{58 이영일, 앞의 책, p. 186. 명단 중 함완섭은 본인의 인터뷰(2001. 10.14)로 밝혀진 사실이다. 홍성기 감독은 공군 촬영대 소속의 스태프와 배우들과 함께 우리나라 최초의 본격 항공영화인 〈출격명령〉(1954)을 만들었다.} 육군 본부에

情炎에 불타는 두女人의 殉愛譜! 倫落의 女性이 찾어가는 사랑의 眞理는!!

監督 金漢日

原作 朴啓周

眞理의 밤

脚色 劉斗演
撮影 林炳鎬

古紀映畫文芸大作 第二回作品

子蘭林
蘭星鍾鎬輝
愛蘭基勝東
鄭尹下金張

仁鶯

尹嚴李

主題歌 女子의 友情 사랑합니다
센추리 레코-드 吹込

世紀映畫株式会社 製作 配給

진리의 밤 김한일 1957 Night of the Truth(Jilli-ui Bam) Kim Han Il

는 촬영기사 김명제, 녹음기사 조종국이, 해군에도 이필우를 중심으로 한 촬영대가 활동했
다.⁵⁹ 59 임병호, 「8·15 광복기의 한국영화」, 『영상기술』 제5호, 1992년 6월호, p. 118.

4 ——

동란기는 영화제작을 뒷받침하는 기술 인력이 구축되는 중요한 시기였다. 특히 국방부
정훈국 촬영대에는 다수의 한국영화 기술인들이 소속되어 활발한 제작활동을 펼쳤다. 자신의
전문분야를 막론하고 영화의 전반적인 과정에 모두 능숙해야만 했던 환경 속에서 그들의 기술
력은 자연스럽게 배양되었다. 촬영기사들은 촬영해 온 필름을 직접 현상하고 편집하는 등 후
반작업을 모두 담당해야 했고, 편집기사들과 현상기사들은 카메라를 들고 전선으로 촬영을 나
가는 과정을 거쳤다. 사실 1950년대 한국영화의 발전은 군영화의 발전과 맞물려 있었다고 해
도 과언이 아니다. 영화의 전반적인 과정에 능숙한 국방부 소속의 영화기술인들에 비해 다른
기술인들은 실력에 있어 차이가 날 수밖에 없었고 동란기 이후 국방부 정훈국 촬영대원들은
한국영화계를 대표하는 기술인들이 되었다. 다른 한 축이었던 미공보원 출신의 영화기술인들
도 이에 구분되는 인맥을 구성, 한국영화 기술 지형의 양대 산맥을 형성하게 된다.

There were many organizations producing films during the war. The United States Information Service in Korea was one of them as a branch of the United States Information Agency and it was equipped with the better-developed filmmaking facilities. There were also domestic Korean organizations that were equipped with large numbers of workers. Their manpower was more advanced than their facilities and the technology they used. Examples of these domestic Korean organizations were: the filming crew of the Troop Information and Education Center under the Ministry of Defense, the Public Information Bureau, the Film Unit of the Air Force, the Navy, and the Army Headquarters, and Hyupdong Film Studio. Film engineers were spread out all over Korea, including in Jinhae, Busan, Daegu and other refugee cities, and these were the places where the above institutions were located and where work continued.

The United States Information Service was previously known as the US army 502nd military unit located in the old building of the Governor General of Chosun. It moved into this location after the liberation, and began making and releasing the bimonthly newsreel, 〈Report of Korean Progressing〉, under the charge of an Army captain. It was the only place in Korea equipped with the better-developed filmmaking facilities such as a Mitchell camera, a RCA electric recorder, a Moviola and a GE exposure meter. According to Lee Kyung Soon, a recording engineer, right-wing filmmakers formed the Kukdong Film Company after removing themselves from the left-wing oriented Korean Film Union. These right-wingers later attached themselves to the US army 502nd military unit. Among them were the cinematographer Lee Pil Woo, who was versatile in dealing with film shooting, recording and development, as well as Lee Myung Woo and You Jang San. Kim Bong Soo and Kim Hyung Geun were also part of the new company as developing engineers. The US army 502nd military unit became the core producer of newsreels in Korea and grew with the reinforcements of more

순애보 | 한형모 | 1957 | A Love Story(Sunaebo) | Han Hyung Mo

가거라 슬픔이여(가거라 슲음이여) | 조긍하 | 1957 | **Let Go Your Sadness(Gagura Seulpeum-Iyo)** | Cho Geung Ha

cinematographers like Kim Hak Sung, Yang Se Woong, Im Byung Ho and Hong Il Myung.

Most of the film engineers in the US army 502nd military unit were either students or previous junior workers of Lee Pil Woo. Lee Pil Woo was one of the Korean film pioneers who played an important role in the history of film technology. Thanks to him, the US army 502nd military unit had become a center for advanced film technology engineers of Korea. While working on the 〈Report of Korean Progressing〉, they also produced other films by using the facilities of the United States Information

Service. The US army 502nd military unit was the only place where simultaneous sound recordings were conducted. The 〈Report of Korean Progressing〉 was the direct beneficiary of this modern technology. This advanced technological support gained from the US army 502nd military unit inspired many other film engineers before and during the Korean War.

When the war started, the United States Information Service moved down to Jinhae and built a makeshift sound recording studio and film lab in the Navy Officer's Club. According to Lee Young Il(「History of Korean Cinema」, p. 185), Im Byung Ho, Im Chin Hwan and Bae Sung Hak worked there as cinematographers, and Kim Bong Soo, Kim Hyung Geun, Seo Eun Seok, Lee Tae Hwan and Lee Tae Sun were there as film lab engineers. Recording engineers like Lee Kyung Soon, Choi Chil Bok and Yang Hoo bo, and film editors like You Chae Won, Kim Hung Man and Kim Young Hee were also members of the new makeshift facilities. The fact that You Chae Won participated in the United States Information Service became known much later from the testimony of Kim Young Hee(16 November 2001). All of this evidence shows that the US army 502nd military unit was strengthened by the many people joining it during the war.

It was specifically the United States Information Service that started making newsreels after the war began. In Jinhae, which was a refugee city at the time, the 〈Report of Korean Progressing〉 was still produced on an irregular basis and on a much smaller scale. It was made into two versions: domestic and international. Thirty copies of each version were made and distributed. Later on, the old Japanese Navy Correspondence Building in Sangnam, Changwon-gun, was restructured to provide proper production facilities. This enabled the United States Information Agency to make regular sources of domestic news(Kim Won Sik, 「Bright and Dark Sides of 15 years of Liberty News」, 「Shin Donga Magazine」, July 1967, p. 290). This time period was known by the Korean film community as the Sangnam United States Information Service days or the

나그네 설움(나그네 서룸) 이선경 | 1957
Sorrow of the Wanderer(Nagne Seol-um) Lee Sun Kyong

인생화보 이창근 | 1957
Life Like a Picture Album(Insaeng Hwabo)
Lee Chang Geun

Sangnam Studio days in order to differentiate these productions from the Jinhae United States Information Service days. The ⟨Report of Korean Progressing⟩ was renamed as ⟨Liberty News⟩ on 1 May 1953. ⟨Liberty News⟩ was produced once every week, and 35mm copies were made. According to the Ministry of Culture and Public Information 「30 Years of Culture and Public Information」, 1979, p. 27), these larger prints were transferred from the original 16mm footage and reversal films. They were screened in cinemas, being alternated with the ⟨Korean News(Daehan News)⟩. Often, forty copies of the 16mm versions were made and screened in rural villages. Teams of travelling projection groups brought these screenings to hard to reach places. ⟨Liberty News⟩(no. 1) contained domestic stories about the appointment of the Korean Prime Minister Jang Taek Sang and visits to President Rhee from high ranking US military personnel. According to Kim Won Sik, the reel also contained footage from international events as well, including the nuclear bomb experiments, new tanks being sent to Korea, and President Truman's moving into the newly renovated White House(「Bright and Dark Sides of 15 Years of Liberty News」, 「Shin Donga Magazine」, July 1967, p. 290). Most of the overseas news stories focused on what was happening in the USA at the time. The newsreels, which were distributed to various institutions and military headquarters, became precious sources of media information for people wishing to catch up with the progress of the war.

People in the refugee cities such as Busan and Daegu could also watch them in their city cinemas. Along with the newsreels, the partially repaired radio network and the newspapers were also valuable sources of media information for people living in the refugee cities.

2

Han Hyung Mo was a key film person who helped organize the Ministry of

Defense's first filming crew activities. He attached himself to the Korean army from the beginning of the Korean War and actively participated in as many film projects as possible. Hence, Han Hyung Mo is a significant figure in Korean film history. His debut film, 〈Breaking the Wall〉, dealt with the Yeosoo and Soonchun riots. During the shooting, he wore an armband with the words: "Filming Crew of the Korean Ministry of Defense", and advanced into the battlefield. This took place on 4 July 1950. Today, this is the date, which is celebrated as the beginning of the Ministry of Defense's filming crew. Han was in the middle of making a Navy promotional film, 〈Path a Man Has to Take(Sanai-ui Kil)〉, in Mokpo, South Junla Province, when the war broke out. Upon hearing about the war, he left his filming crew behind at the Navy base in Mokpo and went to Daejeon with his Eyemo Camera and 10,000Ja(Korean feet) of film. With the permission of the Ministry of Defense, which was temporarily based in Daejon at that time, Han started working with producers such as Kim Bo Chul and Kim Kwan Soo. Kim Bo Chul had previously produced the anti-communism film, 〈Breaking the Wall〉. Kim Kwan Soo had produced the anti-communism film, 〈For my Country〉 as well as the Police Agency sponsored film, 〈Sun in the Night〉. Han and his colleagues went into the battlefield but soon retreated to Daegu as the war situation was getting rougher. In August 1950, after recruiting Shim Jae Hung, who was the cinematographer of 〈Path a Man Has to Take〉, and Yang Bo Hwan, another cameraman, the Troop Information and Education Center under the Ministry of Defense officially launched its film crew.

After Seoul was recovered on 28 September 1950, the film crew under the Troop Information and Education Center placed itself at the Hubahuba Photo Shop in Eulji-ro 4 Ga under a signboard saying: "Filming Crew for Military Made Films". However, due to 'the retreat on 4 January 1951', Bosoo-dong in Busan became the new headquarter for the crew. An old public bathhouse was found and decorated with equipment that was plundered from the Pyongyang Film Studios. Additional cinematographers, editors

풍운의 궁전 | 정창화 | 1957 | **Palace of Troubled Times(Poongun-ui Goongjeon)** | Chung Chang Hwa

and film developing engineers were recruited as well. The crew's operation and facilities were elevated to the status of Military Film Studio in January 1952. This showed the importance of the filming crew's existence. Kim Hak Sung, Hong Il Myung, Shim Jae Hung, Yang Bo Hwan, Kim Bo Chul, Lee Sung Cun, Byun In Jip were its affiliated cinematographers. Kim Chang Soo, Noh Hee Sam and Yeom Hwa Chun were the film developing engineers, and Yang Chu Nam and Kim Hee Soo were the editors working in this studio. Even though the Ministry of Defense was actually the last to begin newsreel production, the filmmakers belonging to it had the most experience and displayed the most active ideas. On 27 July 1952, the ⟨Defense News⟩ started. According to 『40 Years of Korean Military Made Film History』(published by the Korean Military Public Information Bureau, 1992, p. 528), a total of forty-nine newsreels were made before Seoul

노들강변 | 신경균 | 1957 | Bank of Nodeul River(Nodeul Gangbyon) | Shin Kyong Gyun

was recovered again.

3 ——

The biggest achievement of the Ministry of Defense film crew was ⟨Righteous Advance(Chung-ui-ui Chin-gyuk)⟩ vol. 1(1951) & vol. 2(1952). This is the only film still in existence today among all of the feature films and documentaries produced in Korea during the war. The battle scenes of the Korean army fighting in the ⟨Righteous Advance Vol. 1⟩ were mostly shot by the Ministry of Defense film crew members: Han Hyung Mo, Kim Kang We and Kim Jong Han. Kim Kang We was in charge of shooting at the locations on the East Coast side of Korea. Kim Jong Han was in charge of filming on the West Coast side. Han Hyung Mo shot most of the inland battlefields. (See 「The Historical Background of Launching the Film Crew of the Troop Information and Education Center Under the Ministry of Defense」 in 「40 Years of Korean Military Made Film History」, p. 59).

Some of the films, which were shot with difficulties, were not developed right away. Unfortunately, they were stockpiled in the Hubahuba photo studio waiting to be processed(Yang Chu Nam, 「Recollecting the Production of Righteous Advance」, in 「40 Years of Korean Military Made Film History」, p. 81). These incomplete films were relocated to Busan with 'the January 4th retreat' and processed there. Post-production also started in

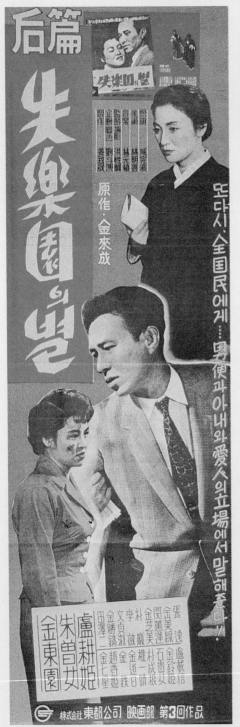

실낙원의 별(후편: 실낙원의 별) 홍성기 1958
Stars of the Lost Paradise Part 2(Sillakwon-ul Byol)
Hong Sung Ki

모정 양주남 1958 Mother's Love(Mojung) Yang Joo Nam

Busan too. The development of the negative films had to be completed in the shabby facilities, which were arranged in the public bathhouse, because there were no advanced recording facilities around at the time. The film crew asked the United States Information Service for help, which was the only place equipped with the sound recording facilities. However, the United States Information Service could not assist any external projects. Han Hyung Mo decided to go to Japan with the negative film of ⟨Righteous Advance Vol. 1⟩.

The post-production of ⟨Righteous Advance Vol. 1⟩ was successful. The play writer, Oh Young Jin, wrote the script and Hong Young Bo was the announcer who narrated it. After the completion of its post-production, ⟨Righteous Advance Vol. 1⟩ had a preview screening at the UN Foreign Press Club in Japan. Apparently, it attracted attention from many foreign reporters and Han received a distribution offer from the Japanese film company. According to Lee Song Chun, Han accepted a deal in exchange of one print copy of ⟨Righteous Advance Vol. 1⟩ for one recording machine, one printer, and a 16mm developing machine, which cost about $20,000 at that time. The high quality of the film had been a great negotiation bargaining tool. This equipment was brought back to Korea and immediately put into use in post-production(「The History of Korean Film Shooting (8)」, 「Film Technology」(no. 16), April 1996, p. 76).

Han Hyung Mo, Kim Chong Han and Kim Kang We, who helped make ⟨Righteous Advance Vol. 1⟩, however, quit their jobs and began their careers as war correspondents for the foreign press. They were both attracted to the promise of a higher salary and better working conditions, such as ample film supplies and access to a vehicle aid(Lee Song Chun, 「The History of Korean Film Shooting (8)」, 「Film Technology」 (no. 16), April 1996, p. 76).

Han Hyung Mo worked for the I.N.S., Kim Chong Han worked for M.G.M. and Kim Kang We worked for Warner Brothers. They all became foreign correspondents for these American companies. Han Hyung Mo later became involved with ⟨Righteous Advance Vol. 2⟩ as an editor. This time, the film was completed with the help of the Sangnam United States Information Service, which provided assistance with the development and sound recording processes(Lee Song Chun, 「The History of Korean Film Shooting (8)」, 「Film Technology」(no. 16), April 1996, p. 59).

The running time of ⟨Righteous Advance Vol. 1⟩ was about eighty minutes long, and the running time of ⟨Righteous Advance Vol. 2⟩ was about fifty-five minutes long. Both contained numerous scenes shot by the Ministry of Defense film crew along with excerpts from foreign newsreels from countries such as the USA. They also contained some documentary footage shot by the North Korean military. It was necessary to incorporate these outside film sources to cover the overall Korean War. The parts shot only by the Ministry of Defense film crew would probably not have been long enough. The North Korean documentaries were confiscated from the Pyongyang film studio. Today, these two volumes of ⟨Righteous Advance⟩ are still frequently used as background footage for the Korean War. Some of the scenes were also inserted into several films made after the war. For example, there is a scene in ⟨As Long As I Live(Yi Saeng-myung Da Hadorok)⟩(1960) which shows the opening sequence where the main actor Kim Jin Kyu was wounded after a battle scene. This battle scene was borrowed from ⟨Righteous Advance⟩.

The story of the making of ⟨Righteous Advance⟩ was like a summary of the wartime Korean film history. A mortar shell injured Kim Hak Sung and Lee Sung Chun while they were filming the scenes of the USA artillery in combat. Behind the scenes stories reveal how difficult it was to complete productions like this in the war conditions. But, it was all worthwhile in the end because of the the significant rewards it achieved.

Apart from the Ministry of Defense film crew, the Public Information Bureau

그대와 영원히 | 유현목 | 1958 | Forever with You(Geudae-wa youngwon-hi) | You Hyun Mok

also started making newsreels in Busan in 1952. The Public Information Bureau released ⟨Special Battle Line News(Teukbyol Jeonson News)⟩ on an irregular basis. According to the Ministry of Culture and Public Information(「30 Years of Culture and Public Information」, 1979, p. 27), in 1953, ⟨Special Battle Line News⟩ was renamed as ⟨Korean News(Daehan News)⟩ and it was produced monthly. The Korean Film Company(Daehan Younhwa-sa), which was a sub-organization of the Public Information Bureau, was in charge of producing ⟨Korean News⟩. Back in 1948, when the Republic of Korea was established, all of the primary ministries and sub-bureaus of the government were organized systematically, as in the case of the Ministry of Public Information and the Public Information Bureau. The Department of Films was organized under the Public Information Bureau and the Korean Film Company was founded in the Department of Films by the ordinance of the Prime Minister. The Department of Films was in charge of planning and shooting, and the Korean Film Company, which is now the National Film Production Center, was fully in charge of all other production procedures. The Department of Films established a film lab in the basement of the Kyungnam provincial office building and two Eyemo cameras and one printing machine were equipped for newsreel making. Ahn Jong Hwa was appointed as the managing director of the Department of Films(Hansung Daily Newspaper(Hansung Ilbo), 17 May 1950). Freelance cameramen were sent to shoot scenes of the front and rear lines. In Daegu, there was also the Air Force Film Crew operating under the Troop Information and Education Center at the Air Force Headquarters. Hong Seong Ki, a director, and Chung In Yeop, a solider in the service at that time, worked as cinematographers. Shin Sang Ok was the director, Han Wan Seup was the lighting engineer, and Jun Taek Yi, Kim Il Hae, Roh Kyung Hee and Hwang Nam were the actors(See Note). According to Lee Young Il, all of these people were members of the Air Force film crew(「The History of Korean Cinema」, p. 186). The Army Headquarters worked with the cinematographer Kim Myung Je and the recording engineer Cho Chong Gook. The Navy Headquarters worked with Lee Pil Woo(Im Byung Ho, 「Korean Films in the Post Liberation Era」, 「Film Technology」(no. 5), June 1992, p. 118).

Note: Ham Wan Seup's name was added later after his name was identified from oral history interviews conducted with veteran filmmakers. Hong Seong Ki made the first aerial film in Korea, 〈Attack Order〉(1954), with the Air Force film crew and actors.

4 —

Once again, it is clear that the war provided Koreans with opportunities to establish production experience with advanced technology and the manpower to support numerous film productions. The filming crew of the Troop Information and Education Center under the Ministry of Defense embraced an impressive amount of Korean film technicians. These were people who were active and engaged with continuous film projects, working to advance the level of film technology and training in Korea. In this way, Korean filmmakers could become specialists in their field. And, because the industry was small, those in film production positions could gain experience in many different tasks. For example, cinematographers got involved with post-production and learned how to develop and edit films. The editors and developing engineers went to the battlefield to shoot scenes.

Ultimately, the development of Korean film history in the 1950s overlapped with the development of the films that were made for the US military. Film crews under the Ministry of Defense went on to become some of the greatest and most experienced film engineers after the war ended. Engineers who were not part of the Ministry of Defense were left behind with lagging technological capabilities. At the same time, while the Ministry of Defense filmmakers began to gather power in the film industry, the film technicians from the United States Information Service also built their own network. These two groups of highly specialized people rose to the top of the Korean film technology field.

공처가 김수용 : 1958 My Loving Wife(Gongchuga) Kim Soo Yong

韓中合作　總天然色

異國情鴛

이국정원 | 전창근 | 1958 | An Exotic Garden(Iguk Jeongwon) | Jun Chang Geun

아름다운 악녀 | 이강천 | 1958
A Beautiful Evil Woman(Areum-daun Aknyo) | Lee Kang Chun

두 남매 | 홍일명 | 1958
Brother and Sister(Du Nam-mae) | Hong Il Myong

눈 내리는 밤(눈 나리는 밤) | 하한수 | 1958
A Night Snow Falling Down(Nun Naerineun Bam) | Ha Han Soo

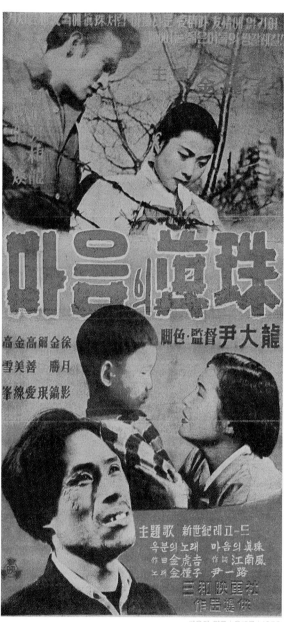

마음의 진주 | 윤대룡 | 1958
Pearls at Heart(Maeum-ui Jinjoo) | Yoon Dae Ryong

4 | 한국영화 제작 기재와 시설

1—

동란기는 미 502부대에서 미공보원으로 이어지는 미국의 선진 영화 기재에 대한 의존에서 벗어나 국방부 정훈국 촬영대 등 한국영화 기술인들의 자체적인 활동이 표면으로 드러나기 시작하는 시기였다. 기록영화 〈정의의 진격〉 녹음을 위해 미공보원을 그만두고 직접 녹음기를 만들었던 협동영화제작소 이경순의 예처럼 영화기술인들은 노후한 기재와 시설마저도 부족했던 환경을 사람의 힘으로 극복해 나갔다. 동란기에 한국영화 기술인들이 활용할 수 있었던 기재의 규모는 다음과 같다.

-한국 내 현존 영화시설[60] 「영화 재건에의 기대」, 연합신문, 1953.3.6.

1. 라보라토리: 상남 미공보원 영화제작소, 국방부 대공사진중대, 국방부 정훈국 촬영대, 진해 협동영화제작소

2. 촬영기: 아이모 타-렛트 신형 2대, 아이모 10대, 미제 빠르보 3대, 16밀리 영화 촬영기 스페셜 5대, 휠모 8대

3. 조명기: 전부 동원하면 약 400킬로와트

4. 녹음기: 전부 4대(35밀리, 16밀리)

5. 필름: 35밀리, 16밀리의 네거, 포시, 사운드 할 것 없이 전무

6. 편집대: 3, 4대

사실 한국영화 제작현장에서 영화 기재와 시설의 빈곤은 항상 따라다니는 문제였다. 6·25전쟁을 겪었다고 해서 기재의 수준이 더 악화되지는 않았다는 것이다. 아래의 해방 후 조선영화인의 손으로 돌아온 기재들과 비교해 보면 6·25전쟁을 거치면서 비교적 기재의 수준이 더 나아졌음을 알 수 있다. 특히 카메라가 증가한 것은 전쟁 중 미군의 도움을 받은 결과일 것이다. 1942년 9월 29일 조선총독부는 조선영화인들의 영화사를 '사단법인 조선영화주식회사'라는 단일회사로 통합시키며 전 한반도의 조선영화인들이 소유하고 있었던 기재를 모두 몰수하였다. 해방 후 이 기재들은 조선영화인의 제작현장으로 다시 돌아오게 된다.

-법인 조영의 시설 및 보유 기재61 이영일, 앞의 책, p. 164. 조명기는 조명기사 함완섭(2001.10.14. 인터뷰)의 증언내용에 기초했다. 현상기의 베르형은 벨 앤 하웰사의 프린터기를 지칭하는 것으로 보인다.

1. 남대문 소재 스튜디오
2. 카메라: 프랑스 데브리사의 빠르보 5대 및 미국 벨 앤 하웰사의 아이모 3대
3. 조명기: 10킬로와트 2대, 5킬로와트 20대, 2킬로와트 30대, 1킬로와트 5대 등
4. 녹음기: 에피아식, 다불용, 기타 3조
5. 현상기: 베르형(벨 앤 하웰 프린터기), 윌리암슨 형, 기타 3조

2 —

  광복이 되자 일제법인 조영에 몰수당했던 프랑스 데브리Debrie사의 빠르보Parvo 카메라 및 미국 벨 앤 하웰사The Bell & Howell의 아이모 카메라 3대가 조선영화인의 손으로 돌아올 수 있었다. 해방기를 거쳐 우리 영화인의 손에 남아 있었던 35밀리 카메라 아이모Eyemo는 전쟁을 기록하기 위해 주로 사용되었다. 한형모가 〈사나이의 길〉을 촬영하다가 전선으로 들고 간 카메라가 바로 아이모이다. 〈정의의 진격〉을 탄생시킨 카메라인 것이다. 1926년에 실용화된 아이모는 일광 로딩 스풀에 35밀리 필름 100피트 롤을 장착한 소형 카메라이다. 처음에는 아마추어용으로 제작되었으나 이후 뉴스영화 촬영에 주로 사용된다. 2차 대전 중에는 미군의 전장 기록에 주로 사용되었다. 작고 가벼워 핸드헬드가 가능했으므로 전쟁 다큐멘터리를 찍기에 가장 적합한 카메라였다.62 민병록, 「세계영상기술발달사」, 문지사, pp. 129~130.
  해방 이후의 극영화 촬영에 주로 사용되었던 빠르보는 사각형의 나무 박스 형태에 덩치도 커서 뉴스용으로는 적합하지 않은 카메라였다. 1908년에 처음 등장했을 때는 들고 다닐 수 있는 가장 작은 카메라였지만 동란기 한국영화인들에게는 크고 불편한 구식 카메라였던 것이다. 동란기 극영화의 대부분은 16밀리 카메라로 촬영되었다. 신상옥의 데뷔작 〈악야〉(1952)와 기록영화 〈백만의 별〉(1954)은 아이모 카메라가 축소된 외관인 16밀리 필모Filmo 카메라로 촬영되었고, 정창화 감독의 〈최후의 유혹〉은 광각, 표준, 망원 렌즈 3개가 타렛 방식으로 장착된 16밀리 스페셜Special 카메라로 촬영되었다.
  앞서 '한국 내 현존 영화시설'에서 모든 종류의 필름이 전무하다는 언급은 당시 필름

부족이 얼마나 심각한 문제였는지 단적으로 말해 준다. 전쟁 중에는 정식으로 필름을 수입하는 회사가 없었기 때문에 미군 부대 근처의 암시장이 필름을 구할 수 있는 유일한 통로였다. 35밀리는 찾아볼 수가 없었고 미군 PX에서 흘러나오는 아마추어용 16밀리 필름이 주였다. 대개 2,3년이 지난 것들이었지만 그마저도 구하기 쉽지 않았다. 〈정의의 진격〉과 뉴스영화를 찍던 국방부 촬영대원들은 필름이 부족해서 외신기자들에게 얻어 쓰기 일쑤였고, 좋은 장면만 찍느라 애를 썼다고 한다. [63 양보환, 「인천상륙작전 종군기」, 『군영화 40년사』, p. 79.] 이후 살펴보겠지만 필름의 심각한 부족은 동란기의 극영화가 16밀리로 제작될 수밖에 없었던 직접적인 배경이 된다.

3 —

　　동란기의 영화현장에서 조명기를 구한다는 것은 더더욱 힘든 일이었을 것이다. 부산에서 오픈 세트로 반쪽짜리 배를 만들어 촬영한 〈최후의 유혹〉, 대구 동산병원에서 실내 장면을 촬영한 〈출격명령〉(1954)은 국방부에서 50킬로와트 조명기를 지원받아 사용했다. 두 영화에서 사용한 조명이 바로 평양 촬영소에서 노획한 조명기로 원로 영화인들은 '소제라이트'라 부른다. 북한군이 후퇴하면서 비교적 가벼운 카메라는 들고 갔지만 무거운 조명기는 버린 것이다. 이른바 소제라이트는 1950년대 한국영화 제작현장에서 꾸준히 사용되었다.

　　흑백자동현상기를 유일하게 보유했던 미공보원을 제외하면 대부분의 한국영화기술인들은 목욕탕 등에 현상실을 만들어 손으로 직접 작업했다. 국방부 정훈국 촬영대의 부산 보수동 목욕탕 현상실, 협동영화제작소의 진해 해병학교 목욕탕 현상실, 공보처의 경남 도청 지하실 현상실이 그것이다. 현상방법은 못을 박은 나무판에 네거 필름을 감아 나무 탱크에 넣고 현상액이 골고루 필름에 침액되도록 아래위로 흔드는 수공업적 방식이었다. 나무판에 감았다고 해서 '와꾸 현상', 아래위로 흔드는 소리를 일본어로 발음해서 '쟈부쟈부 현상'이라고 불렀다. 디졸브 같은 광학작업도 손으로 이루어졌다. 네거 필름의 디졸브되는 부분을 적혈염이 녹은 물을 이용해 앞과 뒤의 커트 부분이 지워졌다가 나타나도록 하는 정교한 수공업적 방식이었다. [64 이성춘, 앞의 글, p. 77.] 편집 역시 16밀리 영사기를 이용하여 필름을 직접 눈으로 보면서 이루어졌다. 스플라이서Splicer가 없어 가위를 사용하거나 심지어 입이나 손으로 자르는 원시적 방식이었다. [65 김영희 인터뷰, 2001.11.16.] 인화기는 일제시대부터 사용되던 벨 앤 하웰사의

돈 김소동 1958 In Money(Don) | Kim So Dong

프린트기를 계속 사용했다.

4 ─

RCA 자기 녹음기 등 최신 녹음 기재가 있던 미공보원을 제외하면 동란기 한국영화의 녹음이 가능했던 곳은 이경순의 협동영화제작소였다. 〈정의의 진격〉 녹음작업이 거부된 것을 지켜본 녹음기사 이경순은 한국영화의 후반작업이 가능한 현상녹음실을 만들기 위해 미공보원을 그만두게 된다. 당시 함께 퇴직한 사람이 김흥만(편집), 김봉수(현상), 김형근(현상), 조백봉(음악), 정주용(축소) 등이었다. 그들은 진해 해병학교 목욕탕을 개조해서 목욕탕은 현상실로, 목욕물을 데우는 가마솥 안은 녹음실로 만든 후 '협동영화제작소'라는 간판을 달고 작업을 시작한다. 특히 이경순은 16밀리 필름식 녹음기를 자신의 손으로 직접 만들었고 이어서 35밀리 필름식 녹음기의 제작에도 성공한다. 공보처의 〈대한뉴스〉와 국방부의 〈국방뉴스〉 등 뉴스영화뿐만 아니라 동란기의 한국영화는 대부분 이곳에서 녹음작업이 이루어졌다. 영화의 완성이 후반작업을 통해 이루어진다는 것은 주지의 사실이다. 〈정의의 진격〉 사건을 계기로 만들어진 이경순의 협동영화제작소는 동란기 한국영화 제작의 토대가 되었다.

당시의 녹음은 무조건 후시 녹음이었고 자기(테이프) 녹음 방식이 아니라 사운드 필름에 직접 녹음하는 광학식이었다. 〈총검은 살아 있다〉(1953) 후시 녹음 과정에서는 성우를 구할 수가 없어서 주인공이었던 윤일봉이 혼자서 5역까지 목소리를 바꿔가며 녹음했다고 한다. 영화음악에 쓸 레코드가 모자라 진해 읍내 다방에서 레코드 몇 장을 빌려왔다는 웃지 못할 에피소드도 전해진다.⁶⁶ 황문평, 「야화 가요 60년사」, p. 247.

나 혼자만이 | 한형모 | 1958 | Only I Can(Na Honja-mani) | Han Hyung Mo

오부자(五父子) 1958 Father and Four Sons(Ohbuja) Kwon Young Soon

1 —

Korean filmmakers had depended on film technology since the US army 502nd military unit was created and even after it shifted to the United States Information Service during the wartime. Clearly, the US had advanced filmmaking facilities and equipment. However, as previously demonstrated, the war enabled filmmakers to gain learning opportunities and display their skills through various filmmaking activities. Numerous Koreans were part of the film crew under the Troop Information and Education Center, which was under the Ministry of Defense. They learned how to use the technology and how to repair it in the field when it needed mending. They were eager to utilize film equipment on their own. For example, Lee Kyung Soon of Hyupdong Film Studio quit the United States Information Service in order to record the ⟨Righteous Advance⟩; he made the recording machine himself. A combination of outdated equipment and a shortage of facilities were traded for manpower. Here are the lists of the facilities available to film technicians during the wartime.

The Current Filmmaking Facilities in Korea, (「Hope for the Filmmaking Restoration」, Yeonhap Newspaper, 6 March 1953):

1. Laboratory: the Sangnam United States Information Service film studio, Anti-aircraft company of the Ministry of Defense, Film Crew under the Troop Information and Education Center under the Ministry of Defense, Jinhae Hyupdong Film Studio

2. Cameras: 2 Eyemo Tarret New Models, 10 Eyemos, 3 Parvos(made in USA), 5 16mm film camera specials, 8 Filmos

3. Lights: altogether about 400kw

4. Recording machines: 4(35mm and 16mm)

5. Raw Film Stock: (no spare 35mm or 16mm film)

장미는 슬프다(Changmi-neun Seulpeuda)　1958
Sad Roses(Changmi-neun Seulpeuda)　Park Sang Ho

첫사랑 송국　1958
The First Love(Chut Sarang)　Song Kook

심정 | 이산경 | 1958 | **Feelings(Simjung)** | Lee Sun Kyong

초설 | 김기영 | 1958 | **The First Snow(Cho Seol)** | Kim Ki Young

6. Editing machines: 3, 4

A lack of film equipment and facilities was not a new problem in the Korean film industry, and it did not seem to get much worse because of the war. Rather, the quality levels of the equipment actually improved compared to the type of equipment imported directly after the liberation. An increase in the number of cameras was due to the aid of the USA military during the war. Before this time, all equipment and facilities in Korea were leftover from the Japanese colonial government, and all were once deprived from the Chosun Film Company. The Chosun Film Company was the unified body of all Korean film companies created by the Governor General of Chosun on 29 September 1942. All Korean production companies were forced to amalgamate into the Chosun Film Company. The leftover facilities are listed below(Lee Young Il, 「History of Korean Cinema」, p. 164) and Ham Wan Seup, the lighting engineer, testified about the lighting equipment:

1. Studio located in the South Gate(Namdaemun)

2. Camera: 5 Parvos of Debris(made in France) and 3 Eyemos of Bell & Howell(USA)

3. Lighting facilities: 2 10kw, 20 50kw, 5 1kw

4. Recording machine: Epia System, Double, and 3 others

5. Developer: Bell and Howell, Williamson, and 3 others

2

The three Eyemo cameras and the Parvo camera were returned to the hands of Koreans after the liberation. The Eyemos were used to shoot documentary scenes of battlefields during the war. As previously mentioned, it was the Eyemo camera that Han Hyung Mo used for making 〈Path a Man Has to Take〉. He then brought it with him to the front lines. It was this camera that shot 〈Righteous Advance〉. Historically speaking, the Eyemo was widely utilized in 1926 as a small camera. It could accommodate 100 feet of 35mm film in a loading spool in the daylight. It was originally made for amateur filmmakers, but later on it was used for shooting newsreels, because it was compact and easy to handle. It was frequently used to shoot footage of the USA soldiers on the battlefields. It was the most popular camera for making war documentaries due to its small size and its ability to be handheld(Min Byung Rok, 「History of World Film Technology Development」, Munji Press, pp. 129-130).

The Parvo camera was used for making feature films in the post-liberation era. Because of its large size and its square wooden box shape, it was not appropriate for making newsreels. Though it was first introduced as a small portable camera in 1908, it became too big and too old to use during the wartime. Thus, most of the feature films shot during the wartime was filmed with 16mm cameras. Shin Sang Ok's first film, 〈The Evil Night〉(1952), and 〈Star of One Million〉(1954), a documentary, were filmed with the 16mm Filmo camera, which was smaller than the Eyemo camera. Chung Chang Hwa's 〈The Final Temptation(Choihoo-ui Youhok)〉 was filmed with a special 16mm camera with a wide angle, standard, and telescopic lens attached with a terret.

As previously mentioned, there was a major shortage of raw film stock available to the Korean film industry. The film shortage problem was far more serious than one can imagine. There were no companies importing film in an official way during the war. The black market near the USA army camps was the only way to acquire film stock. Furthermore, 35mm film was never seen at all and 16mm film(for amateurs) could only be obtained sometimes because they were snuck out of the US army PX. However, most of them were two or three years old, and even then they were hard to get. According to Yang Bo Hwan(「War Correspondence Diary for Incheon Landing Operation」, 「40 Years of Korean Military Made Film」, p. 79), the foreign press often gave film stock to the

지옥화 | 신상옥 | 1958 | Flower in Hell(Chiok-hwa) | Shin Sang Ok

Ministry of Defense film crew for free for their production of newsreels and ⟨Righteous Advance⟩. The film crew tried their best to shoot in the most economical way, concentrating on the best scenes only. During the war, this shortage of film ultimately resulted in an increase of feature film productions made with 16mm equipment.

3 —

During the wartime, it was difficult to find lighting equipment and studio facilities. When ⟨The Final Temptation⟩ was filmed, the set consisted of one half of a small sized boat in Busan. ⟨Attack Order⟩ was filmed inside the Dongsan General Hospital in Daegu. The Ministry of Defense provided both productions with a total of 50kw lighting machines. This particular lighting machine was captured from the Pyongyang Film Studio and actually they were left behind when the North Korean army retreated to the far northern part of the Korean peninsula. Heavy lighting machines were left behind, but the lightweight cameras were brought with them. Filmmakers called it the 'Soje light(Light Made in Soviet Union)'. This lighting machine was continually used throughout the 1950s for various film productions.

The United States Information Service was the only place equipped with an automatic black and white development machine. Other people had to create solutions from scratch for developing films. Public bathhouses were the best locations to use because of their construction and layout of water pools. Film technicians created a basic development room in the public bathhouse and manually worked on developing prints. The film crew of the Ministry of Defense also made a developing room at another public bathhouse in Bosudong in Busan. Hyupdong Film Studio created a development room in a public bathhouse in the Jinhae Marine Training School, and the Public Information Bureau made a development room in the basement of the Kyungnam provincial office. Lab workers wound the negative films around a wooden

흐르는 별 | 김묵 | 1958 | **A Drifting Star(Heureuneun Byol)** | Kim Mook

자장가 | 허한수 | 1958
Lullaby(Chajang-ga) | Ha Han Soo

영원한 내 사랑 | 윤봉춘 | 1958
My Forever Love(Youngwon-han Nae Sarang) | Yoon Bong Chun

panel, which was fixed by nails, and then put it into a wooden tank containing the development liquid. The tank was stirred up and down in order to cover all of the contents. It was sometimes called 'Waku' for the use of the wooden panel or the 'Jabujabu' phenomenon according to the stirring sound(all Japanese words). Optical printers were also built and manually handled in order to create dissolves and other editing effects. According to Lee Sung Chun in 「The History of Korean Film Shooting(8)」 from 『Film Technology』(no. 16)(April 1996 , p. 59), both sides of the edited parts were erased and made to reappear by using a special chemical called potassium ferricyanide. It was an elaborate manual work. A 16mm projector was used in the editing process, which enabled simultaneous viewing and checking of the film. Kim Young Hee testified on 16 November 2001 that films were often cut with scissors, by hand or even with teeth since no one had access to a film splicer. These were indeed very primitive methods. For film printing, a Bell and Howell printer was still used.

4 —

There were two locations where film sound recordings could be made. The first site was the United States Information Service, which was equipped with a state-of-the-art RCA electric recorder. Lee Kyung Soon's Hyupdong Film Studio was the other site where film sound could be recorded. Originally, Lee Kyung Soon worked for the United States Information Service as a sound engineer. However, when the United States Information Service refused to do the sound recordings for 〈Righteous Advance〉, he and other engineers resigned and established the Hyupdong Film Studio. At this new studio, Kim Hung Man was the editor, Kim Bong Soo and Kim Hyung Keun were the development engineers, Cho Baek Bong was in charge of music and Chung Chu Yong was in charge of noise reduction. They united together and built a development lab and sound recording room for the post-production of films. As previously mentioned, a public bathhouse of the Jinhae Marine Training School was restructured for this purpose. The pools became the development rooms, and the large water boiling pot became a recording room. A sign reading "Hyupdong Film Studio" was hung in front of the bathhouse and they commenced work on the post-production of films. Lee Kyung Soon made a 16mm film sound recording machine himself. Later on, he successfully made a 35mm film sound recording machine. Most of the feature films and the newsreels such as 〈Korean News〉 from the Public Information Bureau and 〈Defense News〉 from the Ministry of Defense were completed at the Hyupdong Film Studio. Hence, the Hyupdong Film Studio occupied a strategically important place in Korea's film history. Its post-production facilities immensely contributed to the completion of many films and it became the foundation of film production in the wartime.

Back then, all sound recording was made directly on to the film after the shooting was completed. It was not the magnetic tape recording method. One interesting story involved the sound recording of 〈Bayonet Is Alive〉(1953). The director had trouble finding actors who specialized in voice characterizations. Hence, the principal actor, Yoon Il Bong, had to alter his voice for the recording of five different roles. According to Hwang Moon Pyung, in his book 『Behind Stories of Korean Popular Songs for 60 Years(Yahwa Gayo Yuksip Nyun-sa)』(p. 247), filmmakers had to borrow several records from a nearby cafe because of the lack of available music records to be used for background music.

콩쥐팥쥐(콩쥐팥쥐) | 윤봉춘 | 1958 | Kongjwi Patjwi, a Story of Step Sisters(Kongjwi Patjwi) | Yoon Bong Chun

순정의 문을 열어라 | 조긍하 | 1958 | Open Your Heart(Sunjong-ui Moon-eul Yurora) | Cho Geung Ha

1

동란기 3년간 수입된 외화 편수는 모두 170편이다. [67 우두연, 「지난 3년간의 문화운동 영화(하)」, 경향신문, 1953.11.14.] 연도별로 살펴보면 1951년 약 35편, 1952년 66편, 1953년 69편이 수입된 것으로 대략 추정해 볼 수 있다.

6·25전쟁 발발 이후 외국영화가 정식으로 수입되어 상영된 것은 1951년 가을부터이다. 불이무역주식회사가 수입하고 배급한 미국, 프랑스 영화가 연달아 상영되었고 몰려드는 관객들을 정리하기 위해 기마경관이 동원되기까지 하는 등 대성황을 이뤘다. 불이무역 영화부와 거의 동시에 수입에 착수한 신한문화사 등도 좋은 성적을 올리자 여기에 자극받은 외화 수입사들이 속출하였다. [68 변순제, 「외국영화는 이렇게 수입된다」, 「신영화」, 1954년 11월호, p. 78.]

영화 수입의 문화적 의의라든가 건전한 국민 오락을 위한다는 도덕적 의미는커녕 상업적 입장으로 보아도 결코 바람직하게 볼 수 없었던 것이 동란기의 외화 수입계였다. 저속하고 질 낮은 영화를 창고 같은 극장에서 상영해도 관객들은 꼬리에 꼬리를 물고 몰려왔다. 수입업자는 작품 선택을 고려할 필요가 없었고 흥행에 관한 방법을 연구할 필요도 없었다. 전쟁 중이라 국민들이 찾아갈 오락기관은 극장밖에 없었기 때문이다. 늘지 않는 극장의 절대수와 줄지 않는 관객의 절대수는 극장주와 수입업자에게 이익을 주었다. 즉 영화가 다른 무역품보다 이익률이 나쁘지 않다는 것이 불과 2년 만에 30사 가까운 외화 수입사가 경쟁을 하게 된 이유였다. [69 「외국영화의 수입」, 한국일보, 1954.7.12.]

이기세의 기신양행과 양근모의 동양영화주식회사 [70 「한국영화약사」, 「영화백과 제1집」, 영화백과편찬위원회, 1976, p. 88.] 등 1920년대 후반부터 외화 수입을 하던 회사들이 동란기에 다시 활동을 시작했음을 알 수 있다. 해방 이후 외화 수입을 시작한 신한영화양행과 극동영화사 [71 조혜정, 「미군정기 영화정책에 관한 연구」, 중앙대학교 대학원 영화학과 박사학위 논문, 1997, pp. 52~53.] 도 각각 신한문화사와 극동영화사로 이어졌다. 기존의 한국영화 제작사들도 외화 수입 대열에 참가하였다. 서울영화사로 〈무궁화〉(1948), 〈목동과 금시계〉(1949) 등을 제작했던 이재명도 대한영화교육연구회를 통해 외화 수입을 시작하였다.

이현수의 불이무역주식회사, 서종호의 남화흥업주식회사, 대한영화교육연구회 대표 이재명의 아세아영화주식회사, 덕신공사 대표 윤명혁의 아카데미영화주식회사, 박원석의 한

어느 여대생의 고백

어느 여대생의 고백 신상옥 1958 Confessions of a College Girl(Oneu Yeodaesaeng-ui Gobaek) Shin Sang Ok

돌아온 항구도라온 항구(일명·야녀) 박경주 | 1958 | I Returned to the Harbour(Doraon Hang-gu) Paik Kyung-joo

형제 | 김성민 | 1958 | Brothers(Hyung-je) | Kim Sung Min

별아 내 가슴에 | 홍성기 | 1958
A Star Comes to My Heart(Byol-a Nae gaseum-e) | Hong Sung Ki

국예술영화주식회사 등 동란기에 외화 수입을 시작한 회사들은 1950년대 후반에도 꾸준히 명맥을 유지하였다.[72] 국내의 외화 수입 체계가 동란기를 통해 형성되었음을 말해 주는 것이다.

72 이영일, 『한국영화전사』, pp. 195~197.

2 ―

해방 후 미국영화를 조선극장에 직배하던 중배는 6·25전쟁이 발발하자 일본의 동경으로 옮겨가게 되고[73] 동란기의 외화 수입 거래는 전부 일본에서 이루어지게 된다. 미국영화의 경우에는 미국영화사 지점을 통해서 직접 계약할 수 있었으나, 영국, 프랑스, 이태리, 스페인, 스웨덴, 서독 등의 유럽 국가는 일본인 영화회사와 계약이 되어 있어 일본인과 계약해야만 했다. 일본영화는 1편도 수입되지 않았지만 대일 수출물이 소비되는 결과를 가져왔고 일본은 중간 이익을 남긴 것이다. 게다가 한국의 수입업자들은 서로 경쟁이 붙어서 부르는 것이 값이었고 이 바람에 한술 더 떠서 끼워 파는 영화들도 다수였다.[74] 근년의 영화가 수입되지 않았다는 것은 차치하고서라도 10년 전에 제작된 낡은 영화가 수입되었고, 과거에 상영된 것이 또다시 수입되기도 했다. 국문자막을 국내에서 할 수 없었던 것도 미국영화를 일본을 거쳐 수입해야만 했던 결정적인 이유가 되었다.

73 강진우 인터뷰, 2001.10.6.
74 「지평선」, 한국일보, 1954.9.17.

외국영화 1편을 수입하기 위해 드는 돈은 흑백영화 최하급이 1천5백 달러였고 보통이 2,3천 달러였다. 〈올리버 트위스트Oliver Twist〉 같은 일급품은 1만 달러까지 들여서 수입되는 실정이었다. 당시 언론들은 그만한 자본이라면 우리도 우리 손으로 남과 같은 영화를 만들 수 있다고 목소리를 높였다.[75] 외화 수입에 들어갈 자본의 일부분만 돌려도 미첼 같은 최신 촬영기나 RCA 녹음기, 다량의 네거 필름을 들여와 국산영화의 발전을 도모할 수 있다는 것이다.[76] 한국영화인들은 세트도 없고 라이트도 없는 조건에서 구닥다리 기재만 가지고 기적적인 작품활동을 벌였지만 자연히 작품의 성과는 외화보다 떨어지고 극장은 쉽사리 외화를 상영하는 악순환이 계속되었다. 국산영화조성책이 강구되어 국산영화가 산다면 외국영화 수입 제한은 저절로 실행될 것이라는 당시 영화인들의 목소리는 1954년 3월 31일 국산영화 입장료 면세 조치 성과를 이루어내게 된다.

75 중앙일보, 1953.12.24.
76 사설 외국영화와 국산영화, 한국일보, 1954.12.26.

3 —

　　동란기 한국의 스크린을 점령한 외국영화 중 미국영화는 전체 상영의 50퍼센트 이상을 차지하고 있었다. 당시 영화평론가들의 말을 빌리자면 대부분이 저속한 작품 일색이었다. 하지만 전쟁과 가난에 지친 사람들은 카타르시스를 주는 슬픈 애정영화, 서부극, 코미디영화 등 미국영화에 빠져들었다. 동란기에 상영된 미국영화를 장르별로 살펴보면 〈애수〉, 〈귀향〉, 〈애련〉, 〈여수〉, 〈마음의 행로〉 등의 연애극, 〈악한 보스콤〉, 〈모호크의 대기〉, 〈서부의 분노〉, 〈광야천리〉, 〈서부대혈맥〉, 〈대황원〉, 〈리오그란데〉, 〈대지의 철마〉, 〈캔사스 기병대〉, 〈황원의 정복자〉, 〈군적〉, 〈북서로 가는 길〉, 〈하이눈〉 등의 서부극, 〈연애진단서〉, 〈여기자〉, 〈말크스의 쌍권총〉 등의 코미디물, 〈싱가폴여행기〉, 〈요절병사와 폭탄처녀〉, 〈캐그니의 출세〉 등의 뮤지컬 코미디, 〈뉴욕의 뒷골목〉, 〈무장도시〉, 〈총탄도시〉 등의 갱 범죄물 등이다.

　　1953년도에 수입된 외화 69편을 국적별로 살펴보면 미국이 37편으로 가장 많고 다음으로 프랑스가 20편을 차지한다. 영국이 2편이고 스페인, 스위스, 이태리, 핀란드, 베네수엘라가 각 1편씩이다. 1954년에는 외국영화 수입 편수가 142편으로 증가한다.[77] 「한국연예대감」의 「(표) 연도별 수입 외화 작품 수」에서 1954년의 114편도 잘못된 기록이 된다. 미국영화의 수입은 더욱 증가한다. 미국영화가 94편(72퍼센트), 프랑스가 20편(12퍼센트), 영국이 14편(8퍼센트), 이태리, 서독, 기타 국가가 14편(8퍼센트)이었다. 미국영화 94편을 제작사별로 살펴보면 패러마운트 13편, MGM 11편, 20세기폭스 14편, 셀즈닉 3편, 컬럼비아 14편, BTO 16편, 유니버설 19편, 유나이티드가 4편이었다.[78] 「이해의 꼬마통계 외국영화」, 동아일보, 1954.12.27.

　　〈정부 마농〉, 〈모록코 수비대〉, 〈싱고아라〉 같은 프랑스 애정영화들은 인기를 끌었지만, 이태리 영화들은 관객의 주목을 받지 못했다. 전시의 관객들에게 있어 영화는 잠시나마 고통스런 현실을 잊는 오락거리에 다름 아니었다. 당시 한국의 사회상을 보는 듯한 전후의 피폐하고 가난한 이태리 사회를 반영하는 영화들이 관객의 외면을 받은 것은 어쩌면 당연한 일일 수도 있다. 당시 〈자전차도적〉이나 〈전진〉 같은 영화를 할 때는 객석이 반도 차지 않았고 〈오만불 소동〉 같은 미국영화를 할 때는 초만원을 이루었다[79] 유주현, 「신수입영화와 국문판자막(하)」, 영남일보, 1952.2.19.고 한다.

그림자사랑 : 김화랑 : 1958 : Shadowy Love(Geurlmja Sarang) : Kim Hwa Rang

청춘비가 : 이규환 : 1958
Elergy of the Youth(Chungchun Biga) : Lee Kyu Hwan

1—

According to You Doo Yeon in his article 「Cultural Movement and Films in 3 Years Refugee Time」, published in Kyunghyang Daily Newspaper on 14 November 1953, a total of 170 foreign films were imported into Korea during the three years of the war period. In 1951, thirty-five films were imported into the country. The number increased in 1952 with sixty-six films, and, again, in 1953 with sixty-nine films.

After the war began, the first foreign films were officially imported in the autumn of 1951. Byon Soon Je noted in his article 「Foreign Films are Imported Like This」, published in the November issue of the 「New Film(Shin Younghwa)」(p. 78), that the film department of the Bullet Trading Company(Bullet Muyeok Chusik Hoi-sa) imported and distributed a large amount of the American and French films. Audiences crowded in many of the cinemas to watch these films. Mounted police were sent to the cinemas to control the crowds of people. The Shinhan Cultural Company(Shinhan Munhwa-sa) started the film importing business and apparently made a good profit out of it. Many other foreign film import companies sprang up, seeking profits from the popularity of the picture shows.

For the film import industry, there existed neither cultural meaning for the imported films nor moral cause for enhancing Korea's national recreation. The film import business can be seen as wanting even from the trade perspective. Many coarse and low quality films were screened in shabby warehouses. Yet, audiences crowded the venues every time. Film importers did not have to think too deeply about which films to import or devise careful marketing plans for them. The films sold themselves, and the crowds loved them. This was because cinema was the only recreational institution available during the wartime for the general population. Though the number of cinemas was limited, large audiences brought great profits to the cinema owners and film importers. On 12 July 1954, the article 「Import of Foreign Films」 in the Hanguk

Daily Newspaper pointed out that the better return on investment in the film business outperformed all other goods and services. As a result, about thirty foreign film import companies competed with each other in a two-year period.

During this time, there were traditional film import companies such as the Kishin Trading Company(Kishin Yanghaeng), which was owned by Lee Ki Se, and the Dongyang Film Company, which was owned by Yang Geun Mo. According to 「The Short History of Korean Cinema」, 「Film Encyclopaedia Vol. 1」(edited and published by The Committee of Publishing Film Encyclopaedia in 1976, p. 88), these companies started the film import business in the late 1920s, but had to close their business for political reasons before the liberation with the forced unification of distribution channels in Korea by the Governor General of Chosun. They resumed their import business during the Korean War. Also confirmed by Cho Hye Jung in her doctoral dissertation in 1997(「A Study on the Film Policy Under USAMGIK Period」, pp. 52-53) the Shinhan Cultural Company(previously known as the Shinhan Younghwa Yanghaeng) and the Kukdong Film Company(previously known as the Kukdong Younghwa-sa) began importing foreign films after the liberation. Korean film production companies also imported foreign films. Lee Jae Myung from the Seoul Film Company(Seoul Younghwa-sa) established the Korean Film and Education Research Center(Daehan Younghwa Gyoyook-hoi) to import foreign films. Earlier, Lee Jae Myung had produced ⟨The Rose of Sharon(Mugunghwa)⟩(1948) and ⟨A Shepard Boy and a Golden Watch(Mokdong-gwa Geum-shigye)⟩(1949). Lee Young Il stated in his 「History of Korean Cinema」(pp. 195-197) that these foreign film import companies continued their businesses in the late 1950s.

The list of other film importers includes: the Bullet Trading Company owned by Lee Hyun Soo; the Namhwa Heungup Company Inc.(Namhwa Heungup Chusik Hoisa) owned by Seo Chong Ho; the Asia Film Company Inc.(Asia Younghwa Chusik Hoisa) owned by Lee Jae Myung(mentioned above); the Academy Film Company Inc.(Academy Younghwa

생명 | 이강천 | 1958 | Life(Saeng-myong) | Lee Kang Chun

Chusik Hoisa) owned by Yoon Myung Hyuk who was also a representative of the Dukshin Company(Dukshin Gongsa); and the Korean Culture and Film Company Inc.(Hanguk Yesul Younghwa Chusik Hoisa) owned by Park Won Seok. As noticed from the evidence above, this foreign film importing structure was formed during the wartime.

2 —

In an interview with Chung Jin Woo(6 October 2001), he mentioned that the Central Motion Picture Exchange had had contracts with the Chosun Cinema for direct distribution of American films and had to be moved to Japan with the breakout of the Korean War. That is, during this time, all Korean import companies had to run their businesses through Japan first. American films could be imported into Korea directly by the branches of the American film companies. However, Korean film importers had to

어머니의 길 | 안현철 | 1958
A Mother's Road(Amoni-ui Gil) | Ahn Hyon Chul

한 많은 청춘 | 권영순 | 1958
Troubled Youth(Hanmaneun Chungchun) | Kwon Young Soon

사십대 여인 | 반석 | 1958 | **A Woman in Her 40s(Sasip-dae Yeoin)** | Ban Seok

사랑의 길 | 장황연 | 1958
The Love Road(Sarang-ui Gil) | Chang Hwang Yeon

수정탑 | 전창근 | 1958 | Crystal Tower(Sujung Top) | Jun Chang Geun

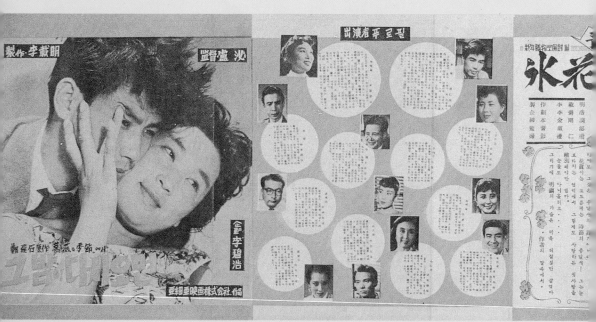

그 밤이 다시 오면 | 노필 | 1958 | When the Night Comes Back(Geu Bami Dasi Omyun) | Roh Pil

사람 팔자 알 수 없다(홀쭉이 뚱뚱이의 사람 팔자 알 수 없다) | 김화랑 | 1958
Never Know What Will Happen to Your Life(Saram Palja Alsu Upda) | Kim Hwa Rang

길 잃은 사람들 | 김한일 | 1958 | Lost People(Gil-ireun Saramdeul) | Kim Han Il

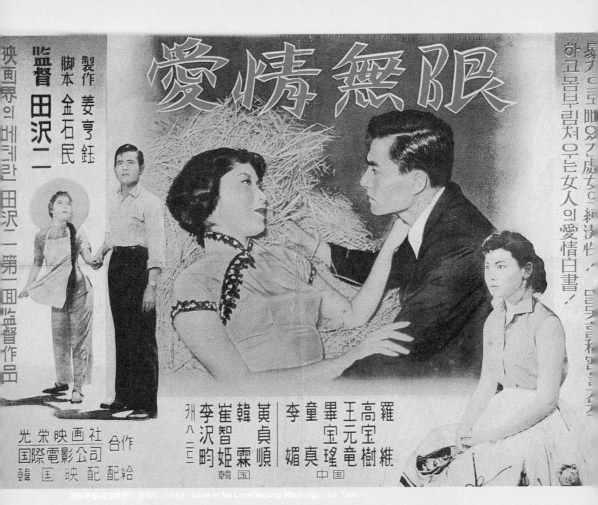

애정무정(애정무한) | 전택이 | 1958 | Love or No Love(Aejung Moojung) | Jun Taek Yi

go through Japanese companies in order to acquire films from other countries such as the UK, France, Italy, Spain, Sweden and West Germany, which already had contracts with Japanese companies. In this way, Japan attained all of the fringe benefits from the foreign films(other than American) being imported into Korea at this time. As mentioned in a column called 「Horizon(Jipyung-sun)」 in the Hanguk Daily Newspaper on 17 September 1954, the competition among Korean film importers became intense and prices for importing films grew higher and higher. In the midst of this inflation, even inferior films were sold as a package deal. Films that were ten years old were also imported as well as films that were being re-released for a second time. Unfortunately, it was not possible to add Korean subtitles in Korea. This was one of the key reasons why American films were also imported through Japan.

The minimum price for importing a black and white foreign film was $1,500, and the average rate for one title was between $2,000 and $3,000. However, a top quality title, such as ⟨Oliver Twist⟩(1948), cost up to $10,000 to import. An article in the Chungang Daily Newspaper on 24 December 1953 claimed that Korea would be able to make the same quality of films if the large amount of money invested in the imports had been given to the Korean film industry. Another article in the Hanguk Daily Newspaper on 28 December 1954 stated that the film industry could be developed easily if part of the money spent on importing foreign films had been reinvested back into the local infrastructure. For example, these funds could have been used to purchase a modern Mitchell camera, RCA sound recording machine, and an inventory of motion picture film stock. Similar attitudes were noticed throughout other newspapers. Though Korean filmmakers did their best to make films under harsh circumstances, with limited sets, shortage of lighting equipment, and outdated facilities, the quality of films produced was far behind those of the foreign films. This was perhaps the key reason why audiences preferred to watch the foreign films to the domestic films. The Korean film community raised their concerns with the government at the time, asking the government to initiate policies to encourage domestic production. Korean filmmakers believed that new government policies were the only way to limit foreign film imports and protect the domestic industry. This idea was realized with the "Tax Law for Admission Fee" on 31 March 1954, which was designed to exempt the admission tax for Korean films. Finally, local productions would receive a break in the form of preferential treatment of their films.

During the War, American films occupied over 50% of the imported foreign film market. Though Korean film critics criticized most of the American pictures for their low taste, audiences loved to watch their tear-jerking melodramas, adventurous westerns and comedies. It is important to remember that these were the same audiences that were strained by the poverty and depressed by the Korean War. It seems that watching these films provided a kind of escapism and catharsis for the audience, making them feel much better during and after the screening. Some of the American films screened during the war(listed by genre) were:

· Melodramas: ⟨Waterloo Bridge⟩(1940), ⟨Homecoming⟩(1948), ⟨Back Street⟩ (1941), ⟨September Affair⟩(1950), ⟨Random Harvest⟩(1942)

· Western films: ⟨Bad Bascomb⟩(1946), ⟨Drums Along the Mohawk⟩(1939), ⟨Sundown⟩(1941), ⟨Red River⟩(1948), ⟨Abilene Town⟩(1946), ⟨Massacre River⟩(1949), ⟨Rio Grande⟩(1950), ⟨Rock Island Trail⟩(1950), ⟨Santa Fe Trail⟩(1940), ⟨Northwest Stampede⟩(1948), ⟨Bad Men of Tombstone⟩(1949), ⟨Northwest Passage⟩(1940), ⟨High Noon⟩(1952)

· Comedies: ⟨Let's Live a Little⟩(1948), ⟨Woman of the Year⟩(1942), ⟨Go West⟩ (1940)

· Musical comedies: ⟨Road to Singapore⟩(1940), ⟨Let's Face It⟩(1943), ⟨Something to Sing About⟩(1937)

· Gangster/crime films: ⟨Johnny One-Eye⟩(1950), ⟨Union Station⟩(1950), ⟨The Crooked Way ⟩(1949)

Looking back at the nationality of imported films in 1953, the USA was at the top with thirty-seven films, and France was second with twenty films. There were two films imported from the UK, and one each from Spain, Switzerland, Italy, Finland and Venezuela. The total number of imported films increased to 142 in 1954(although the

「Korean Entertainment Almanac(Hanguk Yeonye Daegam)」 misstated that there were 114 films imported in 1954). By the end of 1954, the number of imported American films continued to increase: ninety-four films came from the USA(72%); twenty films were from France(12%); fourteen films came from the UK(8%); and fourteen films were imported from Italy, West Germany and other countries(8%). Among the ninety-four American films imported, nineteen were produced by Universal; fourteen came from 20th Century Fox; fourteen were from Columbia; thirteen were produced by Paramount; eleven were from MGM; four films were imported from United; and three were imported from Selznick Pictures. These figures were all cited in the 「Little Statistics for the Foreign Films of This Year」 in Donga Daily Newspapers(Donga Ilbo) on 27 December 1954.

French melodramas such as 〈Manon〉(1949) were also popular among audiences. However, most of the general public ignored the Italian films, which was a completely different reaction than that of the Korean filmmakers. Audiences did not welcome Italian films because of the poor and devastating post-war figures of the Italian society. For audiences who were experiencing the harsh realities of the war, films offered a temporary escape. As You Joo Hyun reported in his article 「New Imported films and the Introduction of Korean Subtitles」 in the Youngnam Daily Newspaper on 19 February 1952, 〈The Bicycle Thief and Paisan〉(1948) were screened in cinemas with less than half of the audience attending. In contrast, the American film, 〈The Noose Hangs High〉 (1948), attracted audiences so large that every screening was sold out.

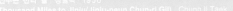

진주는 천리 길 정일택 1958
Thousand Miles to Jinju(Jinju-neun Chun-ri Gil) Chung Il Taek

종각 양주남 1958 Bell Pavillon(Jong-gak) Yang Joo Nam

1

극장은 문을 열어야 한다. 극장문 앞을 그렇게 담백히 떠날 수도 없다. 우리는 이렇
게 문명해 있다. 자국영화를 사랑할 줄도 알고 할리우드 영화를 즐길 줄도 알고 불란서 영화
를 감상할 줄도 안다. 80 오영진, 「영화 1년의 감상」, 부산일보, 1951.12.30.

동란기 피난도시의 영화관에서는 상영의 99퍼센트를 외국영화에 의존하였다. 국내
수입사들이 본격적으로 외화 수입 활동을 시작한 것도 6·25전쟁의 영향이었다. 국내에서
미국영화를 직배하던 중배가 전쟁 발발과 동시에 일본 동경으로 건너갔기 때문이다. 국내 외
화 수입과 배급구조는 동란기를 통해 그 체계를 형성하게 되었다. 1951년 가을 불이무역주식
회사 등 기업형 외화 수입사가 수익을 올리자 군소 수입업자들이 그 뒤를 따랐고 동란기에만
30사 가까운 외화 수입사가 범람하였다. 당시의 영화사라는 명칭은 한국영화제작사가 아니
라 외국영화 수입사를 가리킬 정도로 한국영화 산업의 자본은 외화 수입계에 머물러 있었다.
영화산업 전체가 외국영화의 수입과 상영을 중심으로 형성되어 있었지만 한국영화인
들의 영화제작 활동도 멈추지 않았다. 전쟁이라는 악조건과 원시적인 시설에도 불구하고 그
들은 세계 수준의 영화를 만들겠다는 의지를 잃지 않은 것이다. 하지만 한국영화인들의 기적
적인 작품활동에도 불구하고 작품의 성과는 떨어졌고 극장은 손쉽게 외국영화를 상영하는
악순환이 계속되었다. 외국영화의 수입 편수가 해가 갈수록 증가되었고, 외화 유출은 심각한
사회문제로 대두되었다. 이때 언론의 지면을 빌려 활동하던 영화평론가들은 국산영화 조성
책을 역설하기 시작한다. 국산영화가 산다면 외국영화의 수입 제한은 저절로 실행될 것이라
는 그들의 주장은 환도 후 국산영화 입장세의 면세 조치, 외화 수입 쿼터 등 정부의 정책 결
정에 상당한 영향을 미친다.

2

환도 후의 영화계에는 입장세 면세 조치에 자극받은 흥행 자본이 들어오기 시작했다.
완성이 지지부진하던 〈코리아〉는 외화 수입사인 신한문화사 정화세의 자금으로 완성되어 관
객 동원에 성공했고, 1953년 5월에 제작에 착수했던 〈춘향전〉도 1955년 1월 6일 서울 국도극

장과 부산 동아극장에서 동시개봉하여 한국영화사상 초유의 성황을 이루었다. 〈춘향전〉은 국도극장에서 1주일 상영 예정이었으나 시민들의 요청으로 13일까지 연기되었고 이후 17일, 다시 23일로 연기되었다. 당시 인기 외화가 1주일에 3, 4만 명의 관객을 끈 것에 비해 서울 관객수만 18만을 헤아렸다. 81 한국일보, 1955.1.26. 그동안 국산영화로는 제작비 회수도 어렵다는 것이 일반적인 인식이었지만 〈춘향전〉은 국산영화가 타산을 맞추는 것을 넘어 큰 수익도 올릴 수 있다는 것을 보여준 것이다. 한국영화에서 산업으로서의 가능성을 자각하는 계기가 되었던 〈춘향전〉의 흥행 성공으로 이후 한국영화 제작계에는 자본이 밀려오게 된다. 비록 물밀듯이 들어온 외국영화에 의한 현상이었지만 관객들이 악극, 국극 등의 무대공연에서 영화로 눈을 돌리기 시작한 것도 동란기의 성과였다. 〈춘향전〉의 '영화' 관객도 동란기를 통해 준비되었던 것이다.

1954년부터 1957년까지의 한국영화사를 '성장기' 82 「한국영화자료편람」은 1950년대를 작품 생산·편수에 의존하여 1950년~1953년의 '동란기', 1954년~1957년의 '성장기', 1958년~1964년을 '중흥기'로 구분한다.라고 일컫는다. 일반적으로 1954년 3월 31일 시행된 국산영화 입장세 면세 조치와 〈춘향전〉의 흥행 성공이 그 단초로 제시된다. 하지만 한국영화가 성장기로 진입하는 진정한 동력이 된 것은 사람이었다. 성장기의 도래에는 동란기라는 전 역사가 있었고 그 중심에는 한국영화인의 영화제작에 대한 끊이지 않은 의욕과 노력이 있었다. 특히 영화기술인들은 한국영화 성장의 진정한 토대가 되었다. 선진 영화 기재에 대한 동란기의 갈증은 전후 공보처 산하의 대한영화사, 국방부 정훈국, 미공보원 등 각 기관에 최신 영화 기재 및 시설들이 다량 도입되는 결과를 낳았고, 동란기를 거쳐 준비된 영화기술인들은 한국영화 산업의 디딤돌이 되었다. 동란기는 6·25전쟁의 소용돌이 속에서도 한국영화 성장의 토대가 구축되고 한국영화 산업의 맹아가 나타나는 시기였다.

눈물 박성복 1958 Tears(Nun-mul) Park Sung Bok

1—

The cinemas should run continuously. We cannot simply walk away from their entrance. This is how we have been civilized. We know how to love Korean films, and we know how to enjoy Hollywood films, and we know how to appreciate French Films.

Oh Young Jin, 「Impressions from Watching Films for One Year」 in the Busan Daily Newspaper on 30 December 1951.

In the cinemas located in the refugee cities, 99% of the screenings were dependent on foreign films. That is to say, the bulk of a cinema's profits came solely from screening foreign(predominantly American) films. After the Central Motion Picture Exchange monopolized the Korean film industry, nearly all distribution contracts concerning American film imports were moved to Tokyo, Japan. After the war broke out, domestic film import companies became more active in importing foreign films, albeit from Japan. The war had created an opportunity for these companies, and the film import and distribution system quickly became regularized. Big import companies like the Bullet Trading Company made sizeable profits out of this business, and small to medium sized companies followed. Eventually, about thirty film import companies began operating in Korea. Around that time, film production companies utilized film importing companies, and film investments were concerned primarily with foreign film imports.

Despite all of the activity surrounding foreign films, Korean filmmakers continued to make films. Though the film industry was mainly in operation for the purpose of importing and distributing foreign films, Korean filmmakers kept their filmmaking passion alive. It was their dream to make world-class films. However, their steadfast desires were not enough to stop the vicious cycle. The quality of locally produced commercial films continuously lost ground and cinemas preferred to screen foreign films. As a result, the number of foreign film imports increased, and the diversion of foreign currency became a serious societal problem. Many film critics emphasized the necessity of making new policies, which would encourage local production. Through articles in various newspapers, critics asserted that Korean films should first be rejuvenated, and second be protected from the onslaught of competition from imported foreign films. Eventually, these ideas began to make an impact on the government's policymaking. After the returning of Seoul in 1953, the government worked on creating policies that encouraged growth in the local film industry. Later on, these policies were realized in the form of an exemption of admission taxes on domestic films, and an import quota(quota system) of foreign film imports was also initiated.

2 —

In the early 1950s, the government began to facilitate the redirection of investment capital back into the Korean film industry with the initiation of the admission tax exemption on Korean films. Though the amount of reinvestment funding started off with small amounts, domestic productions saw immediate results. For example, one film project, 〈Korea〉, which previously had been struggling financially, could be completed. Jung Hwa Se, president of a foreign film import company, the Shinhan Cultural Company(Shinha Munhwa-sa), was able to fund this film and release a successful box office hit. Another success story was 〈Chunhyang Story(Chunhyang-jeon)〉(1955) directed by Lee Kyu Hwan, which commenced production in May 1953. On 6 January 1955, it was screened simultaneously at the Kukdo Cinema in Seoul and the Donga Cinema in Busan, making a record-breaking box office hit. At first, 〈Chunhyang Story〉 was supposed to run in the Kukdo Cinema for only one week. However, the many requests from the public enabled it to enjoy a longer run until 23 January. During this time, the number of spectators watching this film in Seoul reached about 180,000. 〈Chunhyang Story〉 was a great success, considering that most popular foreign films had been attracting from 30,000 to 40,000 spectators per week in Seoul(Hanguk Daily Newspaper, 26 January 1955). Initially, there had been general impressions in Korea that filmmakers would have a difficult time breaking even on their project investments. However, 〈Chunhyang Story〉 became one of the first cases to prove that Korean films could return a profit in the domestic market. Clearly, this film created a degree of momentum for the film industry after people realized the potential profitability of local productions. Indeed, investments in the Korean film industry began to soar. This newly found success was also partly due to the fact that audiences seemed to be more interested in and enjoying watching films rather than traditional theatre plays. This was probably due to their cinema experiences accumulated during the wartime through lots of foreign films. Upon these circumstances, audiences were ready to enjoy Korean films and 〈Chunhyang Story〉 could be successfully consumed in this context.

According to the 『Korean Film Material Collection』, the time period between 1954 and 1957 was called the 'growth period'. The starting point of this period stems from the government's initiation of the admission tax exemption for Korean films on 31 March 1954. The growth period also coincides with the success of 〈Chunhyang Story〉 in January 1955. However, the real driving force behind the growth of the local film industry was the significant rise in experienced manpower. (Before the arrival of the growth period, there existed the history of the war and the indefatigable drive and effort of the filmmakers.) It was especially with the efforts of the film engineers that the foundation of the growth period was formed. As previously discussed, the Korean Film Company(under the Public Information Bureau), the Troop Information and Education Center(under the Ministry of Defense), and the United States Information Service all imported advanced film equipment and built new production facilities. They responded in large part to the Korean film community's hunger for working with reliable and adequate film equipment. Prodigies of the Korean film industry were trained through the war, laying the foundation for the development of the future Korean cinema.

3

1950년대 한국영화

1950s Korean Cinema

1—

『한국영화총서』(한국영화진흥조합, 1977)에 의하면 〈춘향전〉(이규환, 1955)이 흥행에 크게 성공하기 전까지, 즉 전쟁 직후부터 1954년 사이에 만들어진 한국영화 편수는 40여 편이다. 이중 전중 기록 또는 홍보를 위한 다큐멘터리 필름이 14편에 이르고, 6편이 통속 애정물, 한국전쟁 영화 5편, 반공영화 4편, 검은 영화(한국의 깡패영화+필름 누아르 또는 갱스터) 3편, 계몽영화 3편, 반공적 검은 영화 1편, 전래영화 1편, 항일영화 1편, 사회성 영화 1편 등으로 이루어져 있다. 다큐멘터리류의 영화들을 제외한다면 전쟁 또는 반공과 연관된 영화제작이 압도적으로 많은 편인데, 이런 류의 영화는 1955년을 기점으로 급격하게 차지하는 비중이 떨어진다. 다른 사회의 영화처럼 이 시기 한국영화 역시 멜로드라마의 압도적인 우세로 이어진다. 그 다음으로는 코미디가 큰 비중을 차지하고 있는데, 이것은 코미디가 갖는 대중 영합성과 사회 구성원 공동의 주제를 말하기 편리한 형식이기 때문이었을 것이다. 1959년을 예로 든다면, 총 111편의 제작 편수 중 멜로드라마가 85편을 차지하고 있고, 그 다음 희극영화가 12편을 차지한다. [83] 『한국영화 자료 편람』(한국영화진흥공사, 1977), p. 47.

제작 편수의 증가는 다음과 같이 이어진다. 1950년 5편, 1951년 5편, 1952년 6편, 1953년 6편, 1954년 18편, 1955년 15편, 1956년 30편, 1957년 37편, 1958년 74편, 1959년 111편, 1960년 87편 등으로, 이후 1970년에 231편이라는 초유의 영화 제작 편수에 이르기까지 1960년대의 제작 편수는 평균 150여 편을 기록하고 있다. 따라서 1958년은 '산업으로서의 모색'이 확고하게 이루어진 시기라고 볼 수 있다. 이 시기는 한국영화의 흥행 성공률이 점차 높아진 것과도 연관이 있지만, 국극 등에 매료되었던 관객들이 점차 서구식 대중문화에 관심을 두기 시작하였던 문화시장의 변화와도 연관이 있을 것이다. 이러한 제작 편수의 양적 증가는 다른 두 가지 측면, 즉 '근대적 사고의 왜곡 또는 투영'과 '하위 대중문화로서의 정착'과 관련을 맺는다. 예컨대 멜로드라마의 주제와 이야기의 내용이 변하면서 하위 대중문화와 만나게 되는 것이다.

산 넘어 바다 건너 | 홍성기 | 1958 | Crossing over the Mountains and Oceans(San Numu Bada Gunnu) | Hong Sung Ki

2 —

　　전쟁 이후 한국영화 부흥의 기폭제는 이규환의 〈춘향전〉(1955)이었다. 거의 2개월에 이르는 개봉기간만 보더라도 이 영화가 얼마나 흥행에 성공했는가를 알 수 있다. 이 영화의 의의는 관객들을 우리 영화로 돌려놓은 주요한 역할을 했다는 데 있다. 이는 국극과 연극 등 다른 연행예술의 관객들이 급격히 감소하는 현상을 초래하였다. 이에 한형모의 〈자유부인〉(1956)도 한껏 가세하였다. 개방적인 사회 분위기와 보수적인 관습 사이에서 삼각관계를 다룬 이 영화는 대중의 저급한 정서에 부응하는 것은 물론 일정한 사회적 토론거리를 제공하기도 하였다.

　　1960년 4·19혁명이 일어나기 전까지 나온 많은 한국영화는 멜로드라마와 조잡한 신파형 멜로물 그리고 코미디 등이 주류 경향을 이루었다. 전쟁 직후의 황폐한 심성과 가난에 찌들린 생활은 영화라는 도피처를 즐겨 택하게 했고 돈벌이만을 목적으로 삼는 영화제작사들은 그런 최루성 드라마와 경박한 코미디 등을 마구잡이로 양산하였다. "일쑤 딴따라라고 부를 만큼 영화계에 대한 사회적 인식이 낮은 탓도 있지만 영화의 급성장만큼 신선한 맨 파워를 확보하는 데 결국 실패한 우리 영화는 전무후무한 졸속 시스템으로 한국영화의 그 많은 양산 욕구를 해결하는 도리밖에 없게 되었다."[84] 이명원, 「한국영화 중흥기의 작품들」, 「한국 시나리오 선집 2권」, 집문당, 1982, p. 424.

　　이는 영화의 대중적 인기와 함께 1954년 한국영화의 입장세 전면 면세 조치에 이어 1959년 문교부가 국산영화에 대한 보상 특혜 조치 '국산영화 장려 및 영화오락 순화를 위한 보상 특혜 실시'에 관한 고시를 제정 공포(문교부 고시 제53호 4월 6일)한 것에도 힘입은 것이다. 즉 당시의 정치적, 사회적, 문화적 공백기를 한국영화가 메웠다는 것이다. 당시의 영화관객들은 한국영화의 주요한 작품들에 대해 아낌없는 찬사를 보내는 것은 물론 저급한 영화조차 따뜻한 감성으로 맞이하였던 것처럼 보인다. 따라서 최소한 1960년대까지 한국영화와 영화관객 사이에는 따스한 전류와 교감 그리고 '추억'이 존재했던 것이다. 하지만 이것이 또 다른 한국영화의 질곡이었다는 것을 간과해서는 안 될 것이다. 즉 정책적 지원과 대중적 인기 속에서 단기수익을 노리는 악성 자본의 유입을 불러왔고, 이는 한국영화의 건강한 발전에 걸림돌이 된 것이다.

모녀(일명: 어머니의 비밀) 최훈 1958
Mother and Daughter(Monyo) : Choi Hoon

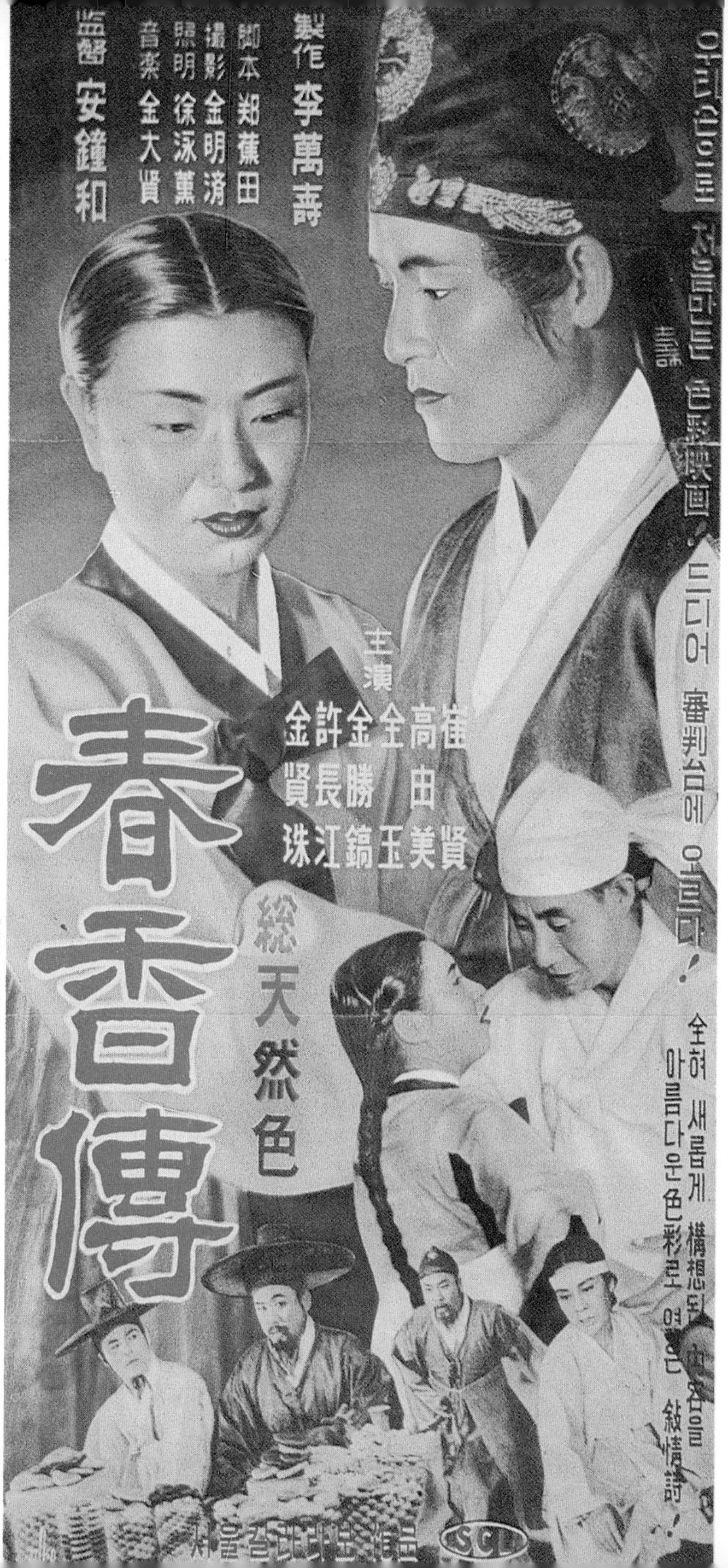

春香傳

製作　李萬壽
脚本　鄭蕉田
撮影　金明濟
照明　徐泳薫
音楽　金大賢
監督　安鍾和

主演
金許金全高崔
賢長勝由
珠江鎬玉美賢

總天然色

아리랑의 첫음마디 色彩映畵 드디어 審判台에 오르다！
壽謠

全혀 새롭게 構想되어 딥터쳐될 것을
아름다운 色] 彩로 여긴 敍情詩

춘향전 안종화 1958 Chunhyang Story(Chunhyang-jeon) Ahn Jong Hwa

서울춤향희史地記念

SCB

1 —

According to the 「Korean Film Collection」, there were about forty films produced between 1950, right after the war, and 1955, when ⟨Chunhyang Story⟩ was released as a success. Among them, fourteen films were documentaries either made for government promotional purposes or for documenting the events of war. The remaining films were commercial feature films. There were six melodramas; five war films about the Korean War; four anti-communism films; three black films(a mixture between the gangster and film noir genres); three enlightening films; one mixture of anti-communism and black film; one film based on a traditional folk tale; one anti-Japanese film; and one social commentary film. Among these feature films, anti-communism and war related themes were the most prominent. However, films focusing on these two subjects decreased rapidly after 1955. Instead, Korean producers and directors began concentrating on making melodramas. Comedy became the second largest genre produced because it was an easy medium, which carried the every-day themes of the common people. According to the 「Korean Film Material Collection」, a total of 111 films was produced in 1959(p. 47) and this included ninety-five melodramas and twelve comedies.

Since 1950, the number of Korean films produced had been on the rise: five in 1950; five in 1951; six in 1952; six in 1953; eighteen in 1954; fifteen in 1955; thirty in 1956; thirty-seven in 1957; seventy-four in 1958; one hundred eleven in 1959; and eighty-seven in 1960. This trend continued to 1970, when 231 films were produced.

The average number of films produced per year in the 1960s was 150. Based on the statistics above, 1958 was the year when the local film industry became firmly established. The rate of successful Korean films had risen because audiences were more open to western styles of popular culture, which revolved around the cinema. As a result, the quantitative growth of the film industry began to mirror "the distortion or reflection of the modern thinking" and "the establishment of the inferior popular culture" of the society. For instance, the change in the main themes and narrative styles of Korean films began to appeal to forms of popular culture rather than high art.

2 —

As previously mentioned, ⟨Chunhyang Story⟩(1955) was one of the key triggers for rejuvenating the Korean cinema after the war. The fact that it ran for two months demonstrates how successful the film was. The significance of ⟨Chunhyang Story⟩ was the role it played in veering the audience's interest toward Korean films. At the same time, there was a dramatic decrease in the number of audiences who attended traditional theatre plays and other types of performances. ⟨Madame Freedom⟩(1956), directed by Han Hyung Mo, also supported this trend. ⟨Madame Freedom⟩ was about a love triangle that develops amid the liberal social atmosphere and conservative customs. The film seemed to cater to the general public's baser sentiments, and, of course, it supplied material for much societal discussions.

Until the April Revolution occurred in 1960, most mainstream Korean films were coarse melodramas and comedies. Immediately after the Korean War, audiences chose to see these films in order to escape from the desolation and poverty they confronted on a daily basis. Profit-driven production companies responded to this trend by haphazardly producing more tear-jerking dramas and frivolous comedies. Although the film industry was experiencing major changes, it was unsuccessful in shaking its reputation as an unsavoury community to work in. In fact, the industry had difficulty securing new manpower to meet its rapid growth. According to Lee Myung Won(「Films Produced in the Second Golden Age」: 「Scenario Collection Vol. 2」, Jimmundang Press, 1982, p. 424), entertainers were traditionally considered to have a lower social status. They were often called "ilsu ttantara", which meant that they were a despised entertainer who had to live hand-to-mouth from day-to-day. In particular, actors and singers were frequently called this. Nonetheless, the film industry had no other recourse but to apply its first and probably last rough-and-ready system to produce as many films as possible to satisfy audience demands.

The newly found popularity of Korean cinema coupled with the execution of the admission tax exemptions for Korean films was followed by preferential measures promulgated by the Ministry of Culture and Education in 1959. The enforcement of the preferential treatment of Korean films and the recreational film sublimation(Notification no. 53) was proclaimed on 6 April 1959. Films were now used to cover the political, social and cultural vacuum in Korea. Audiences loved locally made films and unsparingly praised big productions and even lower quality films were warmly received by most audiences. There were connections and shared memories between audiences and the Korean films they watched, which continued into the 1960s. However, these developments inadvertently created difficulties for the Korean cinema and its growth as an expression of art and culture. Support from the film policies mentioned above, as well as the popularity of Korean films, led to positive outcomes for the local industry. However, as many investors began to think about making quick returns on their investments, productions began to attract speculative investments, which were not good for the overall long-term growth of the industry.

자유결혼 이병일 | 1958 | The Love Marriage(Jayu Kyol-hon) | Lee Byung Il

1—

　전쟁 중에 진해, 부산, 대구 등의 국방부와 공보처 및 군부대에서 홍보 및 기록영화를 만들었던 남한의 영화인들이 본격적으로 작업을 할 수 있었던 것은 전쟁 직후부터였다. 〈악야〉(신상옥, 1952, 김광주 원작)로 데뷔한 신상옥 감독을 비롯하여 이강천, 정창화 등의 감독들이 전쟁 중과 직후에 데뷔하였고, 스태프 및 배우들 또한 그러했다. 이는 남북으로 갈라진 가운데 남한의 영화 인력들이 새롭게 형성되었다는 것을 의미한다. 따라서 전쟁 직후부터 1961년 박정희의 군사 쿠데타 이전까지는 한국영화계가 전쟁의 폐허로부터 새롭게 출발한다는 의미와 함께 새로운 영화인들에 의한 작업이라는 맥락도 함께 놓여 있다.

　이러한 1950년대 영화의 주류적 경향은 단연 멜로드라마였다. 시대를 막론하고 사랑 문제가 서사의 중심축을 이루는 멜로드라마가 대중예술의 주요한 관습적 소재였던 것은 틀림없지만, 우리는 이 속에 드러난 인물들의 행위와 심리 그리고 미장센 등을 통하여 그 시대의 진면목과 정신을 읽을 수 있다. 하지만 영화를 현실 반영의 직접적인 소재로 파악하는 것은 가공의 흔적을 놓치는 일이다. 특히 1950년대 한국영화 제작 현실의 열악함과 제작인들의 정신적 황폐함 그리고 대중문화 상품으로서의 영합성 등을 고려한다면 이 시기 멜로드라마를 읽는 것은 어떤 결론에 곧바로 다가서고자 하는 것이 아니다. 그보다는 그 작품들이 가진 내재적 속성을 당대 문화의 시각과 현재의 영화적 시각에서 바라보는 것이 일차적으로 필요하다고 본다.

2—

　홍성기의 의욕적인 멜로드라마 〈열애〉(1955), 신상옥의 〈꿈〉(1955) 등은 1950년대 중반을 장식한 대표작들이었다. 이후 1956년과 1957년에 접어들면서 본격적으로 멜로드라마가 양산되기 시작한다. 대학 교수와 교수 부인이라는 주목받는 사회적 인물들을 내세워 당대의 사회적 모랄을 묘사한 〈자유부인〉(한형모, 1955)은 그들이 외도하는 것을 소재로 다뤘다. 하지만 이후 그러한 파격적인 설정과는 달리 〈애인〉(홍성기, 1956), 〈애원의 고백〉(홍성기, 1957) 등은 인물설정과 사건 배치의 특수성이나 과장의 성격보다는 전형적인 멜로드라마라는 특징을 지닌다.⁸⁵ 이영일, 「한국영화전사」, 삼애사, 1969, p. 206. 이후 젊은 노동자의 사랑과 인물들의 불우한 환경을 부각시킨 〈잃어버린 청춘〉(유현목, 1957)은 멜로드라마지만 동시에 사회적 문제 의식을 담은 것이었고, 김기영의 〈여성전선〉(1957), 〈황혼열차〉(1957) 등과 이용민의 〈산수화〉(1957) 등은 당시에 화제를 불러일으켰던 멜로드라마들이다.[86] 같은 책, pp. 207~208.

　　이 멜로드라마들은 1958년부터 1960년대에 이르는 동안 성행했던 가련하고 비극적인 여성 인물을 내세운 신파형 멜로와는 다른 것이었다. 적어도 1958년을 정점으로 신파형 멜로와 건강한 여성상과 애정관을 피력하는 멜로드라마는 갈라지게 된다. 1958년 이후의 신파 멜로물의 성향과 그 번성 이유에 대해 이명원은 다음과 같이 말한다. "1958년~1959년에 들어서면서 보다 많이 쏟아져 나온 한국영화의 작품적 특징을 살펴보면 신파물로 불려지는 최루 노선의 강력한 대두를 꼽을 수 있다. 극단적으로 봉건적인 가정제도하에 있어서의 가정비극, 고부지간의 갈등, 남편의 부도덕성에 괴로워하면서 고민하는 아내, 신분이 달라 몸을 숨기는 화류계 출신, 구박받는 의붓자식 등등 더없이 불합리하고 불행한 얘기로 가득 찬 신파물이, 대중으로부터 환영을 받았던 사회심리적 근거를 어떻게 풀이할 수 있을까? 서글픈 사실이지만 대다수의 관객은 남의 행복에 공감하는 힘, 그것을 상상하는 능력마저 잃고 도리어 불행한 운명에만 현실감과 공명을 느끼면서 거기에 눈물을 쏟고 카타르시스를 경험했다고 말할 수 있다.

　　굳이 말하면 전근대적인 사회에서 행복이란 오직 불행을 감수하는 체념과 자기 부정의 능력 속에 그리고 그럴 때 흘리는 눈물 속에 있었기 때문에 우리 영화는 그 눈물을 상업적으로 이용, 신파물의 범람현상을 빚었다고 하겠는데, 그럼으로써 한국영화가 우리 사회의 근대화 과정에 긍정적 역할을 다하지 못했음은 밝힐 나위도 없다."[87] 이명원, 앞의 글, pp. 426~427. 하지만 이러한 현상 지적, 즉 '근대화 과정에 긍정적 역할을 다하지 못했' 다는 주장은 피상적인 고찰일 수 있다. 그것은 '근대화'를 바라보는 시각에 따라 얼마든지 해석이 달라질 수 있기 때문이며, 또 관객들의 신파영화에 대한 태도 역시 '근대를 받아들이는 한국인만의 특성'으로 이해할 수 있기 때문이다.

3 —

　　또 다른 경향은 전쟁이 끝난 후 일시적으로 성행했던 반공영화였다. 1954년에 만들어

춘색시(촌색씨) 박영환 1958
My Wife from the Countryside(Chon-saeksi) Park Young Hwan

화심 신경균 1958 Malicious Intention(Hwasim) Shin Kyong Gyun

화심 | 신경균 | 1958 | Malicious Intention(Hwasim) | Shin Kyong Gyun

진 12편의 극영화 중 3편이 반공영화이며, 전쟁이 끝난 직후에 〈귀향〉(이규동, 1954)이라는 항일영화도 만들어졌다. 이후에도 반공영화와 항일영화는 한국영화의 주요한 테마였다. 하지만 전쟁과 이데올로기적 갈등을 반성적으로 되돌아보는 영화가 극히 적었다. 이후 반공영화는 순수한 반공영화뿐만 아니라 깡패영화, 코미디 등 여러 종류의 영화들과 교접하였다. 깡패영화는 그런 면에서 가장 접합하기 쉬운 형식이었을 것이다. 엄격하게 깡패영화라고 분류할 수만은 없지만 한국에는 나운규의 〈들쥐〉(1927)를 비롯하여 활극적인 영화는 있어 왔다.

정창화의 〈최후의 유혹〉(1953)과 〈유혹의 거리〉(1954)는 어두운 세계를 묘사함으로써 재미를 추구하였지만 다소 계몽적인 내용을 담고 있는 것으로 기록되어 있다. 따라서 '악'의 주체를 공산집단으로 규정하는 것이 대중적으로는 보다 설득력이 있었을 것이라고 추측하는 것은 어렵지 않다. 적대국 소련을 대치항으로 둔 수많은 미국의 영화들처럼 한국의 깡패영화 역시 반공적 요소와 결합함으로써 그러한 체제 이데올로기를 지탱하는 역할을 했을 것이다. 최초의 깡패 반공영화는 한형모의 〈운명의 손〉(1954)으로부터 출발한다. 최초의 반공영화에 해당하는 〈성벽을 뚫고〉(1949)를 만든 이 또한 한형모 감독이다. 이는 그가 철저한 반공주의

자였던 면모와 함께 지배적인 대중 이데올로기를 자신의 영화 속에 차입하는 데 능숙하다는 것을 드러낸 것이기도 하다. 후일 〈자유부인〉(1956, 정비석 원작)을 통하여 당대의 도덕률에 균열을 일으킨 것 또한 세대적 기호를 읽는 능숙함에 기인할 것이다.

4 —

1950년대를 통틀어 멜로드라마 다음으로 성행했던 것은 코미디영화였다. 현재로서는 거의 남아 있지 않은 이 코미디영화들에 대한 평가는 다음과 같다. "그 당시 엎치락뒤치락의 난센스 코미디가 판을 친 것은 밝은 희망과 미래를 잃어버리고 회의와 도피심리에 젖어 있던 사회심리와 맥락을 같이하는 것으로 볼 수 있다. 정력적인 웃음, 생생한 풍자, 현실에 대한 통렬한 비판 등등이 아니라 무의미하고 어처구니없고 실없는 웃음에 난센스 코미디로 불려지는 이유가 있는데 달리 생각하면 그것은 풍자할 대상을 제한받고 있는 우리나라 실정에서 볼 때 어쩔 수 없는 귀결이기도 한 것이다."[88] 이영일, 앞의 글, p. 427.

하지만 이러한 경향을 저속하다고 결론짓는 것으로부터 더 나아갈 필요가 있다. 엘리트주의적 입장에서 그것을 표면적으로 평가하기보다는 '풍자할 대상을 제한받고 있는 우리나라 실정'에서 그 속에 어떠한 하위문화적 흐름이 있는가를 살피는 것과 함께, 이후 〈삼등과장〉(이봉래, 1961) 등 당대 사회와 그 풍속을 다룬, 즉 근대화의 흐름에 대응하는 한국인들의 면모를 살피는 것으로까지 나아갈 필요가 있다. 또 이러한 코미디와는 달리 오영진의 〈맹진사댁 경사〉를 영화로 만든 〈시집가는 날〉(1956)은 한국의 전통적 희극을 되살려낸 작품으로 평가되고 있지만, 사실은 짜임새 있는 드라마, 가벼운 소재를 통한 삶의 묘사 등으로 이루어진 프랑스 연극 드라마의 원용이라고 보는 것이 더 정당할 것이다.

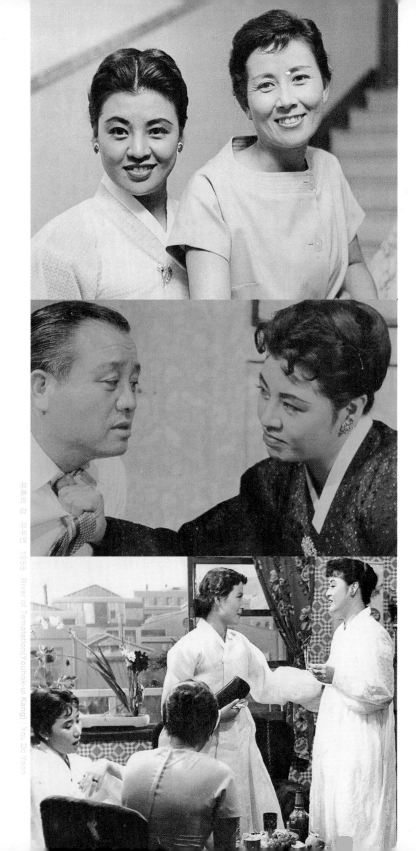

유혹의 강 유두연 1958 River of Temptation(Younhok-ui Kang) You Do Yeon

삼등호텔 | 박시춘 | 1958 | **Three Star Hotel(Samdeung Hotel)** | Park Shi Chun

인생차압 | 유현목 | 1958 | **Seized Life(Insaeng Cha-ab)** | You Hyun Mok

1 —

South Korean filmmakers, who had worked for the Ministry of Defense, Public Information Bureau, and other military film crews in Jinhae, Busan and Daegu, started making their own films after the war ended. Many filmmakers including actors, staff and directors like Shin Sang Ok, Lee Kang Chun and Chung Chang Hwa already have made their debuts before the end of the war. As mentioned earlier, Shin Sang Ok made his debut film 〈The Evil Night〉 in 1952. The level of the industry's manpower was organized in new ways due to the separation of the North and South. The South Korean filmmakers, who had worked together through the war, began to regroup again after the war. They started over with an industry (and a country) in ruins, and continued working together until the 5 · 16 Military Coup of Park Chung Hee in 1961.

One of the main trends of the films from the 1950s was focusing on melodrama. It was natural to see melodramas with love stories as the most pervasive subject matter. These types of narratives, especially through character behaviour and psychology as well as mise-en-scne, provided ways to interpret the society and the sentiments of the time. This approach to viewing films as a reflection of reality was valid as long as the artifice of the production could be acknowledged and accounted for. In actuality, reading melodramas as an exact reflection of society is not an easy task because of the variables involved in filmmaking such as the poor (rising) conditions of the industry, and the devastated minds of the filmmakers and their attempts to cater to the wishes of the audiences. Art was sacrificed for the sake of commercial viability. Thus, it seems important to see the inherent characteristics of the 1950s melodramas through the cultural standpoint of the time and cinematic expectations from the present.

2 —

The representative films of the 1950s included 〈Passionate Love(Yeol-ae)〉(1955) by Hong Seong Ki and 〈Dream(Kkum)〉(1955) by Shin Sang Ok. After 1956, there was a sharp increase in the number and types of melodramas produced. One film in particular, 〈Madame Freedom〉(1955) by Han Hyung Mo, stands out. It surprised a lot of people because it seemed to break the rules of the traditional melodrama narrative. It was about a professor and his wife who stray from their expected paths, both of whom had the kind of social status that attracted public attention. However, other directors were more true to the traditional melodrama genre. As Lee Young Il has noted in 「History of Korean Cinema(Hanguk Younhwa Chunsa)」(Samae Press, 1969, p. 206), the melodramas that Hong Seong Ki directed, such as 〈Lover(Ae-in)〉(1956) and 〈Confession of Imploration (Aewon-ui Gobaek)〉(1957), were typical melodramas without much exaggeration of the characters and their surrounding events. These were much different that Han Hyung Mo's 〈Madame Freedom〉. In addition, Yoo Hyeon Mok made 〈Lost Youth(Iruburin Chungchun)〉(1957), which was more of the traditional melodrama. However, it presented a narrative structure with a new consciousness about social problems. According to Lee Young Il(pp. 207-208), other popular melodramas of the time were Kim Ki Young's 〈A Woman's War(Yeosung Chunsun)〉(1957), 〈The Twilight Train(Hwanghon Yeolcha)〉(1957) and Lee Yong Min's 〈A Wild Chrysanthemum (Sanyouhwa)〉(1957).

The melodramas mentioned above were different from the other melodramas that were produced from 1958 and through the 1960s. Later melodramas wore different colours because of the tragic heroines in the films. The year 1958 can be seen as the dividing point between two trends of melodramas: one style portrayed strong women figures who believed in love, and the other style showed tragic female characters in tearful stories(the later style was called "shinpa"). Lee Myung Won explains some of the reasons for the abundant production and popularity of shinpa melodramas: "Shinpa, a tearful story, was the most distinctive characteristic of the films produced in 1958 and 1959. These stories included: family tragedies under strict feudalism, conflicts between mother-in-laws and a daughter-in-laws, wives tormented by immoral husbands, women ashamed of their prostitute background, and stepchildren mistreated by parents. Such irrational and pathetic stories filled the shinpa melodramas, and audiences eagerly welcomed them. What socio-psychological basis can we use to explain and understand this positive reception? We might be able to argue that most spectators lost their ability to sympathize with the happiness of others along with their ability to accept happy stories. It is sad to say, but audiences identified with the hapless characters and their tragic destiny; and, by crying for them, experienced a form of catharsis(「Films Produced in the Second Golden Age」: 「Scenario Collection Vol. 2」, Jimmundang Press, 1982, pp. 426-427)." "In a pre-modern society, happiness only comes by accepting misfortune, showing the ability of self-denial, and embracing the accompanying tears in the situation. Korean films deliberately exploited these ideals for commercial purposes and produced massive shinpa melodramas. They did not contribute anything positive to the modernization of the Korean society (Lee Myung Won, 「Films Produced in the Second Golden Age」: 「Scenario Collection Vol. 2」, Jimmundang, 1982, pp. 426-427)".

From this statement, the part about the lack of contributions to the modernization process can be seen as a superficial observation. The concept of "modernization" could be interpreted in so many ways, depending on how one looks at it. Moreover, the attitudes of audiences toward shinpa melodramas could be understood as "Korea's national trait to accept modernity".

3 —

Another important trend in the Korean cinema in the mid-1950s was the temporarily prevalent anti-communism theme. In 1954, three out of twelve feature films produced were anti-communism films. Along with them, Lee Kyu Dong directed and anti-Japanese film called 〈Returning to the Hometown(Gwi-hyang)〉(1954). These anti-communism and anti-Japanese themes were treated importantly, but there were few films that provided a retrospective view of the War's ideological conflicts in a regretful way. Anti-communism films often grafted the gangster and the comedy genres together because they were the easiest types of stories to work with. Although not strictly classified as a gangster film, similar action-packed films had been in existence since 1927 with Na Un Kyu's work, ⟨Wild Rat(Deuljwi)⟩(1927).

Anti-communism films also contained socially enlightening contents as well. For example, ⟨The Final Temptation⟩(1953) and ⟨A Street of Temptation⟩(1954), directed by Chung Chang Hwa, entertained audiences with its portrait of a dark underground world while prescribing positive social morals. Looking back, it's easy to assume that the subject of "core evil" as the communist organization was more persuasive to general audiences. However, like the many American films that portrayed the USSR as the evil counterpart, Korean gangster films needed to show an anti-communism element(ideology) that fought against the communists. Han Hyung Mo was the first director who incorporated an anti-communist element in a gangster film. His film called ⟨The Hand of Destiny⟩(1954) was the first anti-communism film made in Korea. Han Hyung Mo was known before the War for his film ⟨Breaking the Wall⟩(1949). It is widely believed that Han Hyung Mo was a thorough anti-communist and he was skillful at adopting the dominant public ideology of South Korea into his films. He was adept to pick up on and apply new social trends, symbols and icons of the time. This was well demonstrated with his later work, ⟨Madame Freedom⟩(1956), which was based on a novel of Jung Bi Seok. As discussed before, this film made a huge impact on the morality of Koreans at that time.

4

Throughout the 1950s, comedies were the second most popular genre after

느티나무 있는 언덕 | 최훈 | 1958 | The Zelkova Tree Hill(Neuti-namu Itneun Undok) | Choi Hoon

melodramas. Sadly, none survive today. However, we know much about these films from the criticism written about them. Most of the critiques from the time read: "The fact that slapstick nonsense comedies are so popular appears to be aligned with the kind of social mentality that is saturated in doubt and escapism without any hope for a bright future. Big laughs, animating satire, bitter criticism of reality, etc., is not to be found in Korean comedies. One can understand why they are called nonsense comedies given their meaninglessness and ridiculousness and attempts at laughs without substance. On the otherhand, it seems natural to see this type of comedy in Korea where the subject of satire is, in reality, limited."(Lee Myung Won, 「Films Produced in the Second Golden Age)」: 「Scenario Collection Vol. 2」, Jimmundang, 1982, p. 427)

Overall, the trend to label popular Korean films as being "coarse" and "low taste"

마도의 향불 | 신경균 | 1958
Burning Incense for Mado(Mado-ui Hyang-bul)
Shin Kyŏng Gyun

by elitists should be reconsidered. Superficial evaluations from any elitist, concerning the inferior flow of culture, would not be helpful in considering the distinctiveness of Korean cinema. Rather, an examination of how Korean audiences were coping with the flow of modernization should be studied. For example, ⟨A Section Chief of the Third Class(Samdung Gwajang)⟩(1961), directed by Lee Bong Rae, is one outstanding production that dealt with the society and customs of the time. In addition, ⟨The Wedding Day(Sijip-ganeun Nal)⟩(1956) is also worthy of note. This is a comedy based on a popular play called ⟨Happy Day of Officer Maeng(Maeng-Jinsa-daek Kyungsa)⟩, and it was praised for reviving the national comedy style found in Korean traditional plays. More to the truth, however, the film seemed to adapt a French theatrical drama and offered a well-structured, full description of contemporary life with light subject matter.

　　〈자유부인〉(한형모, 1956)은 1950년대 멜로드라마의 출발점이자 근대적 사고와 행동
양식들이 극대화된 형태로 나타난 대표적인 작품이다. 서울신문에 8개월 동안 연재된 정비
석 소설을 원작으로 한 이 영화는 '돈'과 '일부일처제'에 대한 질문이기도 하다. 가난한 장
교수(박암)와 아내 오선영(김정림, 실제로 다방 마담[89] 김수남, 〈자유부인〉, 제32회 대중상영화제 「한국영화걸작회고전」,
1994. p. 24.)은 각자 애인을 두고 있다. 장교수는 타이피스트이자 제자인 미스 박의 흠모 어린
애정에 매료되어 있고, 오마담은 옆집 대학생 청년과 파리 양품점 주인인 친구의 남편과 춤
바람이 나 있다. 하지만 장교수의 연애가 로맨틱하고 절제되어 있으며 결국 사고 없이 끝을
맺는 데 반해, 양품점 마담이 된 부인 오선영은 친구 남편과 있던 호텔에 친구가 쳐들어오자
모멸감을 느껴 방황하는 것으로 끝을 맺는다. 장교수의 데이트 장소는 서울 시가지가 바라보
이는 남산 위 언덕이며, 오마담이 남자들과 만나는 장소는 주로 댄스홀이다.

　　특히 오마담에게 춤을 가르쳐준 대학생은 조카 명옥이의 애인이기도 하다. 둘이 춤을
출 때 명옥이가 다른 남자와 들어오고 곧이어 친구의 남편 한대석이 들어와서 오마담은 한대
석과 춤을 춘다. 이 신은 다리를 드러내고 섹시한 춤을 추는 무희의 모습을 스펙클하게 오
랫동안 보여주면서 곧 이어지는 3명의 남자와 2명의 여자 사이에 일어나는 짝짓기로 끝나는
데, 이것은 바로 퇴폐적 난교에 대한 억압된 표현이기도 하였다. '프레젠트', '프렌드', '굿
나잇', '아이 러뷰' 등 낯익은 그러나 참으로 낯선 영어들이 일상어로 불쑥불쑥 튀어나오고
그들은 미국적 가치관에 순응하는 자세로 몸을 내맡긴다. 남자는 "아내하고 춤을 출 바에야
절구통하고 추지"라고 말하고 여자는 "재미없이 남편하고 어떻게 춤을 추냐"고 반문한다.

　　오마담을 동창회에 데려감으로써 새로운 세계를 가르쳐준 친구 인수는 사기꾼에게
몸과 돈을 다 내맡기고는 수정궁 댄스 파티에서 젊은 남자의 품에 안겨 음독 자살을 한다. 번
잡스런 가부장제와 흔들리는 일부일처제의 윤리에 여성들이 저항함에도 불구하고 최후는 다
비극적이다. 반면 남성들은 사회를 책임지는 기둥으로서 온화한 또는 자유로운 그리고 그다
지 책임질 필요가 없는 '천부적으로 부여된 권리'를 즐겁게 누릴 뿐이다. 결국 이 영화는
'돈'이라는 강박적 과제를, 불행을 초래하는 계제로 다룸으로써 여전히 근대 사회적 가치를
거부한다. 또 흥미로운 관음적 시선으로 일부일처제의 윤리가 무너지는 과정을 그리지만, 결

사랑하는 까닭에 | 한형모 | 1958 | Because I Love You(Sarang-haneun Kkadage) | Han Hyung Mo

국은 '건강한 일부일처제의 윤리'를 다시 한 번 강조하는 것으로 끝맺고 만다. 그럼으로써 〈자유부인〉은 이중적이며 왜곡된 당시 사회를 그만큼 이중적이며 굴절된 태도로 그리고 있다. 분명 당시의 서민들은 전쟁 이후 피폐한 생활 속으로 들어온 미국적 가치관을 수긍하면서도 과거의 비근대적 가치관을 고수하는 분열된 모습으로 살아가고 있었을 것이다.

2

〈자유부인〉은 그 모습을 그리는 동시에 여성의 윤리 위반 행위를 서사 정보에 과다하게 배치하는 한편 종국에는 처벌받는 것으로 끝을 맺는다. 당대 윤리 위반의 욕망을 부추겨서 관객을 끌어모으지만 결국에는 교훈적 가치, 비근대적 가치를 설파하는 이중적이며 굴절된 모습을 이 영화 속에서 보게 되는 것이다. 하지만 그러한 교훈적 가치를 당시 관객들은 교

시집살이 장황연 | 1958
Living with In-laws(Sijip-sari) | Chang Hwang Yeon

목포의 눈물 하한수 | 1958
Tears Shed in Mokpo(Mokpo-ui Nunmul) | Ha Han Soo

훈으로 받아들였을까? 관객 개개인들이 체험한 것 역시 교훈적 가치와 욕망의 분출 결과에 따른 응징에 대한 위협인 동시에 현실적 부당함에 대한 저항이라는 이중성과 굴절이었을 것이다. 왜냐하면 시선의 경험은 논리적 경험에 쉽사리 굴복하지 않기 때문이다.

당시로서는 과격한 문제 제기였던 〈자유부인〉의 파토스는 보다 대중적인 차원에서 그 문제를 다루는 〈자유결혼〉(이병일, 1958)으로 이어진다. 3명의 딸이 있는 한 의학박사의 집을 배경으로, 큰딸이 신혼여행 첫날밤에 이제 아무런 감정도 남지 않은 남자의 연애담을 듣고 자신 역시 그랬노라고 고백하자, 남자는 파혼을 하고 미국으로 떠나버리는 것으로 시작한다. 큰딸은 그 후로 두문불출 3년을 보내고, 둘째 딸은 가난한 문학청년형의 가정교사와 사랑을 하다가 집안의 반대에 부딪히자 가출을 감행하며, 셋째 딸은 맞선으로 사귄 전도유망한 사업가 청년보다 아버지의 도도한 조수(전쟁 중에 변심을 당한)를 선택한다. 그리고 큰딸의 남자는 반성을 한 뒤 귀국하겠노라는 편지를 보낸다. 이런 식으로 모든 연애결혼은 성공하고, 기성세대는 이를 수용할 수밖에 없다는 결론을 맺는다.

3

〈자유부인〉이 지녔던 남녀의 대립은 이 영화에서 거의 다 사라지고 단지 비교적 사회 상류층에 속하는 인물들의 자유연애와 결혼만이 주제로 떠오른다. 이것은 직업과 재산을 중시하는 기성세대들의 가치관이 '자유연애'라는 근대적 주제에 우선될 수 없다는 명제를 깔고 있기는 하지만, 그 근대적 주제는 우연한 계기로 이어지는, 치열함을 상실한 플롯 등에 의해 그다지 설득력과 현실감을 불러일으키지 못한다. 하지만 당대의 고답적인 결혼관에 비추어볼 때, 이 영화는 젊은 관객들의 공감을 통한 연대라기보다는 수동적으로 부응하는 것에 불과했다.

하지만 〈자유부인〉과 〈자유결혼〉이 제기했던 그러한 문제 의식조차 〈동심초〉(신상옥, 1959)에 가면 경미한 갈등을 보여주는 데 그치면서 현실 타협적으로 기존의 가치관에 굴복하는 모습을 보인다. 〈동심초〉는 대학생 딸을 둔 과부와 이미 부유한 가정의 딸과 약혼을 한 상태인 전도유망한 청년 사업가와의 사랑을 그리고 있다. 즉 과년한 딸까지 둔 중년 여성의 사랑이라는 소재가 이 영화의 관건으로 등장한 것이다. 양장점을 운영하다가 실패한 전쟁

낙화유수 | 안현철 | 1958 | Falling Flowers(Nakhwa Yousu) | Ann Hyun Chul

딸 칠형제 | 박시춘 | 1958 | Seven Daughters(Ttal Chil-hyungje) | Park Shi Chun

별만이 아는 비밀 | 이선경 | 1958 | **A Secret between Me and the Star(Byol-mani Anuen Bimil)** | Lee Sun Kyong

홀쭉이 뚱뚱이 논산 훈련소에 가다 | 김화랑 | 1959
Holjjuki and Ttungttungi Went to the Military Training Center(Holjjuki Ttungttungi Nonsan Hunryonso-e Gada) | Kim Hwa Rang

과부에게 집요하게 사랑을 표하는 청년 사업가는 결국에는 약혼을 파기하면서까지 그녀에게 접근을 한다. 대학생 딸조차 어머니의 사랑을 이해하지만, 그녀는 당대의 풍속에 굴복하여 재산을 처분한 뒤 빚을 갚고 홀로 시골로 내려가는 것으로 영화는 끝맺는다.

4 ―

평범한 드라마에 불과하지만 청년들의 애정관과 중년의 애정관이 다르다는 것을 역설하는 동시에 약혼 파기까지 하면서 추구하는 남자의 사랑은 순수한 정열에 대한 예찬이기도 하다. 하지만 시대의 도덕률을 존중하는 것으로 이 영화는 타협하고 만다. 이 영화는 〈자유부인〉이 보여주는 남녀 대립과 갈등의 치열함에 훨씬 미치지 못하는 것이다. '전쟁 과부'라는 사회적 소재와 '백마 타고 온 기사'라는 시대적 꿈을 결합한 것으로서, 신파 멜로까지 흐르지는 않았지만 시대윤리를 거스르는 파열음도 내지 않은 것이었다. 이것으로 1950년대의 여성의 애정 권리와 기성의 애정관은 더 이상 전진하지 못하고, 대부분이 불행한 과정과 결말로 점철된 신파 멜로물로 채워지게 된다. 자유결혼 문제가 전면에 등장한 것은 아니지만 주요하게 그 문제가 다뤄진 〈박서방〉(강대진, 1960)에서는 '개인적 사랑'의 문제보다는 '짝짓기'에 대한 근대적 조명이 이루어진다.

〈박서방〉에서 연애를 위해 가출한 첫째 딸의 이야기를 통하여 자유결혼에 대한 문제제기를 한다면, 둘째 딸의 얘기는 자유결혼조차 근대적 가치관인 경제력에 의해 좌우된다는 것을 보여준다. 하지만 아버지인 박서방은 두 딸의 결혼 사건을 기회로 근대적 가치관에 무릎을 꿇고 만다. 즉 건달처럼 보이는 남자와 자유연애를 하도록 허락해야 했고, 돈의 가치에 대해서도 굴복한 것이다. 그리고 결정적으로는 그렇게 보고 싶어 하던 손자조차 이국 땅에서 낳아 길러야 하는, 아들의 외국 파견을 승낙해야만 한다. 〈자유부인〉이 근대적 가치와 여성의 자유연애 사이의 갈등을 통하여 문제 제기 및 대중적 호기심을 불러일으킨 것이라면, 〈자유결혼〉은 보다 계몽적인 차원에서, 사실은 근대적 일부일처제의 원활한 성립을 위한 이데올로기를 제공한 것이었고, 〈동심초〉는 대중적 문제 제기에서 전근대적 윤리로 타협하는, 굴절되는 것이었다. 이런 맥락에서 〈박서방〉은 일부일처제에 대한 치열한 문제 의식은 없었지만, 근대적 제도와 가치를 대하는 당시의 사람들의 표정을 준수하게 읽은 작품이라고 할 수 있다.

1

Melodramas in the 1950s became recognized with the release of 〈Madame Freedom〉(1956). It is representative of films that showed modernized thought and contemporary behaviours. The film was based on a serial novel by Jung Bi Seok, and raised questions about money and monogamous relationships. According to 『The Korean Film Classic Retrospective for the 32nd Daejong Award』(Kim Soo Nam, 1994, p. 24), the story concerned a poor professor named Jang, performed by Park Am, and his wife, performed by Kim Jung Rim (who was in reality an owner and manager of a coffeehouse), both of whom have affairs. Professor Jang becomes attracted to Ms. Park, a typist and one of his students, while his wife, called Madame Oh in the film, flirts with a university student next door and goes out dancing with the husband of a friend and owner of the boutique store where she works as the manager. Jang's romance was portrayed as a romantic and temperate relationship that terminates uneventfully. However, Madame Oh's romance ended up in controversy when her friend's unannounced visit interrupted Oh and her friend's husband in a motel room where they were staying together. Professor Jang had less of a chance of getting caught because his meeting places were usually more discreet around Namsan, a mountain located in the middle of Seoul. Madame Oh's meeting places were usually at public dance halls.

An interesting twist in 〈Madame Freedom〉 is that the university student who teaches Madame Oh how to dance was the boyfriend of her niece, Myung Ok. In one scene when Oh and the university student are dancing together, Myung Ok arrives at the dance hall with another guy. Shortly, her friend's husband, Han Dae Seok, also arrives at the dance hall. Oh quickly changes dancing partners and begins dancing with Han. This spectacle was artfully orchestrated with long and sensual dancing shots of the dance floor showing professional dancers exposing their legs and ends with the partnering of the three men and the two women. We can see how this was an attempt to express symbolically repressed and corrupt sexual desires. Also, familiar but strange English words and expressions, such as "present," "friend," "good night" and "I love you," were commonly blurted by the characters. Those who spoke these words seemed to adopt more of an American attitude or set of values. One man comments that "It is better to dance with a Chulgu than my wife (a Korean stone mortar which shares a similar shape as the Coca Cola bottle)", and one woman asks "How can I dance with my husband when it's no fun".

It was the character In Soo who took Madame Oh to an alumni party and introduced her to a whole new world. A close friend of Oh, In Soo is seduced later on by a con artist and ends up losing everything including her money and her body. The shame was too much for her to handle, and In Soo takes poison and dies while dancing with a young guyat a party. Each female character was portrayed as struggling in an oppressive patriarchical society, and each attempted to destabilize the monogamy system. Society was not so accepting of their efforts, and their prepared ending was tragic. However, for the male characters in the film, society supported their sexual freedom and their hypocritical double standard. The men were portrayed as enjoying "naturally endowed rights" to pleasure with little responsibility. In addition, the concept of money was seen as a trigger for misfortune. In this sense, ⟨Madame Freedom⟩ rejected the values, attitudes and beliefs of the modern society. The film provided an interesting voyeuristic point of view, which attempted to reveal the process of destroying a monogamous system. At the close, the film ended up reinforcing and praising the values of a "sound monogamy system". Hence, ⟨Madame Freedom⟩ did a good job of illustrating a distorted Korean society with double standards. Given that the film received positive responses from the audience, the people at the screenings must have led their lives with similar attitudes as expressed in the narrative. It is possible,

낭만열차 | 박상호 | 1959 | **Romance Train(Nang-man Yeolcha)** | Park Sang Ho

오 내 고향 | 김소동 | 1959 | Oh My Hometown(Oh Nae Gohyang) | Kim So Dong

나는 고발한다 | 김묵 | 1959 | I Lay a Complaint(Naneun Gobalhanda) | Kim Mook

then, that the acceptance of American values, which were introduced to post-war Korean society, provided the more tenacious link to the pre-modern values of the past.

2

The narrative of ⟨Madame Freedom⟩ placed its emphasis on women who violated traditional forms of morality and foregrounded their harsh punishments. As a result, the film centralized ideological statements about the institutions of love, arranged marriages, family, and loyalty. The film's portrayal of the desire to break away from society's conservative morality tempted audiences to come to the cinema. However, in the end, what they watched and experienced were underlying educational lessons, which preached pre-modern values. But did the individuals in the audience back then accept the moral messages of the film only as an educational lesson? It's possible that the audience might have felt threatened by the film and its suggestions about breaking away from conservative social morals (away from arranged marriages) as well as its simultaneous portrayal of desire and repulsion against injustices in real life. At the same time, seeing these concepts unfold on the screen had the power to shape and influence Korean culture in new ways.

The type of pathos seen in ⟨Madame Freedom⟩ continued in ⟨The Love Marriage(Chayu Kyol-hon)⟩(1958) directed by Lee Byung Il, but on a more general level. Love marriage here refers to an unarranged marriage. The story was about three daughters of a medical doctor who has an important status in society. The first daughter marries and goes on her honeymoon trip. On the first night, the husband confesses to having previously loved another. However, when his new bride confessed the same thing, he hastily broke off the marriage and fled to America. She was left alone to spend three years doing nothing. The second daughter left her father's house when her love for a poor and sentimental teacher was strongly objected to by the family. The third daughter overlooked a businessman with a bright future to marry her father's arrogant assistant, who was bitter toward love from having been deserted by his former girl friend during the war. Finally, a letter for the first daughter arrived from America from her renegade husband who sought her forgiveness and wanted to come back to her and to Korea. In the eyes of the parents, all three marriages brought shame to the family because they did not follow the path of the traditional arranged marriage that was prominent in Korean society. However, in the end, all three romances were successful despite the problems and the social stigmas they had to overcome.

3

The gender conflicts found in ⟨Madame Freedom⟩ all but disappears in ⟨The Love Marriage⟩, which explored the concept of free romance and self-selected marriage among the upper class was the main theme. There also seemed to be a strong suggestion that the values and attitudes of the older generation, which emphasized social status, job title, and property ownership, were less important than the idea of 'free romance'. This was a clear example of modern thought. However, this modern thought was not persuasive or realistic in the film because of the story lacked believability. Moreover, the film was a little confusing because it had a loose plot structure. As a consequence, ⟨The Love Marriage⟩ only seemed to satisfy the temporary expectations of younger audiences and did not arouse any long-term sympathy or identification for young people.

The problematical subjects discussed in ⟨Madame Freedom⟩ and ⟨The Love Marriage⟩ were gradually weakened in later films such as ⟨Dongsimcho⟩(1959) directed by Shin Sang Ok. Similar kinds of small conflicts were found in the film, but it ended up compromising and gave in to ideals and thoughts that were more prevalent at the time. ⟨Dongsimcho⟩ is a love story between a war widow, who ran a small tailor shop to

자나 깨나 | 백순성 | 1959 | **Waking or Sleeping(Jana Kkaena)** | Baek Soon Sung

support her daughter's education at a university, and a young businessman, who was engaged to a young woman from a rich family. The young businessman broke off his engagement with the rich woman and approached the widow with sincerity. The widow was only able to achieve an understanding of her pursuer's intentions with the help of her daughter, who knew more about relationships. In the end, the widow sells off her property to pay off her financial debts left over from the war, and leaves the city for the country.

4

⟨Dongsimcho⟩ was a simple story that had less elaborate conflicts when compared to ⟨Madame Freedom⟩. It addressed the differences between the love of the young and the love of the middle-aged. The young man's affection toward the widow

애모 | 신경균 | 1959 | My Love(Aemo) | Shin Kyong Gyun

사모님 | 최훈 | 1959 | Dear Lady(Samonim) | Choi Hoon

슬픔은 여자에게만(슬픔은 여성에게만) | 최문일 | 1959
Sadness Only for Women(Seulpeum-eun Yeoja-egeman) | Choi Moon Il

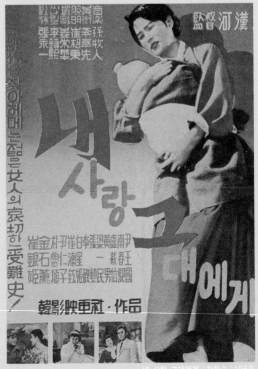

내 사랑 그대에게 | 하한수 | 1959
My Love to You(Nae Sarang Geudae-ege) | Ha Han Soo

그 여자의 죄가 아니다 | 신상옥 | 1959 | It Is Not Her Sin(Geu Yeoja-ui Jwo-ga Anida) | Shin Sang Ok

praised for its pure passion, which was so strong that he was willing to give up a financially secure life and future with a rich and younger woman. However, the film ended with a compromise that suggested that the moral principles of the time should be maintained and respected. Though it was a story about the war widow and her prince charming, it would not be considered a shinpa melodrama with tear-jerking scenes and the story was not developed as provocative as it could be. All other films were a shinpa melodrama with a tragic end for the women characters. There was another film, 〈Mr. Park(Park Subang)〉(1960) directed by Kang Dae Jin, that discussed the idea of free marriage, but it was more focused on "making couples" rather than "individual love".

Generally speaking, these were stories about a woman's right to experience romance and other prevailing concepts about romantic relationships expressed in the Korean cinema during 1950s.

〈Mr. Park〉 is a story about its namesake's three children. The first daughter who left the house to pursue her romance was the one who raised questions about free marriage. The second daughter's situation proposed that even free marriage was dependent on the economic abilities of the couple, which was a modern value. Mr. Park was subdued by these conflicting modern values as he attempted to deal with the unarranged marriages of his daughters. If he agreed to his first daughter's wishes, he would be seen as permitting her to marry a penniless and jobless bum. In the second daughter's case, even though she wanted to choose her own husband, Mr. Park had to accept the financial situation as a primary concern of the marrying couple. Finally, he felt compelled to send his son to work at an overseas office of the company though he wanted to keep him around to enjoy seeing his endearing grandson.

In conclusion, 〈Madame Freedom〉 reflected modern values and the concept of free romance for the women on screen and provoked curiosity and questions about them. 〈The Love Marriage〉 provided an ideology that firmly reinforced the system of monogamy in the modern and enlightened sense. 〈Dongsimcho〉 showed that publicly raised questions about love and relationships could be answered by compromising with pre-modern ethics. And, 〈Mr. Park〉 showed a general public facing the modern ideals and values without raising any strong debates about monogamy as represented in the previously mentioned films.

1

1950년대 영화가 보여준 남성과 여성에 대한 묘사는 1960년대 중반 이후의 영화에 비쳐진 것과는 대조적인 모습을 보여준다. 적어도 이 시기 영화에 나타난 주요한 작품들의 여성은 현실적으로 보다 주체적이며 적극적인 의지의 소유자처럼 보인다. 오히려 남성들은 시대의 희생자이며 불행한 과거를 가졌으며, 비극을 향해 운명처럼 달려가는 모습을 보여준다. 이런 묘사는 아마도 전쟁으로 인한 직접적인 피해(참전으로 인한 신체적 손상 또는 실직 등)를 남성들이 주로 입었으며, 또 가정 경제를 책임져야만 하는 남성의 위치 등을 기반으로 형성된 남성상이었을 것이다. 반면 여성들은 전쟁 이후 남성들의 무기력함을 보완해야만 하는 과정에서 생겨난 발언권과 여성 지위의 향상을 동반한 근대적 가치의 유입으로 보다 적극적이며 주체적인 모습으로 그려졌을 것이다.

하지만 이러한 묘사 뒤에는 다른 이데올로기도 숨어 있었을 것이라고 짐작할 수 있는데, 그것은 여성을 사회 복구에 동원하고 남성의 무거운 어깨를 가볍게 하는 데 노력 동원해야 한다는 '시대적 요구'라고 볼 수 있다. 따라서 이러한 남성과 여성의 묘사가 두 성의 관계를 직접적으로 드러낸 것이라고 볼 수는 없다. 오히려 남성 중심의 사회가 경제적으로 불안해지거나 가족 단위의 경제력이 흔들릴 때에야 여성을 진정한 주체로서 수용한다는 의미로 봐야 할 것이다.

시대적인 배경은 다르지만 〈젊은 그들〉(신상옥, 1955)에서 조선 말기 무너져가는 왕조를 구하기 위한 비밀 결사대에 속한 여주인공은 남장을 한 채 중요한 임무를 수행한다. 〈피아골〉(이강천, 1955)에서 지리산에 숨어든 빨치산 여대원들은 남성에 버금가는 또는 더 강한 면모를 보여주기도 한다. 반면 남성 인물들은 미련할 정도로 잔인하거나 우유부단한 모습을 보여준다. 이상의 2편은 영화가 다룬 배경의 특수성에 기인한 단순한 현상일 수도 있다.

2

〈돈〉(김소동, 1958)에서 여주인공인 옥경은 돈을 '목숨보다 소중한 것'이라고 보지만 마을 고리대금업자인 억조의 돈을 앞세운 유혹은 결코 받아들이지 않는다. 또 남자 주인공인 영호의 염세적이며 적당히 속물적인 태도와는 달리 돈을 벌기 위해 서울로 가는 것을 결심하

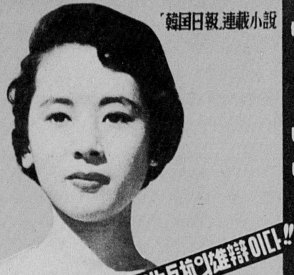

女流文壇의慧星 朴花城女史가一代의心血을傾注한問題의巨作!

"韓国日報連載小說

崔銀珹
金芝美
(一人二役)
金東園
金石薰

石金里・南宮遠
成笑民・張惠卿
盧載信・方秀一
高善愛・全桂賢
孟晩植・崔承伊

"고개를넘으면" 이것은젊은이들이외치는理由있는反抗의雄辯이다!!

고개를넘으면

開封迫頭
国際

"山有花"의

李庸民 監督
朴花城 原作

고개를 넘으면 이용민 1959 When I Go over the Valley(Gogae-reul Numeumyon) Lee Yong Min

는 진취적인 모습까지 보여준다. 〈지옥화〉(신상옥, 1958)에서 양공주로 지내는 여주인공은 기둥서방과 그의 남동생까지 섭렵하는 대범한 모습을 보인다. 하지만 결국에는 응징당하고 만다. 반면 남자 주인공들은 어느 정도는 무능하고 무기력하다가 여성이 자신의 욕망에 배치되는 행동을 하거나 배신했을 때 그녀를 응징하는 모습을 보여줄 뿐이다.

3

〈어느 여대생의 고백〉(신상옥, 1958)에서 부모를 잃고 고학을 하는 여주인공은 우연히 어느 정치가의 잃어버린 딸 행세를 하게 되자 괴로워하면서도 악착같이 공부를 하여 여성 판사가 되는 위치까지 오른 후 자신의 과거를 고백하지만 속았던 부모들조차 이를 받아들이는 설정으로 되어 있다. 〈동심초〉(신상옥, 1959)에서는 어머니의 재가를 찬성하는 진취적인 대학생 딸과 전쟁 과부로서 고군분투하는 어머니의 모습 그리고 그 어머니를 사랑하는, '사랑에 목매달고 있는' 젊은 남자 주인공의 모습이 비교적 대조적으로 묘사되고 있다. 〈무영탑〉(신상옥, 1957)은 백제에서 신라로 건너온 석공 아사달을 사랑하는 신라의 공주와 아사달의 약혼녀인 아사녀의 로맨스를 다룬 영화다. 여기에서 공주의 사랑은 대단히 적극적인 반면 소극적인 아사달은 결국 아사녀에게 상처를 주고 그녀를 자살하도록 한다. 그녀가 죽은 것을 알리는 노파는 혈기등등하게 아사달을 꾸짖는 모습으로 묘사되며, 결국 아사달은 아사녀를 따라 물에 뛰어든다.

4

〈출격명령〉(홍성기, 1954)에서 공군 조종사들로 설정된 남자 주인공들은 여자를 사이에 두고 서로 오해와 반목을 일삼다가 출격 후 서로 도움을 주는 것으로 화해를 한다. 반면 여성들은 사랑을 주도하거나 하다못해 최소한 적극적인 모습을 보인다. 〈잃어버린 청춘〉(유현목, 1957)에서 주인공인 전기 노동자는 술집 여급인 여주인공과의 사랑에 돈이 필요하던 차에 우연히 살인현장에서 돈을 줍고 피해자에게 결정적인 폭력을 가하게 된다. 술집 마담의 적극적인 모습에 비해 여주인공의 적극성이 두드러지는 것은 아니지만, 살인을 저지른 후 초조하게 방황하며 결국 붙들리고 마는 남자 주인공의 모습은 '꽉꽉한 전후 근대 사회'를 살아

꿈은 사라지고 | 노필 | 1959 | Disappeared Dream(Kkumeun Sarajigo) | Roh Pil

가는 남성들의 짓눌린 어깨를 보여주는 것이었다.

5——

　〈자유결혼〉(이병일, 1958)에서 어머니의 권력은 아버지의 권력보다 훨씬 크며, 완고
한 할아버지조차 자식과 손자들의 주장에 결국은 굴복하고 만다. 또 여성 인물들과 남성 인
물들의 태도 또한 큰딸의 경우를 제외하고는(여기에서 큰딸은 극복되어야 할 소재이며, 타의에
의해 극복될 뿐이다) 여주인공들이 보다 적극적인 태도를 보인다. 〈곰〉(조긍하, 1959)에서 아
내를 잃은 무기력한 남자 주인공에 비해 그 아이들을 돌보는 여선생이 문제를 해결하는 데
주도적인 역할을 한다. 하지만 두 사람의 결혼은 커다란 신분상의 차이와 경력에 의해 이루

꿈은 사라지고 | 노필 | 1959 | Disappeared Dream(Kkumeun Sarajigo) | Roh Pil

어지지 못한다. 〈십대의 반항〉(김기영, 1959)에서 여성들은 남자 부랑아들의 뒤치다꺼리를 하
는 것으로 묘사되고 있지만, 개개인의 성격이나 역할에서는 결코 남성 인물들에 비해 소극적
이거나 무능하게 묘사되지 않는다.

6 ——

〈구름은 흘러도〉(유현목, 1959) 역시 여주인공들이 개척자적인 모습을 보이며 영화를
주도하고 있다. 〈이 생명 다하도록〉(신상옥, 1960)에서 전쟁에서 하반신 마비가 된 남자 주인
공의 삶은 여주인공에 의해 구원받고 인도된다. 노골적으로 여성의 사회 복구를 요구하는 이
데올로기가 개입된 작품이다. 〈지상의 비극〉(박종호, 1960)은 부두 노동자들의 진정한 대변자

가 자본가들의 하수인인 노동자들에 의해 무너지는 과정을 그리고 있는 작품인데, 여기에는 그들을 바라보는 아들과 딸들의 모습이 거의 동등하게 배치되어 있다. 이 작품 속에서 어른 이나 아이 할 것 없이 남녀는 불평등하거나 어느 한쪽이 소극적인 모습으로 묘사되지는 않는 다. 다만 남성 인물들의 왜곡성과 파괴적인 모습이 두드러질 뿐이다. 〈하녀〉(김기영, 1960)는 노골적으로 여성의 괴력을 다룬 작품이다. 주인공 아내 또한 순종적인 모습이 아닐뿐더러, 그 집에 들어온 하녀에 의해 가정은 파괴된다. 물론 이 작품은 인간의 본능을 과장되게 그리 고 심리적 모험을 강조하고 있다는 특징을 갖고 있기는 하다.

7 —

　드라마 속 남성과 여성의 역할과 성격에 관해 보았지만 이것을 곧바로 능동적인 여성 상의 제시 또는 성차별적 요소가 없었다는 논지로 직결시킬 수는 없을 것이다. 영화에서 묘 사된 성격과 역할보다는 영화가 담고 있는 여러 사회문화적 요소들은 인물을 통하여 발현되 고 인물을 통하여 입장이 나타나기 때문에, 우리는 이러한 분석에서 좀더 나아갈 필요가 있 다. 따라서 '문화산업의 형성을 향한 모색'이라는 1950년대 영화의 지향 가운데 드러난 '근 대적 사고의 영화적 굴절 또는 투영' 그리고 '하위 대중문화로서의 정착'에 대한 것을 본격 적으로 살펴볼 필요가 있게 된다.

백만장자가 되려면 | 정일택 | 1959 | To be a Millionaire(Baekmanjangja-ga Doiryo-myon) | Chung Il Taek

The description and portrayal of women and men in the films of the 1950s can be differentiated from those in the mid 1960s. Women characters in the 1950s were more independent, energetic(active) and portrayed more in a positive way than their counterpart male characters who were portrayed as lethargic and helpless victims of the time. It was common for male characters to have met with misfortune in their past as well as a future destined for tragedy. On the one hand, men were wounded by the war in both a physical and mental sense. They were shot at, blown up and injured in different ways, and they lost their jobs and their homes. At the same time, they had the responsibility of supporting a family. On the other hand, women took on active roles in the process of compensating for the recklessness of the men in their lives. This became prominent for female characters after the war and the introduction of modern values, which attempted to elevate the status of women and help them achieve more positive and independent characteristics.

It should be noted that there have always been hidden ideologies behind the descriptions of male and female characters in the Korean cinema. Women were "required to participate in society at the time" to alleviate the heavy burdens of their men and help in the restoration of society. It was not a general relationship between the two genders. This implied that women could be accepted as independent subjects when the male-oriented or family-oriented society was economically troubled.

In 〈The Youth(Cholmeun Geudeul)〉(1955), a historical film directed by Shin Sang Ok, a female character was portrayed as a member of an underground organization wearing men's clothes to carry out an important mission in order to save the Chosun Dynasty. 〈Pia Village(Piagol)〉(1955) was another film that portrayed female communist guerrillas as being stronger than the male guerrillas who were hiding out in Jiri Mountain. The male characters described here were more indecisive and much more brutal, without any justification, than the women. It is possible to say that these two films particularly shared a uniqueness with their background settings.

2

〈In Money(Don)〉(1958), directed by Kim So Dong, Ok Kyung, the female character, believed that money was "more precious than life". However, she eventually rejects Uk Cho, the usury of her village who was trying hard to attract her with his money. Unlike Young Ho, the main male character of the film who kept a snobbish and pessimistic outlook on life, Ok Kyung leaves for Seoul to make a fortune. In 〈Flower in Hell〉(1958), Shin Sang Ok created a female character, which was surprisingly open-minded toward the character's love relationships. A prostitute for foreigners(Yang Gong-ju), the principal character has a love relationship with her pimp,and later on with his younger brother. These male characters in her life were portrayed mostly as incompetent and helpless until a woman betrayed them or acted against their will, at which point they brutally punished her. In the end, Shin Sang Ok's female character is killed.

3

Shin Sang Ok created various interesting women characters in his films. 〈Confession of A College Girl(Oneu Yeodaesaeng-ui Gobaek)〉(1958) was a story of mistaken identity. The principal female character lost her parents and was forced to live on her own. She then happened to be mistaken as the missing daughter of a politician. While she agonized over cheating the politician, she continued her studies and became a successful female judge. 〈Confessions of a College Girl〉 ended with a confession about her past deeds to her fooled parents, the politician and his wife, and their acceptance of her as their real daughter. 〈Dongsimcho〉(1959) was another film with notable representations of women. It contrasted three characters: a widow struggling with her life, her grown up daughter studying at a university and a young man with dying love for the student's widowed mother. 〈A Pagoda With No Shadow(Muyoung-top)〉(1957) was another, which was based on an old folk tale about a mason, Asadal, who came to Shilla Dynasty from Baekje Dynasty in order to build a pagoda. It focused on a love triangle between Asadal, the princess of Shilla, and Asadal's fiance, Asanyo, from Baekje. While the princess's love for Asadal was rather aggressively described, Asadal did not firmly express his love for Asanyo. This was sadly illustrated in his failure to save her from drowning. An elderly lady appeared at the death scene, which was close to the end of the film, and she scolded Asadal so severely that he ended up drowning himself.

4 —

The male characters in 〈Attack Order〉(1954) were air force pilots. The central conflicts in the pilots' lives revolved around women who held the active role in leading their relationships. After responding to orders to attack the enemy and flying their missions over the battlefields, they helped each other and reconciliated their lives again. 〈Lost Youth(Iruburin Chungchun)〉(1957), directed by Yoo Hyeon Mok, portrayed a man, an electric engineer, who experienced the toughness of a post-war modern society. The electric engineer was in love with a waitress at a bar and desperately needed money to continue their relationship. He happens to witness two people fighting for money and the electric engineer is compelled to murder the wounded victim to take his money. After the murder, he becomes nervous and slowly wanders around until he is caught by the police. To the contrary, the female characters in 〈Lost Youth〉, such as the engineer's girlfriend and the female owner of the bar, were much more strong-minded than the engineer and the other male characters in the film.

고바우 조봉행 1959 Gobau(Gobau) Cho Jung Ho

청춘극장 | 홍성기 | 1959 | Youth Theatre(Chungchun Kukjang) | Hong Sung Ki

살인의 신부 | 김수용 | 1959 | Three Brides(Samin-ui Shinbu) | Kim Soo Yong

인생대학 일년생 | 윤봉춘 | 1959
The First Year of a Life College(Insaeng Daehak Ilnyon-saeng)
Yoon Bong Chun

5

In ⟨The Love Marriage⟩(1958), the mother figure governed more authority than the father figure, and the stubborn grandfather could not win over the claims of his children and grandchildren. With the exception of the first daughter, who was influenced externally, most of the female characters in the film were more positive and active than the male characters. ⟨Bear(Gom)⟩(1959) by Cho Geung Ha, portrayed a female teacher who took care of the kids belonging to a single father who had lost his wife. The teacher provided much support and helped the single father solve many problems. However, the two are unable to marry because of the differences in their social positions and an unfavourable past. In ⟨A Defiance of Teenagers(Shipdae-ui Banhang)⟩(1959), directed by Kim Ki Young, women took care of male juvenile delinquents behind scenes. However, the individual characteristics and roles these women played were as distinctive and competent as the male characters.

6

The women in ⟨Even the Clouds are Drifting(Gureum-eun Heul-lodo)⟩(1959), directed by Yoo Hyeon Mok, were portrayed as frontier type characters that lead the film's narrative. ⟨As Long As I Live(I-saengmyeong dahadolog)⟩(1960) directed by Shin Sang Ok, involves a male character whose lower half of the body was paralysed in the war. His life was saved and guided by a strong female character who unselfishly took care of him. A direct request for a woman to sacrifice herself was clearly implied in this film as its leading ideology. ⟨A Tragedy on Earth(Jisang-ui Bigeuk)⟩(1960), by Park Jong Ho, portrayed truthful spokesmen of poor wharf labourers who had fallen from attacks by other labourers. These other dominating and menacing workers were controlled by wealthy businessmen who only cared about profiteering from the workers on the wharf. Regardless of their different age and gender, the men and women characters in

인생복덕방　박성복 ｜ 1959
Life Estate Agency(Insaeng Bokduckbang) ｜ Park Sung Bok

점은 아내　이강천 ｜ 1959
Young Wife(Julmeun Ahnae) ｜ Lee Kang Chun

그 여자는 행복했던가 | 송국 | 1959
Was She Happy(Geu Yeoja-neun Haengbok-haet-dunga)
Song Kook

사랑 뒤에 오는 사랑 | 강찬우 | 1959
Love after Love(Sarang Dwie Oneun Sarang)
Kang Chan Woo

this film were treated as equals, and they shared the same level of activeness. However, some of the male characters were portrayed as being more destructive and exaggerated. 〈Housemaid(Ha-nyo)〉(1960) by Kim Ki Young created two distinctive female characters in the story. This film bluntly dealt with the strange and strong will of one woman who was intent on stealing a man away from his wife, who was also considered disobedient by her husband for speaking her own mind. Both women were not traditional, and the new housemaid got what she asked for that is, the break-up and destruction of the family. This film showed the dark nature of human beings in an exaggerated way and by emphasizing the psychological adventure characters sought.

7

Various male and female characters and roles from the films in the 1950s have been discussed above. Though it may appear that many of the female characters were treated fairly well, it would be hard to conclude that women were always active characters operating without sexual discrimination. It was the characters rather than the roles they played that represented the social and cultural elements expressed by the directors and the scriptwriters of the time. Since the characters bore the attitudes toward contemporary society and culture, a closer analysis of this aspect should be followed up. Ultimately, we should remember that the films of the 1950s were attempts at establishing the cultural industry. While achieving this aim, reflections of modern thinking and the settlement of the culture among the lower class were also being processed at this time, which also deserves more attention.

1

1950년대 한국 지식층들 사이를 떠돌던 개념은 당시 사회를 극복하려는 의지인 동시에 반공 냉전 의식과 각종 통제들, 친미 기득권 계층과 민중 간의 갈등 그리고 문화적 콤플렉스 등에 적극적으로 저항하지 못하는 자학적 의지의 표출이기도 하였다. 그것은 바로 실존주의였다. 일간신문에 프랑스 실존주의자의 글이 번역되어 몇 차례 연재될 정도로 지식 사회에 자극을 줬던 실존주의가 한국에 수용된 경로와 태도는 분명하게 밝힐 수 없지만, 강팍한 집단체제에서 개인으로 도피하는 출구이기도 하였다. 이러한 실존주의를 주도했던 문학계에서 그것이 구체적으로 드러나는 것은 리얼리즘과 모더니즘의 형식을 통해서였다. 물론 1950년대에는 리얼리즘보다 모더니즘이 더 주류를 이루었고, 이 모더니즘 속에는 현실 비판이라는 테제가 잠재되어 있었다.

하지만 이 시기 한국영화는 그러한 것들과는 직접적으로는 어떤 관계도 맺지 않고 있었다. 매체 특유의 대중 지향성과 영화창작 계층들의 무지 또는 불필요하다는 생각에 의해, 당대의 시대정신과 직접적인 관련은 결코 맺지 않는다. 설혹 현실 비판이 있다고 하더라도 그것은 '한국 영화의 문맥' 속에 놓여 있는 것이었다. 따라서 한국영화는 오히려 대중문화의 현상, 대중들의 세계관과 밀접한 연관을 맺고 있는 셈이었다. 그렇다면 여가 문화를 단지 즐길 뿐인 일반 대중들의 문화적 관심은 무엇이었을까? 그것의 첫째는 영원한 주제인 사랑과 시각적 즐거움에 관한 것이었고, 그 다음으로 또는 그 속에는 고단한 현실을 살아가는 자기 모습을 되돌아보는 것이었다. 그것은 바로 '모더니티'라는 개념으로 응축되는 것이기도 하다.

2

모더니티란 양가적 개념인 동시에 감정상태라고 본다. 인간의 이성과 과학기술 그리고 합리성에 대한 신뢰라는 의미의 모더니티와 근대 문명을 비판적인 시각으로 바라본다는 의미의 모더니티는 자연스럽게 모순적인 태도와 감정을 포함하고 있기 때문이다. 특히 한국의 경우에는 그것이 외부에서 강제되거나 불안한 상태로 수용되었기 때문에 한국인들의 모더니티에 대한 태도는 불균질하거나 모순적인 것이었다. 물론 이러한 논의는 대단히 제한적이다. 이런 한계에도 불구하고 이 작품들 속에서 모더니티는 결코 통일된 경향이나 분명한 특징으로 드러나지는 않는다는 것을 밝힐 수밖에 없다.

남녀 차별 현실을 비판하며 여성의 자유 권리를 주장하다가 결국에는 파멸하는 여성을 그린 〈자유부인〉(1956)이 있는가 하면 서구식 자유연애와 결혼을 설득력 있게 교훈적으로 그린 〈자유결혼〉(이병일, 1958)은 비슷한 소재와 주장을 하는 것 같지만 실제로는 근대 의식을 제각각 받아들인 것이었다. 한편 〈출격명령〉(홍성기, 1954)은 전쟁을 소재로 한 것이지만 남성들의 관계 속에서 여성들이 배분 또는 교환되는 모습을 보여준다.

탄광촌의 한 가족이 겪는 고난과 이후의 해피 엔딩으로 이루어진 〈구름은 흘러도〉(유현목, 1959)는 당시 현실을 대체로 긍정적으로 바라본다. 하지만 〈십대의 반항〉(김기영, 1959)은 부랑아로 살아가는 아이들의 모습을 노골적으로 보여주면서 그러한 현실을 방관하는 기성세대에 대한 날카로운 비판을 드러내고, 〈잃어버린 청춘〉(유현목, 1957)은 역시 가난한 전기 노동자의 불행한 살인 사건과 사랑의 실패를 드러냄으로써 세상을 바라보는 비관적 시선을 감추지 않는다(〈워터 프론트〉(엘리아 카잔, 1954)를 원용했다는 혐의가 가기는 하지만 부두 노동자들의 계급적 대립을 다루되 아이들의 시각에서 풀어간 〈지상의 비극〉(박종호, 1960)은 세대 간의 갈등과 사회 현실의 모순을 놀라울 정도로 적극적으로 드러낸 작품이다).

3 ──

〈어느 여대생의 고백〉(유현목, 1958)은 '가난─선의의 사기─출세─고백과 화해'라는 장르적 공식fomula을 따르고 있다. 법학을 전공하는 유정이라는 여대생은 그간 학비와 생활비를 대주던 할머니가 돌아가시자 당장 하숙비 걱정을 해야 할 처지가 된다. 유정의 친구는 우연히 아버지의 오래된 짐 속에서 어느 비련의 여자가 남기고 간 일기장을 입수하게 되는데, 그 일기장에는 현재 유명한 국회의원인 최림을 사랑하여 임신까지 했지만 결국엔 사랑에 실패하여 자살을 한 과거가 기록되어 있었다. 일기장의 일부를 찢어낸 후 친구는 최림에게 전화를 해서 유정을 소개한다. 유정은 최림의 도움으로 학업을 마치고 고등고시에 수석합격을 해서 최초의 변론까지 성공적으로 수행한다. 하지만 유정을 수상하게 여긴 최림의 아내는 집요하게 유정의 과거를 추적해서 결국 그것이 사기극이라는 사실을 밝혀낸다. 하지만 유정 역시 그 사실을 고백하려던 참이었고, 그것은 둘만의 비밀로 접어둔 채 행복한 결말로

고종 황제와 의사 안중근 | 전창근 | 1959
The King Kojong and the Patriot Ahn Jung Keun(Kojong Hwangje-wa Euisa Ahn Jung Keun) | Jun Chang Geun

달려간다. 이 영화는 연애가 개입된 멜로드라마는 아니다. 오히려 가난의 문제를 배경으로 성공의 희망을 제시하는 과도적 근대기 신파영화의 양식을 취하고 있다고 보아야 할 것이다.

이처럼 1명의 감독이 여러 작품에서 세상을 다르게 바라보는 흔적을 남기는가 하면, 감독과 소재에 따라 모더니티를 수용하는 모습은 모두 제각각이다. 실제 사회는 돈을 중심으로 모든 것이 결정되고 있지만 영화에서는 여전히 그러한 근대적 가치보다는 인간관계를 강조하는 작품도 있다. 〈곰〉(조긍하, 1959)에서 아내의 부정을 터무니없이 의심하다가 결국 아내를 죽음으로 내몬 곰이라는 별명의 노동자는 사회의 냉대와 자학의 감정 때문에 술만 마시며 아이들을 전혀 돌보지 않는다. 하지만 아이들의 담임 선생님인 옥경이가 아이들을 돌보고 곰을 설득하여 결혼을 하려고 한다. 그러나 대중영화가 가지고 있는 지배적 가치관, 즉 중년 노동자와 미혼 교사라는 계급적 차이를 극복한 사랑을 허용하지 않는 프로그램에 의해 옥경이 병을 얻어 죽는 것으로 영화는 끝을 맺는다. 이 속에 흐르고 있는 도도한 계몽성 안에는 개척자적 근대 의식도 들어 있지만 실제로는 '인간관계'를 강조하는 비근대적 의식이 채우고 있었다.

가는 봄 오는 봄(일명: 그리움은 가슴마다) | 권영순 | 1959
Spring Goes, Spring Comes(Ganeun Bom Oneun Bom) | Kwon Young Soon

4 ──

하지만 모더니티를 수용하는 이러한 혼란스러움 속에서도 근대 사회에 대한 저항은 많은 작품들 속에서 드러난다. 비록 통일된 경향이나 분명한 특징은 아니지만 말이다. 〈돈〉(김소동, 1958)에서 아버지는 아이들의 자유연애를 결국에는 수용할 수밖에 없고, 인간됨의 가치만 믿었던 그는 둘째 딸의 혼사와 연관된 일에서 '근대인'에 의해 톡톡히 쓴맛을 본다. 결국 아버지가 스스로의 유교적 결혼관을 접거나 다른 근대적 질서를 수용하는 것으로 끝을 맺기는 하지만 영화 전편을 통하여 강조되는 것은 근대적 가치에 대한 저항이다. 〈자유부인〉에서도 경제력이 있어야 한다는 여주인공의 주장과는 달리 수업료를 받지 않고 강습을 베푸는 남성을 대조적으로 묘사함으로써 '돈 가치 추종'을 거부하는 맥락이 드러난다. 물론 〈어느 여대생의 고백〉(신상옥, 1958)처럼 고아가 된 여대생이 법관이 되기까지 '돈 때문에' 거짓말을 할 수밖에 없게 된 내용을 담고 있는 영화가 없는 것은 아니다.

그렇지만 신분의 차이를 극복하고 사랑에 성공하는 커플을 포함한 〈자유결혼〉, 돈 때문에 결혼을 미루다가 결국 순간적으로 돈에 눈이 어두워 사고를 치고 비극을 향해 내달리는 〈잃어버린 청춘〉, 신분의 한계를 뛰어넘고 코믹하게 결혼에 성공하는 과정을 그린 〈시집가는 날〉(이병일, 1956) 등은 모두 '돈 가치'에 저항, 부정 또는 최소한 다른 가치를 드러냄으로써 대안을 제시하는 태도 등의 모습으로 나타난다.

부언하자면, 당시 영화의 미장센은 조금이라도 기회가 되면 서구적 장면을 연출했다. 이는 서구생활 문화에 대한 지대한 동경을 반영한다고 볼 수 있다. 〈출격명령〉의 파티 장면은 서양인들의 파티 그 자체이며, 〈자유결혼〉에는 코카콜라를 마시는 모습과 골프를 치는 젊은 남녀의 모습 등이 연출된다. 1950년대 영화들의 이러한 모습은 대중들의 모더니티에 대한 태도만큼이나 혼란스러운 것이었다. 그리고 그 태도는 직접적으로 드러나는 것이 아니라, 대중문화적 기호와 얽히면서 보다 하향 평준화된 형태로 표현된다. 즉 모더니티에 대한 양가적 태도와 감정은 당시 한국영화의 양식적 특징과 어우러지면서 구체적으로 표현된 것이다.

태양의 거리 | 김화랑 | 1959 | Street of the Sun(Taeyang-ui Geori) | Kim Hwa Rang

사랑이 가기 전에 | 정창화 | 1959 | Before My Love Is Gone(Sarang-i Gagi Jeon-e) | Chung Chang Hwa

여인숙 | 김화랑 | 1959 | A Tavern(Yeoin-sook) | Kim Hwa Rang

육체의 길 | 조긍하 | 1959 | A Road the Body Followed(Yukche-ui Gil) | Cho Geung Ha

다시 찾는 양지 | 안현철 | 1959
The Sunshine Regained(Dashi Chajeun Yangji) | Ahn Hyon Chul

인생극장 | 박구 | 1959 | A Life Theater(Insaeng Kukjang) | Park Koo

1—

During the 1950s, the Korean intelligentsia experienced anti-communism debates, increased governmental control, and conflicts between the pro-Americans, who had vested rights in the Korean film industry, and the general public. They also showed the will to overcome miserable social situations and, at the same time, the helpless surrounding of their own cultural inferiority complex. From France, existentialism was introduced to Korea through newspaper articles and it opened a new way of thinking. It could now be seen that individuals had the ability to stand ahead independently of strict collectivism. This existentialism was realized under the realism and modernism movements in the literary world. Although modernism was more prevalent than realism, criticism of reality was latent within modern thought.

However, Korean films of this time period had no direct relationship to any of the ideologies mentioned above. Accepting that film was a mass media for the general public rather than, say, a literary work, there were some filmmakers who did not feel the necessity to put all of their thoughts into their work. Even though the criticism of realism existed in its own filmic context, it was much closer to the general point of view of the people than as a representation of popular culture. Compared to the other arts, films were more easily consumed by the general public who was the audience of Korean cinema. Audiences were interested in watching love themes because they conveyed enjoyable visual stimulation. In turn, audiences were given a chance to look back and reflect on their own portraits of living in a harsh reality. It's possible to identify this as the concept of modernity being adapted to the cinema.

2—

Modernity was seen as an emotional status, which had a double standard. Expressions of modernity in this time period had two conflicting meanings and attitudes. First, there was the trust in human reason, technology and the overall rationality of society. Second, there was the critical view with which to see modern civilization. Outside forces introduced modernity to Korea when the country was unstable. Thus, Korea, more than most other nations and countries, developed a series of interesting attitudes toward modernity that were not homogeneous or in harmony with each other. Common sense views of modernity were not shown in films as a conforming tendency or an outstanding feature.

If we revisit the tale in 〈Madame Freedom〉(1956), we can see how it criticized the reality of sexual discrimination by insisting that women should achieve the rights to act and live freely in society. In the end, the woman was cast aside and destroyed by society for being provocative. 〈The Love Marriage〉(1958) also presented an educational lesson about Western style romances and free marriages(unarranged marriages). Both of these films seemed to convey the same subject matter and claims modernity, but in different ways. Alternatively, 〈Attack Order〉(1954) showed how women and their relationships with men were distributed around like objects in the background of the war.

Yoo Hyeon Mok described the reality of Korea in a positive way in his work, 〈Even the Clouds are Drifting〉(1959), through a family of a mining town that experienced difficulties and happiness at the end. 〈A Defiance of Teenagers〉(1959) by Kim Ki Young critically portrayed a story of juvenile delinquents and the older generation's disinterest towards them. 〈The Lost Youth〉(1957) contained a critical view of the world from the point of view of a poor electrician who committed an unintended murder and failed in love. 〈A Tragedy on Earth〉(1960), similar to 〈On the Waterfront〉(1934) directed by Elia Kazan, dealt with class conflicts between wharf labourers. The director used a juvenile narrator, which offered a child's point of view of these conflicts. Class struggles and social conflicts were well displayed in this film.

3

In 〈Confessions of A College Girl〉(1958), Yoo Hyeon Mok used a formula in the story that revolved around poverty, involuntary deception, success, confession, and reconciliation. When You Jung's grandmother died, she was left to worry about paying tuition fees and living expenses in order to complete her law degree. A friend of hers accidentally finds the diary of an abandoned woman who left her baby behind and killed herself after the failure of her romance and affair with a well-known congressman, Choi Rim, who was the father of the baby. You Jung's friend called Choi Rim on the telephone and introduced You Jung to him as his long lost daughter, as a ploy to get Choi Rim to give You Jung money to finish her degree. Their deceit worked, and You Jung passed the bar exam with the top score. Soon after, she successfully conducted her first court case. Choi Rim's wife, who had long suspected the real identity of You Jung, confronted her and discovered the truth. You Jung was about to tell the truth to Choi Rim, but his wife had beat her to it. The film actually has a happy ending because Choi Rim's wife decides to keep You Jung's true identity as a secret. This was not a classical melodrama but a pre-shinpa melodrama that showed that poverty could eventually lead to success.

There were other films that expropriated the ideals of modernity. For example, one director showed different perspectives of the world through his diverse films. Notions of money (or a lack there of) largely drove the realism portrayed in many films. However, there were others that emphasized human relationships over money, which was quickly becoming the core of modern values. 〈Bear〉(1959) was about a labourer (named bear) who suspected that his wife was cheating on him. His wife had so much guilt and was so devastated at the accusation that she killed herself. Bear was deeply hurt by the cold society that blamed him for the death of his wife and his own guilt drove him to constant drunkenness. As a result, his children were neglected. Their

나비부인 | 박성호 | 1959 | Madam Butterfly(Nabi Buin) | Park Sung Ho

elementary school homeroom teacher, Ok Kyung, found out about Bear's situation and attempted to encourage him to live a better life and look after his children. As mentioned before, Bear and Ok Kyung are unable to marry and the film ends with Ok Kyung dying from an illness. It's hard to imagine this middle-aged labourer with children getting together with a single female teacher in terms of their differences in social class. A relationship like this could not be accepted or allowed within the predominating traditional values. The enlightening part of the story showed a pioneering concept of modernity, but the human relationships surrounded by pre-modern concepts were emphasized more.

4

Resistance against modern society was also represented in many films. ⟨Money⟩ (1958) portrayed a father who learns to accept the free romances of his children. While preparing the second daughter's wedding, the father is forced to cast away his traditional point of view of marriage, articulated in Confucian philosophy, and is faced with the bitter taste of the modern way of thinking. This kind of resistance against modern values was shown consistently throughout this film. Another film, ⟨Madame Freedom⟩, showed a woman who insisted that economic power was the most important thing in life. Her insistence was in contrast to a man who gave free dancing lessons to the public, which we can read as resistance against a materialistic society that is only concerned with financial status. In addition, ⟨Confessions of a College Girl⟩ portrayed a female college student who lied to get money so she could achieve her dreams.

Alternatively, ⟨The Love Marriage⟩ told the story about a couple who successfully married in spite of the differences in their social classes. ⟨The Lost Youth⟩ showed a man who made huge sacrifices in mistaken ways in order to get the money he needed for a wedding. Also, ⟨The Wedding Day⟩(1956) comically described the marriage process of a couple, which overcame the differences in their social classes. The ideals and values within each of these three films resisted focusing only on money-oriented beliefs.

The other significant trend and issue to be identified in the films of the 1950s was the frequent use of a mise-en-scne that contained a western living style. This was an illustration and a reflection of the yearning for western culture. The western style party scene in ⟨Attack Order⟩ and the scene of Coca Cola being drunk during a game of golf in ⟨The Love Marriage⟩ are examples of this. The type of modernity represented in the films of the 1950s was more about confusion. Meanings were mixed with icons of popular culture and downgraded to the level of a lower culture. A double standard toward modernity was well aligned with the different styles of Korean films.

유관순 | 윤봉춘 | 1959 | **You Gwan Soon(You Gwan Soon)** | Yoon Bong Chun

흥부와 놀부 | 김화랑 | 1959 | **Heungbu and Nolbu, a Story of Brothers(Heungbu-wa Nolbu)** | Kim Hwa Rang

6 | 1950년대 한국영화의 서사형식

1—

1950년대 한국영화의 서사형식과 스타일을 찾는 문제 또한 난감하기는 마찬가지이다. 이 시기에 어떤 사조나 경향이 유행하지도 않았으며 더더구나 영화 언어적 인식이 극도로 미비했던 시기였기 때문이기도 하다. 예술 차원에서 모더니티를 거론할 때 자연스럽게 따라붙는 '모더니즘'의 양식을 찾는 것 또한 쉬운 일이 아니다. 모더니즘 영화양식은 고전적인 편집을 의도적으로 무시하거나, 고전적 서사형식의 파괴 그리고 스타일상의 각별한 장치 등으로 압축할 수 있지만 다른 한편으로는 모더니티의 비판적 요소 즉 사회를 부정적, 비판적으로 바라보는 시선까지 포함하고 있는 것이다. 하지만 이 시기 영화들이 모더니즘의 요소를 가지고 있는 흔적은 결코 찾아볼 수가 없다. 따라서 이 부분의 서술은 서사형식과 스타일상의 특징을 간략하게 언급하는 데 그칠 수밖에 없다.

2—

우선 장르 혼합적인 경향을 먼저 언급한다면, 〈지옥화〉(신상옥, 1958)를 들 수 있다. 이 영화는 미군 기지촌을 배경으로 파격적인 상황설정과 스펙터클이 연출된, 개성 뚜렷한 작품이다. 돈 벌기 위해 상경한 형이 양공주와 동거를 하며 범죄행각을 벌이자, 형을 고향으로 데려가고자 온 동생이 양공주의 유혹에 넘어가 삼각관계를 형성하는 것으로 플롯이 짜여져 있다. 멜로드라마의 틀을 이루고 있긴 하지만, 한국형 갱스터의 모습도 들어 있고 부분적으로는 뮤지컬 같은 볼거리도 제공하고 있다. 이 영화의 전반부는 서울의 삭막한 환경과 미군부대 지역의 생활상을 비판적으로 묘사하는 것으로 시작하지만 그 이후부터는 주인공 양공주를 관음의 대상으로 묘사하고 있으며, 그녀를 그릇된 욕망의 상징처럼 드러나게 한다. 형과 형수와 시동생 사이의 삼각관계라는 당시로서는 파격적인 설정에도 주목할 수 있겠지만, 결국 형과 형수가 파멸하는 결말로 갔기 때문에 그러한 진전된 설정조차 양공주라는 희생양을 통해서만 가능한 것이다.

이외에도 영화에는 주목할 만한 장치들이 빈번히 등장한다. 비록 양공주이기는 하지만 형수와 시동생 간의 애욕이 전개되고 뮤지컬 같은 공연이 전개되는 미군부대 안에서 물품을 훔치다가 발각되어 총격전이 벌어진다. 아마 할리우드 영화의 영향과 프랑스 영화의 영향

별은 창 너머로(별은 창 넘어로) 홍성기 | 1959
The Sunshine Coming through the Window(Byol-eun Chang-numuro)
Hong Sung Ki

춘희 신상옥 | 1959 La Traviata(Chunhee) | Shin Sang Ok

구름은 흘러도 유현목 | 1959
Even the Clouds Are Drifting(Gureum-eun Heul-lodo) You Hyun Mok

칠일간의 애정 장황연 | 1959
Love for Seven Days(Chil-il Gan-ui Sarang) | Chang Hwang Yeon

청춘일기 | 이병일 | 1959 | The Youth Diary(Chungchun Ilgi) | Lee Byung Il

이 있었던 것으로 짐작되는데, 그것은 장르 혼합적인 성격에서 찾을 수 있을 것이다. 즉 미군 기지촌이라는 설정은 대단히 현실적인 것이기는 하지만 뚝섬에 수영하러 간 주인공들의 요염한 수영복과 자태 등은 할리우드에서 빌려온 것이고, 그들이 사는 기지촌에 대한 묘사는 프랑스 시적 리얼리즘 영화를 떠올리게끔 한다. 하지만 이것보다 더욱 놀라운 일은 미군부대에 인물들이 잠입하는 장면에서 벌어진다. 부대의 파티장에는 삼삼오오 양공주들이 미군과 어울리고 있는데 이곳에서 공연되는 집단 쇼는 할리우드 뮤지컬을 연상시킨다. 게다가 그것을 여러 숏으로 보여주는데 총 5분이 넘는 구경거리이다. 이후 물건 도난 사건으로 벌어진 추격전은 교차 편집으로 이루어져 있는데 그것을 보여주는 총 지속시간과 여러 숏들에서 할리우드 갱스터 필름을 연상시킨다.

3 —

    서사형식의 차원에서 본다면, 우선 〈구름은 흘러도〉(유현목, 1959)를 예로 들면서 설명하는 것이 좋을 듯하다. 어느 벽촌 광산의 빈곤한 가정에서 살아가는 4남매의 이야기를 다룬 이 영화는 오빠가 몸이 약해 실직을 하자 형제들이 뿔뿔이 흩어지지만 주인공인 소녀는 끝끝내 희망을 잃지 않고 살면서 결국에는 행복해진다는 얘기이다. 재일교포 소녀 야스모토 스에코安本末子의 일기가 원작인데, 원작은 해피 엔딩이 아니라고 한다. 상대적으로 정교한 구성임에도 불구하고 이 영화는 할리우드의 고전적 서사형식을 지향하는 모습을 보여준다.

    "우리나라의 시나리오, 특히 각색 시나리오는 철저하도록 해설에 가까운 서술형식에 뿌리박고 있는 것이다. 때문에 이 서술형식이 도달한 곳은 언어감각이 지니는 이미지와 의미 표상이 아니라, 그저 사건을 엮어서 그 스토리를 이야기 줄거리식으로 만들어놓은 데 불과하다. (…)시나리오란 이야기 줄거리가 아니라 언어감각에 입각한 이미지와 의미표상이 주로 연상력을 가져야 할 것이다. (…)때문에 두 동생 남매를 남겨놓고 돈벌이 하러 떠나는 4남매 가족의 이별 장면에도 그렇게 심각한 인생의 저면이 부각되지 못했을뿐더러 클라이맥스를 해피 엔드로 끌고 간 것을 보더라도 완전히 이 각색이 감출 수 없는 스토리 추종의 결함을 빚어내었고, 또 그럼으로 인해서 이 작품은 통속화를 면하지 못했을 것이다."[90] 최일수, 「구름은 흘러도」, 「시나리오 문예」 제4집, 1959, 12; 전양준, 장기철 책임 편집, 「닫힌 현실 열린 영화」, 제3문학사, 1992, pp. 83~84에서 재인용.

    여기에서 보듯 당시 영화들의 서사형식은 스토리를 플롯으로 만들어가는 과정에서 정보 제시의 방식이나 그 결과물로서의 체계에 대해 분명한 입장이 있었던 것은 아니라고 볼 수 있다. 인물과 사건과 환경을 중심으로 플롯을 구성하는 것에 그쳤다는 말이다.

4 —

    하지만 최일수의 비평처럼 이 영화의 플롯이 그렇게 엉성한 것은 아니다. 다른 영화들이 거의 에피소드 뭉치들의 연결로 이루어진 상황을 감안한다면, 이 영화는 비교적 플롯 체계를 염두에 둔 것이라고 볼 수 있다. 게다가 극적 전개를 위해, 또 해피 엔딩을 위해 플롯을 구성했기 때문에 주제와 소재가 허구적으로 조작되는, 즉 할리우드의 관습적 서사를 지향한 측면을 지적할 수 있을 것이다. 앞에서 프랑스 연극 드라마의 영향을 받은 것으로 얘기했

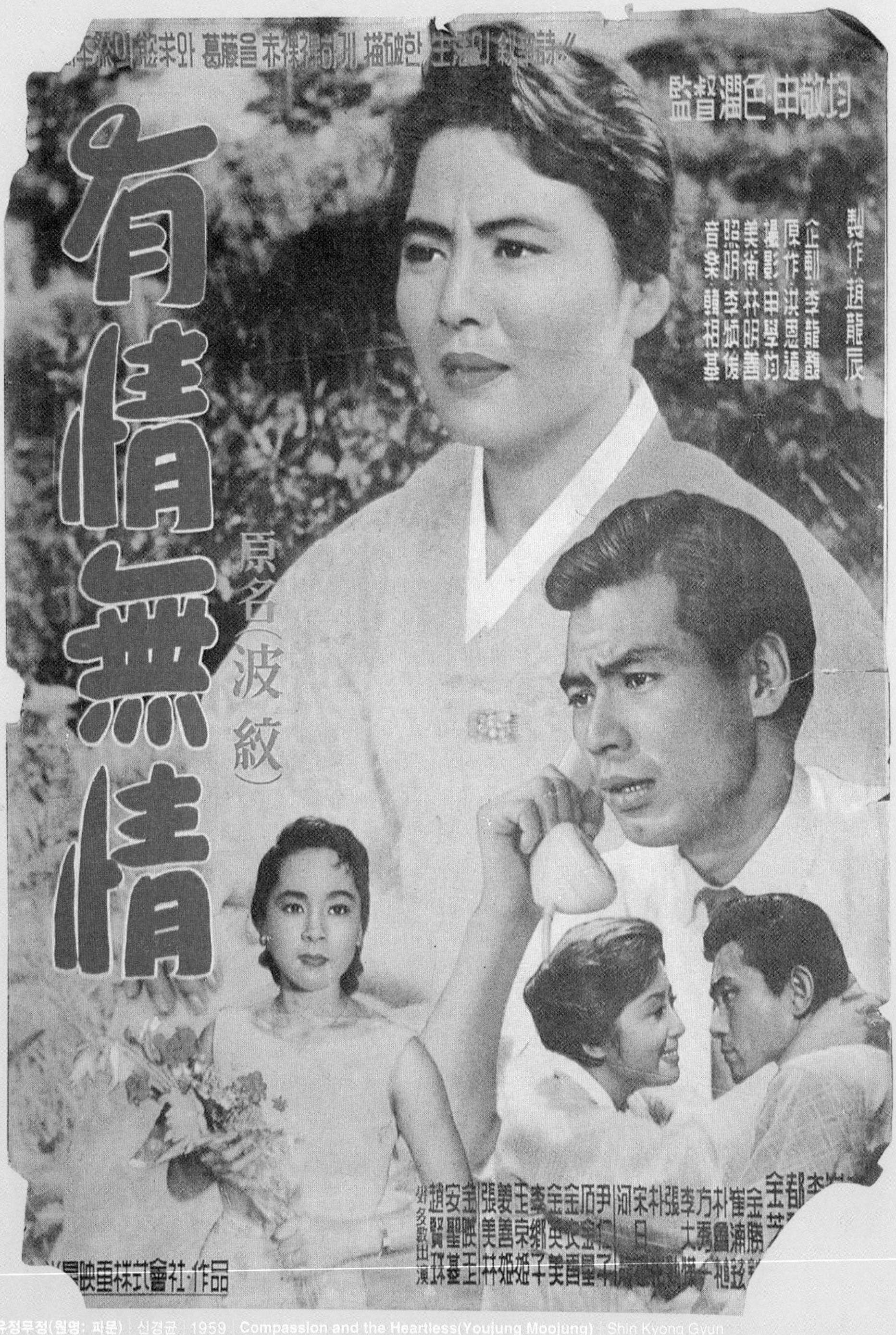

유정무정(有情 無情, 波紋) 신경균 1959
Compassion and the Heartless(Youjung Moojung) Shin Kyong Gyun

던 〈시집가는 날〉(이병일, 1956)이나 〈잃어버린 청춘〉(유현목, 1957), 〈어느 여대생의 고백〉(신상옥, 1958), 〈동심초〉(신상옥, 1959) 등의 경우에도 서구 드라마의 틀을 빌린, 그래서 압축적이며 선형성이 분명한 영화라고 할 수 있다. 하지만 이것은 비교적 단선적인 플롯이라는 의미일 뿐 정보전달 과정을 지칭하는 내레이션의 차원에서 볼 때는 산만하고 중복적인 내레이션을 취하고 있다(그리고 부언하자면, 최일수의 서사와 이미지에 대한 인식은 당시로나 현재로나 비교적 수준 높은 서사와 스타일에 대한 비평적 인식을 보여준다).

　　언급한 작품들을 제외한 다른 대부분의 작품에서 발견되는 서사형식은 공통적으로 중심 사건의 느슨한 진행과 에피소드들의 결합이라는 특징으로 요약할 수 있을 것이다. 특히 〈십대의 반항〉, 〈지상의 비극〉 등에 등장하는 여러 인물들이 각자마다 플롯의 중심을 이루며 이 사이에는 다른 지엽적인 에피소드들 또한 배치되어 있는, 할리우드 서사와는 전혀 다른 모습을 보여준다. 〈지상의 비극〉에는 노동운동을 하다가 실패한 덕호와 그의 아들 요한 그리고

구름은 흘러도 유현목 1959   Even the Clouds Are Drifting(Gureum-eun Heulleodo) Yoo Hyun Mok

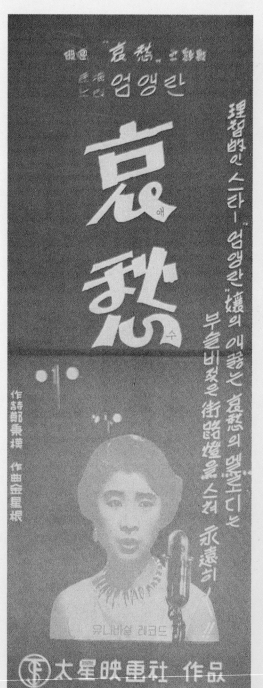

애수 | 강원주 | 1959 | **Sorrow(Ae-soo)** | Kang Won Joo

비극은 없다 | 홍성기 | 1959
No More Tragedy(Bigeuk-eun Upda) | Hong Sung Ki

결혼조건 | 강찬우 | 1959
Condition for Marriage(Kyolhon Jogeon) | Kang Chan Woo

복도 많지 뭐유(복두 많지 뭐유) | 백호빈 | 1959
You've Got Lucky(Bokdo Manji Mwo-yu) | Baek Ho Bin

포주를 하고 있는 처 윤옥 그룹과 어용 노조원인 십장 기영과 그의 딸 행자와 처 경숙 그룹, 그리고 부두 하역 감독을 하는 광철, 노동자 칠성, 구두닦이 준철, 준철의 누나인 창녀 난이, 난이의 구두 닦는 애인인 용규 등이 등장한다. 내러티브는 어느 인물에 특별한 중심이 주어지지 않고 사건의 성격에 따른 배분만으로 각자의 독립적인 사건과 행위를 보여주는 산발적인 플롯 구조를 취하고 있다. 물론 끝에 가서 사건들이 결합되기는 하지만 끝까지 종결되지 않은 상태로 인물과 사건은 열려 있다.

5 —

〈자유부인〉 역시 복잡한 에피소드 결집형의 서사이며, 〈피아골〉은 주인공의 욕망을 알아차리는 데 한참 시간이 걸릴 정도로 다른 지엽적인 사건들이 많다. 〈돈〉 역시 영화 전체의 '수수께끼—해결' 구조를 파악하는 것은 중반 이후에 접어들어야 가능하며, 〈지옥화〉는 주요한 플롯이 중간에 바뀌었다가 다시 처음의 플롯으로 돌아오는 구조를 가지고 있다. 앞에서 비교적 단선적이며 선형적인 내러티브를 취하고 있다고 했던 〈잃어버린 청춘〉도 지나치게 빈번한 플래쉬백의 사용으로 산만하기는 마찬가지이다.

1950년대 영화들은 시점 숏을 준수할 뿐 아니라 강조형의 클로즈업, 숏/역전 숏 등의 공식을 대체로 준수하고 있다. 그렇다고 해서 이 시기 한국영화들이 할리우드의 고전적 스타일을 완성했다는 의미로 받아들이기는 힘들다. 조악한 형태로 별다른 영화 언어적 인식 없이 부분적으로 고전적 스타일을 답습하는 데 머물렀다고 볼 수 있다. 이상으로 보건대 1950년대 한국영화의 서사형식이나 스타일은 한국의 전통적인 서사형식이나 특별한 시지각적 인식을 드러낸 것이라고 할 수는 없다. 다만 복선적인 플롯 구조가 주제 의식을 강화할 때도 있지만, 대부분의 경우에는 주제가 지닌 아우라aura를 전달하는 데 방해가 될 뿐이었다. 물론 작품 한 편 한 편을 분석해 들어간다면, 그 작품만이 지닌 긍정적 또는 부정적인 특징들을 발견할 수 있을지도 모르지만, 서사형식과 스타일로 국한해서 개관하는 차원에서 본다면 당시의 한국영화는 미지의, 미개척의 분야였던 셈이다.

1

In terms of narrative structure, there weren't many outstanding features and styles in the 1950s films. There were no discussions relating to the concept of film as a language. Structures of modernism in art were not easily found or explored. Modernity would have included critical views of society with various stylistic approaches such as the neglecting of traditional editing, breaking the classical narrative structure, and the use of unique stylistic devices. However, there did not seem to be any Korean films that contained stylistic elements of a modern aesthetic. This chapter discusses a few of the common narrative structures and styles.

2

〈Flower in Hell〉(1958) is one exceptional case that employed a mixture of different genres. The background of this film was set in a brothel located near the American Army camp in Seoul. A man from the countryside comes to Seoul in order to make money. He has no place to go, so he starts living with the prostitutes who worked for foreigners. Then he marries one of the prostitutes. During his stay in Seoul, the man commits many minor crimes. Eventually his brother comes to the city to ask him to go back to the countryside with him. In the meantime, however, his brother is seduced by his wife, who was still working as a prostitute, and a bizarre love triangle is formed. Within this melodramatic structure, scenes with gangsters and music were inserted for entertainment. Starting from the dreary environment of Seoul and the bleak living standard around the US Army camp, the film portrayed the prostitute as an object of voyeurism and the wrong desire. The shocking love relationship between the three characters, a brother, his prostitute wife, and her brother-in-law, was controversial considering the time period. This advanced story was only possible with a female character as the prostitute for foreigners and with the brother and his wife ending up

십대의 반항 | 김기영 | 1959 | A Defiance of Teenagers(Sipdae-ui Banhang) | Kim Ki Young

황금의 상처 | 홍일명 | 1959 | Golden Injury(Hwang-geum-ui Sangchao) | Hong Il Myong

세 쌍동 | 이창근 | 1959 | Triplet(Se Ssang-dong) | Lee Chang Geun

with total self-destruction.

There are a few interesting filmic devices worth noticing in this film. For example, the sexual tension between the wife and the brother-in-law was skilfully dealt with. The film was riddled with abruptly starting musical scenes. Characters stole things from the US Army camps, and gunshots and chasing scenes followed. The film seemed to contain a mixture of influence from the Hollywood and French films. The use of a real prostitute village around the US Army camp provided a realistic background to the film. One can see how the vivid description of the prostitute village was similar to the French realism films. On the contrary, the close-up shots of the main characters wearing swimsuits were used to pronounce their sexiness, a style that was clearly adopted from the Hollywood films. When the main characters sneak into the US army camp, they are surprised to see a live musical show, the type reminiscent of the 1930s Hollywood musicals. This scene lasted five minutes and was edited with many quick cuts. The chasing scene that followed the stealing scene was edited together in a parallel style, again, reminding us of the types of Hollywood gangster films, which had fast-paced chase scenes with lots of quick cuts between exciting parallel actions.

3 —

Another one of You Hyun Mok's films, 〈Even the Clouds are Drifting〉(1959), is also a good example for discussing narrative structures. This film is based on a true story that a Japanese girl had recorded in her diary. It is the story about four brothers and sisters living together in a remote mining town. Tragically, the family had to separate after the oldest brother lost his job due to his poor health. The youngest sister, also the main character, keeps hoping for a better future. She eventually finds happiness at the end, which was a different ending from the original story. This particular film seems to follow the Hollywood classical narrative structure.

장마루촌의 이발사 | 최훈 | 1959 | The Barber at Jangmaru Village(Jangmaruchon-ui Ibalsa) | Choi Hoon

오늘도 내일도 · 이영 · 1959
Today and Tomorrow(Oneuldo Naeildo) · Lee Young

끝없이 하염없이 · 김영창 · 1959 · Forever(Kkut-upsi Hayom-upsi) · Kim Young Chang

Regarding ⟨Even the Clouds are Drifting⟩, Choi Il Soo commented in 「Scenario Series Vol. 4」 in December 1959, that "The scenarios of Korea, especially with adapted scenarios, are complete narrative structures that fit into the explanatory style. This narrative style applies only to the story telling and not the image or the expressions of the symbols through the film language. ⋯ Scenarios should be associated with images and meaningful symbols from the film language. ⋯ Because of this narrative strategy, the sadness behind the superficial separation scene of the family was not expressed well. The made uphappy ending, which was very different from the original story, created a big fallacy in the whole context. This attempted to prioritize a story oriented film structure, and made the film seem appealing to the general public."

As witnessed from this statement, narrative film plots were mostly structured around characters, events and background. There were no other driving forces behind narrative development and structural design.

4 —

Choi also provided other quality criticisms about the story and images in the film. He criticized its loose plot, but thought that it was still better than the other films produced around the same time. For Choi, this film followed the conventional narrative constructions of Hollywood films, which made up their own themes and subject matter. This was perhaps the reason why the happy ending was used to progress the film's drama forward to a concluding resolution. As for the adaptation of western style dramas, ⟨The Wedding Day⟩, ⟨The Lost Youth⟩, ⟨Confessions of a College Girl⟩, and ⟨Dongsimcho⟩ all seemed to be influenced by French dramas and should be discussed together as a cohesive whole. The condensed linear development of story devices can be witnessed in these films. Though the narratives were a little repetitive in terms of providing background information, their simple linear plots are identifiable.

독립협회와 청년 이승만 | 신상옥 | 1959
Independence Club and Young Rhee Syung Man(Doknip Hyuphoi-wa Chungnyon Rhee Syung Man) | Shin Sang Ok

Many other films not mentioned above also shared common narrative characteristics, such as the slow progress of a main event and the adding of many episodes. ⟨A Defiance of Teenagers⟩ and ⟨A Tragedy on Earth⟩ were two such films that portrayed several main characters at once, all carrying on and dealing with their own episodes and situations, which showed a differentiation from Hollywood film narratives. For example, in ⟨A Tragedy on Earth⟩, there were numerous main characters: Duk Ho, a failed labour movement leader from the past; Yo Han, his son; Yoon Ok, his wife and part pimp; Ki Young, a foreman and fake labour member; Han Ja, his daughter; Kyung Sook, his wife; Kwang Chul, a wharf manager in charge of unloading materials; Chil Sung, a labourer; Nani, his elder sister and a prostitute; Yong Gyu, her boyfriend and a shoeshine boy; and Jun Chul, also a shoeshine boy. There is no central narrative found in this film, and not a single character is chosen to be more important than any of the others. The film showed the independent behaviours of each character according to a series of independent events. The narratives were scattered in accordance with the characteristics of each event. Although the events shown through the film became unified as one in the end, the characters and their own events were left open to interpretation.

5

Other Korean films were hard to make sense of because of their disorganized plots. ⟨Madame Freedom⟩ was also part of the collection of complicated episodes, and ⟨Pia Village⟩ showed too many marginal events before the main character revealed his desires. ⟨Money⟩'s basic plot, mystery and solution became clear half way through the film, and ⟨Flower in Hell⟩ had a circular plot, whose starting plot changed in the middle and came back to the original one at the end. ⟨The Lost Youth⟩, though it had a simple and linear narrative, scattered the delivery of the story with its frequent use of flashbacks.

The Korean films of the 1950s followed basic principles of shooting. Point of view shots, close-ups, and shot reverse shots were all employed to help move their narratives forward. It would be difficult to say that these films completely relied on and used the classical Hollywood style. Rather, these films partially employed the classic Hollywood style by adapting it in different ways. The narrative style and structure of the 1950s films did not have any particular characteristics such as a "traditional Korean narrative style". Foreshadowing plot structure was often used to strengthen the main filmic themes. However, when used, this obstructed the aura of the central theme because it seemed to confuse the audience. Generally speaking, until now, most of the films from the 1950s have been left out of discussions about the unique use of the narrative structures and style.

여사장 | 한형모 | 1959 | Female Executive(Yeo-sajang) | Han Hyung Mo

1950년대 한국영화는 1960년대 한국영화에 어떤 흔적을 남겼을까? 비록 1950년대 영화들에 묘사된 인물들의 모습, 즉 현실에 짓눌려 있으며 근대 의식을 수용하는 동시에 거부하는 분열적인 태도가 1960년대 초기 대표작들까지 이어지기는 하지만 그것은 현실의 고정적인 반영에 더 가까운 것이라고 보는 편이 낫다. 특히 서사형식과 스타일이 비정형의 형식으로 스토리 중심이나 전달 중심으로 구성되었다는 것을 감안한다면 1960년대 영화의 의식적인 사회 비판과 스타일에 대한 자각 등은 외국영화의 자극이나 감독 내부의 자각에 의해 이루어진 것이라고 볼 수밖에 없다(가까운 예로 1990년대 새로운 한국영화의 대표작이라고 꼽히는 홍상수의 〈돼지가 우물에 빠진 날〉이나 〈강원도의 힘〉을 잉태할 직접적인 조건을 1980, 1990년대 한국영화가 가진 것은 아니었다는 것을 상기할 필요가 있다). 오히려 1960년대 영화의 개화는 앞에서 말한 이유뿐만 아니라 무너져가는 이승만 정권 말기의 사회적 동기와 문학 등의 다른 예술에 의해 더 많이 영향을 받았을 것이다. 하지만 그럼에도 불구하고 1950년대 영화들이 1960년대에 전수한 '그 무엇'을 밝히는 일은 과제로 남아 있다.

이름 없는 별들 | 김강윤 | 1959 | Stars with No Names(Ireum-upneun Byoldeul) | Kim Kang Yoon

동심초 | 신상옥 | 1959 | Dongsimcho(Dongsimcho) | Shin Sang Ok

What legacy would have been inherited from the films made in the 1950s? The characters portrayed in the 1950s were burdened by the harsh realities of society. They were also confused by the introduction of modernity and could not easily decide to accept it or refuse it. Similar characters have also been found in the films of the early 1960s. They too offered reflections of the social realities of the time, which were not that different from those of the 1950s. However, unlike the reception of films from the 1950s, the conscious social criticisms and awareness of the film style began to get noticed in the 1960s. Considering that storytelling in the 1950s was importantly perceived at the time of the films' release, their narrative structures and styles had no relationship to their legacy that is, their narrative styles were not passed on to the films of the 1960s. This was a trend that was influenced more from the directors themselves than from the external impact of foreign films. We can see similar issues today with the contemporary cinema in Korea. Director Hong Sang Soo does not owe the success of his films, such as 〈The Day a Pig Fell into the Well〉 and 〈The Power of Kangwon Province〉, to the legacy of Korean films from the 1980s. The changes seen in the films of the 1960s would have been influenced by the social causes against Rhee Syung Man's dictatorship as well as other concerns that simultaneously shaped the art and literary fields. There must be something more from the films of the 1950s than a legacy of characters. Our search for a larger legacy from this time must continue.

1945년

— 8·15 광복.

— 「조선영화건설본부」 〈해방뉴스〉 1·2보 제작.

— 「조선영화동맹」 결성 12월 16일.

1946년

— 미군정청 영화 법령 제68호 4월 12일 및 제115호를 공포 10월 8일.

— 고려영화사 제작, 최인규 감독, 전창근 각본·주연 작품 〈자유만세〉 상영 10월 22일.

— 「조선영화동맹」 등 문화예술단체의 영화법 철폐 성명 발표 10월 23일.

1947년

— 김소동 감독의 조선영화과학연구소에서 제작한 최초의 16밀리 유성영화 〈목단등기〉 개봉.

1948년

— 미 502부대에서 최초의 컬러 16밀리 문화영화 〈희망의 마을〉 제작.

— 뮤지컬 드라마 〈푸른언덕〉에서 사운드 필름에 동시녹음.

1949년

— 홍성기 감독 데뷔작 〈여성일기〉 극영화 최초로 컬러 16밀리 제작.

— 촬영기사 한형모 반공극영화 〈성벽을 뚫고〉로 연출 데뷔.

1950년

— 윤용규 감독의 〈마음의 고향〉(1949) 한불문화교류 위해 프랑스 영화 〈꿈속의 노래〉와 교환.

— 6·25 전쟁.

— 부산에서 한국영화평론가협회 발족 9월 10일.

1951년

— 국방부 정훈국이 제작한 〈정의의 진격〉 1부 부산 동아극장, 대구 자유극장 개봉 6월 20일.

1952년

— 신상옥 감독의 데뷔작 〈악야〉 피난지 대구에서 완성.

1953년

— 최초의 대학 영화과가 설치된 2년제 서라벌예술학교 설립, 학장은 〈월하의 맹서〉(1923) 감독 윤
백남.
— 정창화 감독 〈최후의 유혹〉으로 감독 데뷔.

1954년

— 국산영화 장려책으로 국산영화 입장세 면세 조치 단행 3월 31일.

1955년

— 이규환 감독의 〈춘향전〉 흥행 성공, 서울 국도극장과 부산 동아극장에서 동시 개봉 1월 6일.
— 『국제영화』, 『영화 세계』 영화월간지 발간.
— 미공보원에서 제작한 〈주검의 상자〉로 김기영 감독 데뷔, 미첼 카메라와 마그네틱 레코더로 동시
녹음 촬영.
— 한국 최초의 여성 감독 박남옥 〈미망인〉으로 데뷔.

1956년

— 한국영화인단체연합회 결성.
— 아세아재단에서 미첼 카메라, 휴스턴 자동현상기 등 시가 6만 불 상당의 영화 기재 기증.
— 한형모 감독의 〈자유부인〉이 국도극장에서 개봉 6월 9일 45일간의 흥행기록을 수립.

1957년

— 5개 작품 선정 후 1편당 외화 수입 쿼터 1편을 부여하는 우수국산영화 선정제도 신설.

— 아세아재단에서 기증받은 기재로 한국영화문화협회 발족, 정릉 스튜디오 설립.

— 부산극장에서 부일영화상 제1회 수상식 개최.

— 이병일 감독의 〈시집가는 날〉(1956) 제4회 아세아영화제에서 특별희극상 수상.

— 16밀리 리버설 컬러 필름 작품 〈선화공주〉 개봉.

1958년

— 동양 최대 규모의 안양촬영소 건립(수도영화사 대표 홍찬).

— 최초의 시네마스코프 영화 〈생명〉 개봉 7월 16일.

1959년

— 문교부 「국산영화장려 및 영화오락순화를 위한 보상 특혜조치」에 관한 고시 제정 공포 4월 6일.

— 반공예술인단과 한국영화제작가협회 공동주최로 제1회 영화의 날 제정.

1945

— Korea gained Liberation from Japan 15 August.

— The Chosun Film Construction Headquarters(Chosun Younghwa Geonsul Bonboo)

produced 〈Liberation Newsreels〉 Parts 1 & 2.

— Establishment of the Korean Film Union(Chosun Younghwa Dongmaeng) 16 December.

1946

— The United States Army Military Government In Korea(USAMGIK) promulgated the

Military Government Ordinance No. 68, 'Regulation of the Motion Pictures' 12 April

and No. 115, 'Film Law' 9 October.

— 〈Hurrah! for Freedom(Jayu Manse)〉, produced by the director Choi In Kyu and written

for the screen by Jun Chang Gun, was released 22 October.

— Cultural organizations including the Korean Film Union issued a statement against

the film law and requested its abolition 23 October.

1947

— The first 16mm Sound film, 〈Mokdan Dunggi〉 was produced and released by the

director Kim So Dong and his institution, Chosun Film & Science Research

Centre(Chosun Younghwa Gwahak Yeongooso).

1948

— The US Army's 502nd military unit produced the first color 16mm cultural film,

〈Village of Hope(Himang-ui Maul)〉.

— The simultaneous sound recording on film was made for the musical drama 〈Green

Hill(Purun Unduk)〉.

1949

— Hong Sung Ki debuted with 〈A Woman's Diary(Yeosung Ilki)〉, the first color 16mm feature film.

— Han Hyung Mo, previously known as a director of photography, debuted as a director with 〈Breaking the Wall(Sungbyuk-ul Ttulgo)〉, an anti-communism feature film.

1950

— 〈The Hometown in My Heart(Maum-ui Gohyang)〉 by Director Yoon Yong Gyu was exchanged with the French film 〈Chanson du Rêves(Kumsok-ul Norae)〉 for the cultural exchange between Korea and France.

— The Korean War broke out.

— Korean Film Critic's Association was established in Busan 10 September.

1951

— 〈Righteous Advance(Jungui-ui Jin-kyuk) Vol. 1)〉 produced by the Troop Information and Education Centre under the Ministry of Defense film crew was released at the Dong-a Cinema in Busan and Jayu Cinema in Daegu 20 June.

1952

— Shin Sang Ok debuted with 〈Evil Night(Akya)〉, which was made in Daegu, a refugee city.

1953

— Serabol Art College was established with a two-year course in Korea's first department of film, and Yoon Baek Nam, the director of 〈Flight Under the Moon (Wolha-ui Maengseo)〉, became the school's first president.

— Chung Chang Hwa debuted with 〈The Final Temptation(Choihoo-ui Youhok)〉.

1954

— 'Tax Law for Admission Fee' 31 March, an exemption of the admission tax for Korean films, was established in order to promote Korean films.

1955

— 〈Chunhyang Story(Chunhyang-jeon)〉, directed by Lee Kyu Hwan, was released simultaneously at the Kukdo Cinema in Seoul and Dong-a Cinema in Busan 6 January, and enjoyed a successful run.

— Monthly film magazines such as 『International Films(Kukje Younghwa)』 and 『Film World(Younghwa Segye)』 were published.

— Kim Ki Young debuted with 〈A Box For A Corpse(Jugum-ui Sangja)〉 with the production support of the United States Information Service. The simultaneous sound recording was carried out with a Mitchell camera and magnetic recorder.

— The first female director Park Nam Ok debuted with 〈Widow(Mi-mang-in)〉.

1956

— The Korean Association of Film makers(Hanguk Younghwa-in Danche Yeonhap-hoi) was established.

— The Asia Foundation donated film equipment including a Mitchell camera and Houston automatic developer worth about $60,000.

— 〈Madame Freedom(Jayu Buin)〉 directed by Han Hyung Mo was released at the Kukdo Cinema(June 9) and had a long run for 45 days.

— A new system of annually recognizing the best 5 Korean films was launched. The production companies of these 5 films were each awarded the rights to import one foreign film.

— The Korea Film & Culture Association(Hanguk Younghwa Munhwa Hyuphoi) and Jungnung Studio were established with the support of film making equipment donated by The Asia Foundation.

— The first Buil Film Award ceremony was held at Busan Cinema.

— 〈The Wedding Day(Sijip-ganun Nal)〉(1956) received a special comedy award from the 4th Asia Film Festival.

— 〈Princess Seonhwa(Seonhwa Gongjoo)〉 was made with 16mm reversal color film and released for general distribution.

— Asia's largest studio, Anyang Film Studio was built(Sudo Film Company's chief representative, Hong Chan).

— The first cinemascope film, 〈Life(Saengmyung)〉 was released 16 July.

— The Ministry of Culture and Education declared 'the enforcement of the preferential treatment of Korean films and the recreational film sublimation' 6 April.

— A national Film Day was enacted by the Anti-Communism Artist Group and the Korean Film Producer's Association(Hanguk Younghwa Jejakga Hyuphoi).

찾아보기

영화명

감독명

Index

Name of Directors

A

B

C

H

한국영화의 풍경 1945 – 1959
Traces of Korean Cinema from 1945 to 1959

초판 1쇄 | 2003년 12월 20일
초판 2쇄 | 2007년　1월 17일

기획 및 발간 | 한국영상자료원(KOFA)
사진 · 포스터 | 한국영상자료원
글 | 이효인, 정종화
번역 | 심애경, 브라이언 예시스(감수)

펴낸이 | 전성은
펴낸곳 | 문학사상사
주소 | 서울특별시 송파구 오금동 91번지(138-858)
등록 | 1973년 3월 21일 제1-137호
편집부 | 3401-8543~4
영업부 | 3401-8540~2
팩시밀리 | 3401-8741~2
한글도메인주소 | 문학사상
홈페이지 | www.munsa.co.kr
이메일 | munsa@munsa.co.kr
지로계좌 | 3006111

ⓒ 한국영상자료원, 2003

* 잘못 만들어진 책은 구입하신 서점이나 본사에서 바꾸어 드립니다.
* 값은 표지 뒷면에 표시되어 있습니다.

ISBN 89-7012-622-8 03680